Teacher Preparation in Career Pathways

Other Titles of Interest

Teacher Preparation in Career Pathways

The Future of America's Teacher Pipeline

Edited by Karen Embry Jenlink

ROWMAN & LITTLEFIELD EDUCATION
A division of
ROWMAN & LITTLEFIELD PUBLISHERS, INC.
Lanham • New York • Toronto • Plymouth, UK

KH

Published by Rowman & Littlefield Education
A division of Rowman & Littlefield Publishers, Inc.
A wholly owned subsidary of The Rowman & Littlefield Publishing Group, Inc.
4501 Forbes Boulevard, Suite 200, Lanham, Maryland 20706
www.rowman.com

10 Thornbury Road, Plymouth PL6 7PP, United Kingdom

British Library Cataloguing in Publication Information Available

Library of Congress Cataloging-in-Publication Data

Teacher preparation in career pathways : the future of America's teacher pipeline / edited by Karen Embry Jenlink.
p. cm.
Summary: "edited collection: in schools, colleges, and universities today, the emergence of the teacher career pathway model as a means of addressing persistent challenges in teacher workforce development and school staffing in America signals a transition within the profession"— Provided by publisher.
Includes bibliographical references.
IISBN 978-1-60709-870-6 (hardback) — ISBN 978-1-60709-871-3 (paper) — ISBN 978-1-60709-872-0 (ebook)
1. Teachers—Training of—United States. I. Jenlink, Karen Embry. II. Jenlink, Karen Embry.
LB1715.T4255 2012
370.71'1—dc23
2012012412

Printed in the United States of America

4/15/13

This work is dedicated to Della Washington, a legendary teacher and mentor.

Contents

Preface

This book project formed as a result of innovation, collaboration, and dissemination among teacher preparation programs and school districts across the country. Its foundation began while I was serving as dean of the School of Education at St. Edward's University, a Hispanic-serving Catholic institution of higher education in Austin, Texas. A first-generation college student whose path to teaching was circuitous and met with resistance from my parents, I found myself—as a dean—passionate about increasing access and visibility for first-generation and historically underserved students to consider education as a professional career choice. I also understood firsthand the necessity of financial aid in achieving one's dreams to earn a college degree.

Austin, like many urban centers across the United States, faced persistent staffing challenges in critical teaching fields and experienced a revolving exodus of new teachers to suburban school districts, where student demographics and working conditions differ from those of inner-city schools. To address these staffing challenges, the School of Education at St. Edward's University approached the Austin Independent School District with the idea of "grow your own" approach to teacher recruitment and retention. Working with Austin Community College, Austin Interfaith, Capital Idea, and St. Edward's University, the partners formed the first teacher pipeline, Project Access (later named the Teacher Pipeline), to recruit and prepare teachers from a candidate pool of bilingual and special education paraprofessionals who were employed in the Austin Independent School District.

The success of the Teacher Pipeline led to the exploration and development of two other urban teacher pipeline programs at St. Edward's University during my tenure as dean—Jumpstart and the Robert Noyce Teacher Scholarship Program—both designed to increase access to teacher preparation for high-performing, first-generation, and historically underserved students by linking teacher workforce demand in the Austin region with university-based teacher preparation across secondary and postsecondary (Grades 9–14) educational partnerships. With funding from the Sid W. Richardson Foundation of Fort Worth, Texas, faculty from St. Edward's University and Austin Community College visited programs in other states that offered firsthand glimpses of emergent and well-established teacher pipeline programs in the design and development of career pathways. These "grow your own" programs offered innovative approaches for preparing teachers through academic career pathways among high schools, community colleges, colleges, and universities. In 2009, returning to my family in Nacogdoches, Texas, and accepting an offer from Stephen F. Austin State University to prepare leaders in higher education, I realized the need for a book to capture and document this emerging trend in teacher preparation and to empirically examine its success in responding to persistent challenges of teacher capacity, representation, and quality.

Teacher Preparation in Career Pathways: The Future of America's Teacher Pipeline grew out of this research and collaboration with teacher preparation programs across the country that are addressing the challenges of providing a diverse, highly skilled teacher workforce through innovative approaches for preparing teachers in career pathways among high schools, community colleges, colleges and universities. The voices of teachers and university faculty, public school and college administrators, and teacher candidates join with policymakers and educational stakeholders in this book and collectively reveal a new narrative for transforming teacher preparation in the 21st century.

Acknowledgments

In many respects, serving as editor of an anthology is a journey, and there are many individuals to whom I am indebted for their guidance and support in the undertaking of this journey. First, I wish to thank the authors for their investment of time and energy in sharing valuable experiences and for the perspectives they contributed to the book project over the past 2 years. Their narratives illustrate a slowly evolving transformation occurring in teacher preparation across the country in schools, colleges, and universities, and their voices offer personal documentation describing the emergence of the teacher career pathway as a model for teacher workforce development in 21st-century schools.

Second, I would like to recognize the support of my institution, Stephen F. Austin State University, and my colleagues who are involved in teacher and leadership preparation. Specifically, I wish to acknowledge Laurie Stone Rogers and Brooks Knight, who as doctoral research assistants provided assistance on the book project. I am indebted to Laurie especially for her communication with the authors and for hours of copyediting with the revisions.

Third, I would like to acknowledge my appreciation to Rowman & Littlefield Education for finding the book project to be of importance to the larger educational community and for encouraging scholarly inquiry in teacher preparation. A special thanks is extended to Tom Koerner for his senior counsel and to the editorial staff for its support in shaping a high-quality work.

And most important, I wish to express my appreciation to my husband and colleague, Patrick M. Jenlink, with whom this project began as a conversation during our first book. I thank Patrick for his tireless support throughout the process. Whether quietly listening, engaging in critical conversation, or proofreading my writing with a keen eye, his unwavering support became the lighthouse that helped me stay the course and see the journey home.

Introduction

Teacher Preparation in Career Pathways: The Future of America's Teacher Pipeline consists of nine chapters divided into three parts. In recent years, the emergence of "grow your own" approaches to teacher recruitment and preparation has risen sharply in response to the challenges of critical shortages in teaching fields, changing demographics, and increased teacher attrition due to retirement and the high-stakes testing environment that prevails in schools today.

Once largely represented by a dual paradigm of university-based and alternative preparation programs, the profile of teacher preparation in America is rapidly shifting in relation to staffing challenges in high-need schools and a heightened emphasis on workforce development in high schools—which includes high school redesign, early college high schools, career pathways spanning middle school postsecondary education, and the emergence of Grade 9–14 educational initiatives that overlap high school with college coursework in efforts to increase access, representation and success of underrepresented and first-generation students in postsecondary education.

The first part, "Teacher Career Pathways: A Historical Context," consists of the overview and the first chapter, "Preparing a Diverse, Highly Skilled Teacher Workforce in America," which establish a historical, social, and political context to the emergence of the teacher career pathway model across four decades of educational reform. This part explores the teacher career pathway model as a 21st-century workforce solution to address persistent teacher shortages in critical fields and in hard to staff schools. It also examines the effects of the economic recession and the challenges of forecasting accurate teacher supply and demand in relation to changing student demographics in secondary and postsecondary education. Finally, it argues for the need for responsive teacher preparation in recruiting and retaining a more diverse teacher workforce.

The second part of the book, "Addressing Teacher Supply and Demand in the 21st Century," consists of five chapters that portray a variety of teacher career pathway programs implemented at local, regional, and state levels. The programs presented are characterized by their focus on recruiting, preparing, and retaining a diverse teacher workforce through the recruitment of historically underserved high school and college students who have an interest in becoming teachers. These career pathway programs represent the scope and scale of innovation occurring within teacher preparation today.

In chapter 2, "Urban Teacher Enhancement Program: A Promising Career Pathway Model for the Preparation of Teachers in Urban Schools," Deborah Voltz describes the Urban Teacher Enhancement Program (UTEP) at the University of Alabama at Birmingham, where she is dean and professor. The Urban Teacher Enhancement Program was designed to address the needs in urban educator recruitment and retention. The program includes a number of critical elements that support responsive teacher education—specialized recruitment and screening strategies, enhanced program content and delivery mechanisms, and a network of candidate support—each of which is collaboratively planned and implemented by teams of educators from the university and local high-poverty urban school districts.

In chapter 3, "Infect Your Own: Delaware's ASPIRE—Academic Support Program Inspiring Renaissance Educators," Melva L. Ware, director of ASPIRE, offers insight into the challenges in preparing students for postsecondary opportunities, particularly students from ethnic minority backgrounds. The teacher career pathway program ASPIRE offers several unique features that are explored in this chapter: the summer internship, engaged campus community outreach, and an achievement-focused and diverse core group of teacher education majors. ASPIRE is considered a model in Delaware in realizing its goals to achieve a more diverse and highly effective teaching workforce.

Chapter 4, "Grow Your Own Illinois: Taking Action in Chicago Neighborhood Schools," explores a third urban regional pipeline. Anne Hallett, director of Grow Your Own Illinois, describes a community-based solution to high rates of teacher turnover. In Grow Your Own Illinois, community organizers wanted highly effective teachers for their own neighborhood schools and decided to invest in people who pass the "zip code test," primarily those who live in the low-income communities where they plan to teach. To achieve this, they developed relationships with colleges of education, school districts, and other community groups. Together, they began the work of developing a robust, equitable, and innovative teacher preparation program that now has candidates in 16 locations in Illinois: 8 in Chicago and 8 in other high-need communities.

In chapter 5, "The Online Completer Program: A Regional Teacher Pipeline With 22 Community Colleges in Rural East Texas," assistant professor Dawn Michelle Williams and instructor Paula Griffin describe the Online Completer Program at Stephen F. Austin State University, which provides an avenue for individuals living in rural, isolated areas to complete their associate and bachelor degree and obtain their teaching certification while continuing to work as paraprofessionals in schools. In this chapter, the authors identify and examine a variety of challenges that many nontraditional students face in successful postsecondary transfer, including distance from the university, work schedules, financial issues, and parenting responsibilities. The role of technology is discussed in terms of facilitating online teacher preparation, including the use of webcams for student teaching observations.

In the concluding chapter of this part, chapter 6, "CERRA: A Statewide Pipeline for Teacher Recruitment, Preparation, and Induction in South Carolina," Gayle Sawyer, director of CERRA (Center for Recruitment, Retention, and Advancement), offers an exemplary model of statewide programming and collaboration among stakeholders, which strategically addresses the need for, and the needs of, educators. For over 20 years, CERRA has provided systemic leadership in identifying, attracting, placing, and retaining well-qualified individuals for the teaching profession in the state of South Carolina and in addressing the changing needs for teachers from underrepresented populations in critical subject fields and in underserved geographical areas in South Carolina. CERRA is purposefully placed as the last program within this part as a leading example of a long-term, sustainable teacher career pathway program that has successfully gone to scale in addressing South Carolina's statewide issues of teacher mobility, attrition, and leadership succession.

The third part of the book is entitled "Closing the Gaps Through Teacher Career Pathways." In the three chapters within it, authors representing diverse stakeholders' perspectives speak to the issues surrounding educational policy and practice critical to closing the gaps in postsecondary transfer and degree attainment. This part is followed by the coda, which summarizes the teacher career pathway model and raises questions regarding its role and agency in transforming the pipeline of teacher preparation in 21st-century schools.

In chapter 7, "Building the Teacher Pipeline for College Access, Readiness, and Success," authors Heather Zavadsky, director of research and implementation for the Texas High School Project, and Kelty Garbee, describe three program models—Early College High School, T-STEM Academies, and UTeach—which demonstrate how school districts and colleges can strategically create career pathways that will engage students, increase their earning potential, and infuse their communities with needed skills. The authors not only highlight applications to the structures within these models that support students and teachers but also show how they may positively affect the teacher labor market.

In chapter 8, "The Role of Social Capital in Student Persistence and Retention in Career Pathways: A Theoretical Framework," Gregory M. Bouck of Caddo Parish Schools, Shreveport, Louisiana, brings a critical lens to contemporary research associated with postsecondary transfer and explores the theoretical underpinnings of student engagement, persistence, and success within 2- and 4-year institutions of higher learning. In its creation of teacher career pathways, the community college—specifically, the experiences of community college students transferring to 4-year universities—provides the backdrop for this review of literature.

In chapter 9, "Teacher Career Pathways and Educational Policy: A Quick Fix or Long-Term Solution?" Leslie Huling and Virginia Resta, professors at Texas State University, examine demographic and societal trends that affect the sustainability of teacher career pathway programs. The authors examine policy support for different models of teacher career pathway programs, specifically those targeted at recruiting teacher aides into teacher certification programs and those targeted at recruiting secondary teachers.

The third part concludes with a coda, "An Emerging Portrait of Responsive Teacher Preparation," which offers a synthesis of the core ideas presented in the book. Specifically, it extends considerations for educational stakeholders—including deans, superintendents, principals, faculty, and teachers—regarding the future influence of this emerging model of responsive teacher preparation, a model that is gaining traction and visibility within the teacher pipeline in America today.

I

Teacher Career Pathways: A Historical Context

Public school districts in this country will not and cannot ultimately fulfill their promise to American society- and the ever-increasing expectations placed on them by their communities- without an adequate and reliable supply of well-prepared and effective classroom teachers. And those teachers will not be found unless universities renew their institutional commitment to meeting this critical human capital need. The leaders of our universities must step up to this challenge if we are to achieve the nation's ambitious educational goals.

—O'Keefe and Pelz-Paget (2009, p. 6)

During the latter part of the 20th century, teacher preparation in the United States underwent unprecedented reform. A confluence of economic, political, social, and cultural factors converged, simultaneously shaping the others and ultimately resulting in a myriad of alternative pathways to teacher certification and licensure (Cochran-Smith, 2004). Amid these factors, the idea of a career pathway for teacher preparation emerged. Taking numerous forms based on state and local teacher demand and the various licensure routes, teacher career pathway programs today offer students a professional career path leading from high schools and community colleges into 4-year universities to earn a college degree and become certified to teach in America's public schools (Bragg, 2007; Fuller & Nolen, 2010; Jenlink & Eames, 2009).

The antecedents of the teacher career pathway model are situated in 20th-century educational reforms. Spanning secondary and postsecondary education, these reforms included an increased emphasis on standards and accountability, a heightened focus on career and technical education in high schools and community colleges, and the deregulation of teacher certification to address persistent shortages in critical teaching fields. Today, teacher career pathway programs resonate with historical struggles to address teacher quality, diversity, and capacity through responsive teacher preparation. Teacher career pathways are increasing access and representation within the teaching profession by strategically targeting historically underrepresented student populations for teacher workforce development to meet local, regional, and statewide teacher supply and demand, particularly in critical teaching fields.

HISTORICAL ORIGINS

The historical origin of the teacher career pathway model is largely based on 20th-century reforms in vocational education. In *What Work Requires of Schools: A SCANS Report for America 2000* (Secretary's Commission on Achieving Necessary Skills, 1991), early lessons from industry pointed "to the need for a student pipeline in which high schools students choose technical fields early and lay a solid foundation that enables them to transition smoothly to articulated two-year postsecondary programs in those fields" (Hull, 2005, p. 10). Thus, specialized career pathways emerged within the field of career and technical education to ensure a well-prepared pool of graduates that were ready for postsecondary education or job training after high school.

Career and technical education career pathways today offer several configurations that span secondary and postsecondary educational settings. A 2+2 career pathway represents an articulated degree plan that is designed to support a seamless transition from high school into postsecondary education leading to a technical degree (e.g., an associate of arts). A 2+2+2 career pathway includes overlapping high school with postsecondary education. In such a career pathway, high school students can earn college credit through dual-enrollment programs, transition to a 2-year technical or community college to earn an associate's degree, and then complete a bachelor's degree in an accredited 4-year college or university. A 2+4 career pathway omits the 2-year college with an articulated degree plan that maps high school credits toward earning a bachelor's degree in an accredited college or university.

Declining student achievement and postsecondary degree attainment amid rapidly changing student demographics further highlighted the issue of teacher quality as central to ensuring America's success not only in the classroom but also in the global marketplace. Beginning with establishment of national academic standards for mathematics in 1989, the latter part of the 20th century was marked as a time of standards setting with the intention of equipping America with a highly skilled workforce. The development of 22 national industry standards and 16 academic standards established minimum competency levels of knowledge and skills that qualified individuals as being workforce ready (Mid-Continent Regional Educational Laboratory, n.d.). Within the national movement to implement the academic and industry standards frameworks, increased accountability with new monitoring responsibilities emerged, and high-stakes testing systems were developed as the means to assess student academic achievement benchmarked against new standards.

Catalyzed by the requirements of the No Child Left Behind Act for determining what counted as a "highly qualified teacher," alternative routes to teacher licensure sprang up in response to a highly politicized agenda aimed at deregulating teacher licensure. As Cochran-Smith (2004) stated,

> what's driving teacher education . . . are the intersections and collisions of three major trends: intense and singular attention to teacher quality as individual teacher effectiveness in raising test scores, the emergence of a highly regulated deregulation as the federal agenda for reforming teacher preparation, and the ascendance of science as the presumed solution to most educational problems. (p. 7)

Finally, changes in federal and state policy regarding teacher licensure and uneven teacher supply and demand—particularly in critical shortage fields of science, mathematics, bilingual education, and special education—also influenced the design and emergence of teacher career pathway programs across the country (Bragg, 2007). The development of technical career pathways, the implementation of academic standards, and the establishment of alternative routes to teacher licensure offered opportunities to open up avenues of exploration and collaboration in the design of new models of teacher preparation to address the staffing challenges in diverse school districts and states with rapidly changing student demographics. Across nearly four decades of educational reform, what emerged is an innovative, responsive model of teacher preparation, forged across secondary and postsecondary educational settings that, by design, seeks to transform the profile of the dominant White female teacher workforce, which has historically characterized teacher preparation and practice in America. The formative, shaping influences of these educational reforms offer a significant historical context for examining the teacher career pathway model.

REFERENCES

Bragg, D. D. (2007). Teacher pipelines: Career pathways extending from high school to community college to university. *Community College Review, 35*(1), 10–29.

Cochran-Smith, M. (2004). Taking stock in 2004: Teacher education in dangerous times. *Journal of Teacher Education, 55*(1), 3–7.

Fuller, E., & Nolen, A. (2010). *An emerging understanding of the Arkansas teacher pipeline.* Retrieved from http://aacte.org/index.php?/Research-Policy/Recent-Reports-on-Educator-Preparation/an-emerging-understandin-of-the-arkansas-teacher-pipeline.html

Hull, D. (2005). *Career pathways.* Waco, TX: Center for Occupational Research and Development.

Jenlink, K. E., & Eames, S. (2009, April). *Closing the gaps through an urban teacher career pathway targeting underrepresented high-performing youth.* Paper presented at the American Educational Research Association, San Diego, CA.

Mid-Continent Regional Educational Laboratory. (n.d.). *History of the standards.* Retrieved from http://www.mcrel.org/standards-benchmarks/docs/history.asp

Okeefe, M., & Pelz-Paget, N. (2009). Foreword in The Sid W. Richardson Foundation, *Delivering a high quality teacher workforce for Texas: Reconsidering university-based teacher preparation in Texas, renewing commitments, and improving practice in the twenty-first century.* Fort Worth, TX: The Sid W. Richardson Foundation. Retrieved August 8, 2011, from www.sidrichardson.org/SRFEducationReport.pdf

Secretary's Commission on Achieving Necessary Skills. (1991). *What work requires of schools: A SCANS report for America 2000.* Washington, DC: U.S. Department of Labor.

Overview

Although we now appear to have consensus about the importance of teacher quality, there is no parallel consensus about how to define it: How to conceptualize teacher quality in ways that account for the complexities of teaching and learning, how to identify which characteristics of teacher quality are linked with desirable educational outcomes, how to decide which educational outcomes are desirable in the first place, and how to recruit, prepare, and retain teachers who provide rich academic learning opportunities but also prepare their students for participation in a democracy.
—M. Cochran-Smith (2004, pp. 3–4)

Gaining momentum in the 21st century, teacher pipelines as career pathways offer a "grow your own" model for building a new teacher workforce in America—a teacher workforce that will not resemble the predominantly White female teacher candidate pool of the past. This is a new teacher workforce, one that is recruited and prepared within the student population in America's schools.

This teacher workforce is built from a diverse pool of high-performing candidates who begin their teacher preparation in high school or at a local community college and complete teacher licensure while earning a bachelor's degree. Some are already working as paraprofessionals in schools in which they will be hired as teachers. Others are high school juniors and seniors who will teach in the same schools they are currently attending, thereby strengthening their local communities through education while remaining close to their families.

Forged during the latter part of the 20th century, teacher pipelines as career pathways began to emerge in various locales across the United States in response to regional and statewide teacher shortages in diverse educational settings (Bragg, 2007). Some developed regionally in hard-to-staff urban school districts, and others formed within rural schools in geographically isolated communities (Locklear, Davis, & Covington, 2009). The teacher pipeline as career pathway is a model of social agency, increasing access to teacher education as a professional career choice for first-generation and historically underrepresented students. Today, in the 21st century, the teacher career pathway model is gaining traction, visibility, funding, and recognition as a strategic and sustainable response to persistent and systemic problems regarding teacher quality and teacher supply and demand.

Through the teacher pipeline model, high-performing historically underserved and under-represented students in high school and community colleges are strategically recruited and offered initial preprofessional experiences in public school settings (Woullard & Coats, 2004). Financial aid in the form of scholarships, grants, tuition discounts, and state and federal funding enhances student opportunity to attend a 4-year university and earn a bachelor's degree with teacher certification. Dual credit, early college high schools, and tightly articulated agreements that span high school with community college and university degree plans allow students to map and accelerate a college degree in less than the usual 4 or 5 years, often resulting in additional cost savings.

In teacher career pathway programs, students are provided with authentic career exploration through service learning and early preprofessional experiences, such as tutoring after school, thereby enhancing teacher retention and reducing the likelihood of students changing careers after achieving teacher certification. Shifting away from the traditional recruitment of teacher candidates in institutions of higher learning, teacher pipelines increase access to higher education and promote teacher quality through the strategic recruitment of a diverse pool of talented and high-performing candidates who are invited to consider a career in education while attending high school or a community college. Rigorous academic requirements, coupled with strong academic support and individual case support services, ensure retention and student success to degree completion (Harkness, DeLoach Johnson, Hensley, & Stallworth, 2011; Hoffman, Vargas, Venezia, & Miller, 2007; Woullard & Coats, 2004).

Recently, well-established teacher pipelines in certain school districts are joining in educational leadership preparation to address regional shortages in school leadership through "grow your own" approaches. In these programs, teacher pipelines are evolving into leadership feeder programs as graduates become mentors and teacher leaders and are supported to move into leadership roles within their local school districts. Today, the model of teacher pipelines as career pathways is distinguished as a 21st-century model of professional workforce development and social agency with the ability and capacity to addresses the persistent challenges of school staffing, teacher shortages, and teacher quality in schools today.

REFERENCES

Bragg, D. D. (2007). Teacher pipelines: Career pathways extending from high school to community college to university, *Community College Review, 35*(1), 10–29.

Cochran-Smith, M. (2004). Taking stock in 2004: Teacher education in dangerous times. *Journal of Teacher Education, 55*(3), 3–7.

Harkness, S. S., DeLoach Johnson, I., Hensley, B., & Stallworth, J. A. (2011). Apprenticeship of immersion: College access for high school students interested in teaching mathematics or science. *School Science and Mathematics, 111*(1), 11–19.

Hoffman, N., Vargas, J., Venezia, A., & Miller, M. S. (2007). *Minding the gap: Why integrating high school with college makes sense and how to do it.* Cambridge, MA: Harvard Education Press.

Locklear, C. D., Davis, M. L., & Covington, V. E. (2009). Do university centers produce comparable teacher education candidates? *Community College Review, 36*(3), 239–260.

Woullard, R., & Coats, L. T. (2004). The community college role in preparing future teachers: The impact of a mentoring program for preservice teachers. *Community College Journal of Research and Practice, 28,* 609–624.

Chapter One

Preparing a Diverse, Highly Skilled Teacher Workforce in America

Karen Embry Jenlink

The future of millions of children in the United States, especially ethnic and minority and low income children, rests in the hands of policymakers, community leaders, and educators they will never meet. The quality of teaching these children will receive depends increasingly on the reforming and restructuring of teacher preparation and professional development programs in every state.
—Futrell (1999, p. 318)

Issues of teacher supply and quality are pressing concerns for educators across the nation, transcending the boundaries of a single state. Yet, because education is a state responsibility, truly effective strategies for addressing these issues will come from the work of local and state leaders.
—O'Keefe and Pelz-Paget (2009, p. 5)

Issues surrounding the current workforce influence teacher preparation. Students, too, have changed, and bring to schools numerous challenges for today's teachers. Examining teacher preparation thus is informed by what we know about the teacher workforce.
—American Association of the Colleges of Teacher Education (2010, p. 6)

The antecedents of the teacher career pathway models emerging in high school and college and university partnerships today extend the educational reforms of the 20th century forward to address societal issues of equity and social justice within emergent and rapidly changing demographics and educational settings. Closing the achievement gaps among diverse student populations, increasing college rates among first-generation and historically underserved and undocumented students, and addressing America's underprepared population of secondary students who are not ready for college or the workforce after four decades of mandated educational reforms are issues central to economic stability and the sustainability of our educational system within a democracy (Futrell, 1999; Hoffman, Vargas, Venezia, & Miller, 2007; Howell & Tuitt, 2003; Kazis, Vargas, & Hoffman, 2004; No Child Left Behind [NCLB], 2002).

In recent years, a heightened focus on the preparation of secondary students for success in college and the world of work beyond high school featured prominently in the emergence of innovative approaches to seal the leaks in the preK–16 education pipeline. With significant funding from federal and private foundations, including the Bill and Melinda Gates Foundation, models such as Early College High School have shown promise in contributing significantly to the increase of first-generation student success in postsecondary institutions (Kazis, 2004). Dual-enrollment programs, largely offered by partnerships between highs schools and 2-year colleges, offer students the opportunity to begin earning college credit in high school through articulation agreements (Hoffman et al., 2007). Career pathway programs resemble earlier career and technical education career pathway models, such as Tech Prep, except that newer emerging models in the 21st century are more heavily focused on college readiness, academic education, and preparing students for careers based on a broader set of employable skills, not narrowed to skills specialized to industrial or applied technology (Bragg, 2007).

Teacher career pathways are in a position to serve a role of cultural and social agency within innovative programs that integrate high school with 2- and 4-year colleges and universities. First, teacher career pathways facilitate a college-going culture by directly recruiting first-generation and historically underserved students to consider a career in education while enrolled in middle or secondary school (Holland & Farmer-Hinton, 2009). Second, student transfer and success are enhanced within academic career pathway models as first-generation and underserved students are afforded supportive frameworks that provide academic support, financial aid, and mentoring within a preK–16 educational system (Hoffman, et al., 2007). The emphasis on building a college-going culture and increasing access among historically underserved and underrepresented student populations in postsecondary education is integral to building capacity in a diverse teacher workforce (Futrell, 1999).

Addressing persistent issues of equity and social justice in closing the achievement gap, academic career pathways, including teacher career pathways, are redefining the course of preK–16 educational reform in the 21st century (Bragg, 2007). Academic career pathways encourage innovation in policies and practices that "will reduce the unacceptably high cost of our nation's failure to prepare large numbers of young people for further education, productive careers, and active citizenship" (Kazis, 2004, p. 1).

Chief among these is the ability of middle and secondary schools and postsecondary institutions to work collaboratively to increase postsecondary student success and opportunity for economic and professional advancement through the attainment of a degree in postsecondary education (Hoffman, et al., 2007; Woullard & Coats, 2004). The economic disadvantage that is set into motion and perpetuated when students who complete high school do not go on to complete a college degree decries a moral imperative for the implementation of strategies that will increase postsecondary matriculation and foster student success. College graduates today earn, on average, 70% more as compared to high school graduates. Moreover, the number of jobs requiring degree or certificate completion continues to rise in the 21st century (Kazis, 2004).

In this chapter, I examine the role of teacher career pathways as a model of responsive teacher preparation, and I explore its role as cultural and social agency in securing a diverse, highly skilled teacher workforce in America. The chapter is divided into four sections. The first section provides a historical backdrop for the teacher career pathway model, exploring the response in teacher education to national educational reforms across the latter part of the 20th century and beginning of the 21st century.

In the second section, I offer a brief history of career and technical education, and I explore the shaping influences from career and technical education on the emergence of teacher career pathway model. The third section provides a contemporary context for examining the role of teacher career pathways as social agency, examining demographic trends in licensure and employment in teacher workforce compared with student enrollment and postsecondary degree attainment.

Finally, within the fourth section, teacher career pathways are linked to teacher workforce development, examining projections for teacher supply and demand in relation to student demographics and enrollment growth in 21st-century schools. Throughout the chapter, I underscore the potential of the teacher career pathway model for transforming teacher preparation into a responsive model for teacher workforce development in the 21st century.

TEACHER CAREER PATHWAYS: A HISTORICAL CONTEXT

Background

The emergence of teacher pipelines as a career pathway model evolved slowly across four decades of national education reforms to improve schools in a postsegregation era. Evidenced throughout this reform movement are legal cases and legislated mandates to restructure schools and teacher licensure. Moving forward from the historic struggles to end segregation in our public schools, beginning with the landmark case *Brown v. Board of Education* in 1954 to civil rights legislation in the 1960s, legislated policy mandates focused heavily on addressing educational inequities and increasing educational attainment for all children. During the 1970s and 1980s, funded research studies such as *A Nation at Risk* (National Commission on Excellence in Education, 1983) established the need for policies that would serve to mandate a rigorous curriculum for every child in America and ensure the preparation of a uniform teacher workforce well prepared to teach diverse student populations and secure America's future as a globally competitive superpower.

Entering the 21st century, rapidly shifting demographics and growth in student populations, coupled with pending teacher shortages, formed the backdrop for a new slate of educational reforms designed to address persistent issues of students achievement, public school accountability and teacher quality (Darling-Hammond, 2000). The national hallmark of these reforms was the Reauthorization of the Elementary and Secondary Education Act. Also known as NCLB, the act introduced a new formula for determining what counted as a "highly qualified teacher," embedded clinical practices in educator preparation, and established standards and accountability test frameworks for teacher preparation.

Coupled with increased funding to community colleges and the promotion of alternative routes to licensure, NCLB promulgated a neoliberalist agenda aimed at deregulating teacher licensure. As Cochran-Smith (2004) noted, what's driving teacher education . . . are the intersections and collisions of three major trends: intense and singular attention to teacher quality as individual teacher effectiveness in raising test scores, the emergence of a highly regulated deregulation as the federal agenda for reforming teacher preparation, and the ascendance of science as the presumed solution to most educational problems. (p. 7)

Thus, it is against a backdrop of four decades of educational reform that emerging systems of educator preparation in general, and teacher pipelines and the teacher career pathway model featured in this book in particular, are framed within the larger discourse on educational policy and practice.

Teacher Preparation Reform in the 20th Century

In the 1960s, federally funded programs such as Project Head Start and the National Teacher Corps established a social justice reform agenda within the educational system, notably moving teacher preparation closer in proximity to student learning. Project Head Start promised an early start to educational success by offering more services earlier to underserved youth (ILHeadstart, n.d.). During the same time, the National Teacher Corps project shifted the domain of teacher preparation from the university setting to school-based enterprise that linked teacher preparation with student achievement (Futrell, 1999).

In 1983, the National Commission on Excellence in Education issued its landmark report *A Nation at Risk* and sounded the call to alarm the American people regarding the "virtually unbroken decline" of student performance since the 1950s. The report demonstrated that on international comparisons of student achievement on standardized tests and literacy rates, students graduating from American schools and colleges were consistently ranked lower and outperformed by their counterparts in other countries and by American students in prior decades. In *A Nation at Risk*, the American public was portrayed as developing an "emerging sense of national frustration . . . described as both a dimming of personal expectations and the fear of losing a shared vision for America."

National frustration over the fact that fewer young people were being prepared in the educational system to be successful in college or work prompted the search for defining excellence in the individual learner, in schools and colleges, and in society. With the twin goals of equity and high-quality schooling as the drivers for educational reform, the quest for excellence focused on student achievement, college and career readiness, economic productivity, and lifelong learning. *A Nation at Risk* sparked controversy over the American educational system and generated a national debate that continues today over standards and accountability and student achievement as they relate to the preparation of teachers and teacher quality. At the heart of the controversy, enduring questions of the effectiveness of current teacher preparation practices run deep.

Teacher Educators' Response to *A Nation at Risk*

In response to the failing circumstances in schools identified in *A Nation at Risk*, the need to overhaul the educational system of teacher preparation, as Futrell (1999) argued, loudly resonated in subsequent state-of-education reports delivered by the Holmes Group, the Carnegie

Forum on Education and Economy's Task Force on Teaching, and the Renaissance Group. The Holmes Group, a group of education deans, foresaw the need to reform schooling in America while reforming the education of educators. Its first report, *Tomorrow's Teachers* (Holmes Group, 1986), established a set of actionable targets for the "transformation of teaching from an occupation into a profession" (p. 10). These targets confronted persistent challenges associated with teacher preparation in the United States, including low quality, weak accreditation policies, and a lack of professional identity. In addition, the group pointed to the responsibility of teacher preparation programs in addressing the decline of student achievement identified in *A Nation at Risk*.

The Holmes Group is chiefly recognized as being responsible for creating the professional development school model and is credited with shifting teacher preparation from the university campus to the public school setting. In 1995, the group issued a report entitled *Tomorrow's Schools of Education*, which further catalyzed the growing movement to implement professional development schools, establishing field-based preparation programs in clinical settings within schools for the purpose of preparing teachers to work in diverse schools with diverse learners.

Like the Holmes Group, the Renaissance Group (1993)—consisting of university presidents, provosts, and deans—initiated a plan to effect widespread reform for university-wide support for teacher education. From its inception in 1989, the Renaissance Group's influence served to focus the improvement of the quality of educator preparation. The platform of the Renaissance Group was characterized by collaboration with preK–12 schools, extensive field experiences, integration of subject matter content with pedagogy, technology innovation, diverse schools, assessment of learner outcomes, and a continuum of teacher professional development shared by the individual, the university, and the school system.

Development of Professional Teaching Standards

A third reform effort, the National Board for Professional Teaching Standards (NBPTS), emerged during the last decade of the 20th century to respond to concerns over teacher quality and to design improved measures for a preparing a quality teacher workforce. Premised around a set of core propositions concerned with what teachers should know and be able to do, the NBPTS purported to define and measure teaching excellence through a rigorous examination process. The NBPTS sought to address the issues of low teacher quality by developing an advanced credentialing system with national board certification across 16 subject areas that would serve to develop and distinguish high-quality teachers within the teaching profession (Carnegie Forum on Education and the Economy, 1986). Subsequent to the efforts of the Holmes Group, the Renaissance Group, and the NBPTS, numerous state reform initiatives emerged that dramatically influenced legislation and policy development aimed at transforming teacher education in the 21st century.

Teacher Preparation Reform in the 21st Century

At the beginning of the 21st century, NCLB ushered in an era of sweeping legislative educational reform redirecting the emphasis of teacher preparation away from colleges and universities and toward alternative forms of licensure. These changes left deep, lasting imprints on teacher preparation reform. NCLB, like its precursor, the Elementary and Secondary Education Act of 1965, focused national attention on equal access to education and on enforcing high standards and accountability within the current system of education in the United States. NCLB contained a section on improving teacher quality, and it introduced tough sanctions for placing teachers who were "out of field" in classrooms on emergency or temporary certificates. As enacted, NCLB eliminated provisional certificates and closed state and district loopholes that shortchanged students by placing "out of field" teachers in hard-to-staff classrooms.

NCLB enacted sweeping educational reform in the systems of standards and accountability, with increased emphasis on student performance, as demonstrated through high-stakes testing. NCLB will be long remembered in teacher preparation reform for attempting to define what constituted a "highly qualified" teacher and for subsequently legislating requirements for public schools to demonstrate that all teachers in core academic subject areas meet the requirements of "highly qualified." According to NCLB, to be considered "highly qualified," teachers in core subject areas must be fully certified and licensed within their state, hold a bachelor's degree from a 4-year institution, and demonstrate competence within a core academic discipline. Competence within the academic discipline is demonstrated by holding an academic major in the undergraduate degree within the subject area, holding a graduate degree in the subject area, or holding national board certification in the subject area.

Teacher Educators' Response to NCLB

Originally designed to "reward success and sanction failures," NCLB intended to promote innovative teacher reforms in certification and licensure in an effort to improve teacher quality and enhance student achievement. With large-scale funding attached to the legislated reforms, addressing the enduring issue of low teacher quality quickly became politicized within the economic requirements for states to develop assessment systems that would measure teacher performance based on gains in academic achievement, offer incentives (such as merit-based pay for teachers in high-need schools), and provide mentoring to support teacher retention.

The sanctions imposed by NCLB created a market-based context that supported the development of alternative certification, providing alternative routes for teacher licensure to comply with legislated mandates for placing a "highly qualified" teacher in every classroom. According to the National Center for Alternative Certification (2009), during the NCLB era, the number of alternatively certified teachers nearly tripled, increasing from just over 16,000 teachers in 1999 to over 45,000 in 2009. Colleges and schools of education concurrently experienced significant drops in traditional teacher certification programs. In 2003, the number of teachers certified in traditional university-based programs dropped from an all-time high of 172,000 to 142,133. Six years later, in 2009, the available data showed slightly over 44,000 teachers completing certification in traditional university-based preparation programs. With multiple routes to licensure, deregulation in teacher preparation had begun (Cochran-Smith, 2004).

OVERVIEW OF CAREER AND TECHNICAL EDUCATION

For over 200 years, the development of technical education—formerly, vocational education—in America remained closely aligned with industrial development and increasing demands for a highly skilled labor force (Barlow, 1976). As part of the secondary education reforms within the last quarter of the 20th century, the term *career education* emerged. The term encompasses lifelong education and links the development of work-related skills to the general education curriculum. With support from the U.S. Congress and the American Vocational Association, the Carl D. Perkins Vocational and Applied Technical Education Act of 1990 and the related School to Work Opportunities Act of 1994 served as the catalysts that launched Tech Prep, a nationwide vocational education initiative that linked secondary education with postsecondary education in 4+2, 3+2, and 2+2 career pathways (Hull, 2005).

Career and Technical Education Pathways

Tech Prep was originally implemented for the purpose of immediately placing high school graduates in the workforce. High school students in Tech Prep were positioned through carefully sequenced coursework in technical fields, toward entering the workforce after 2 years of postsecondary education or training in a specialized field. The key features of Tech Prep included articulation agreements among 2- and 4-year colleges and technical schools, highly specialized curricula developed around a common core of academic proficiency, joint training of high school and postsecondary faculty, and professional development for secondary guidance counselors.

Career pathways, as models of workforce development, became highly visible as part of the technical high school curriculum reform initiative Tech Prep and closely coupled postsecondary education with long-term regional, state, and national economic development. Community colleges and 2-year technical schools played key roles in the successful implementation of the Tech Prep model, as nine model Tech Prep sites and eight educational consortia were established, building a national emerging model of career education (Office of Vocational and Adult Education, n.d.).

The reauthorization of the Carl D. Perkins Vocational and Applied Technology Education Act in 2006 focused the Tech Prep model on increasing academic achievement in career and technical education, improving state and local accountability, and strengthening the connections among secondary and postsecondary partners in education (Threeton, 2007). It also created a separate funding stream for the promotion of innovative secondary and postsecondary partnerships, leading to improved academic proficiency among technical students and seamless student transition through articulation agreements spanning secondary and postsecondary institutions.

Teacher Career Pathways

The design for the teacher career pathway model was adapted from, and replicates several elements of, vocational and technical career pathway models within career and technical education (Bragg, 2007; Jenlink & Eames, 2009). Highly specialized career pathways models, especially in science- and technology-based occupations, continue to dominate the field of career and technical education. Unlike purely technical fields, teacher career pathways often exist as hybrid models that fuse career and technical programs within high schools in a professional academic career pathway that leads to attainment of a bachelor's degree and teacher licensure (Bragg, 2007). Hybrid models such as teacher career pathways have been slower to emerge in the professional disciplines but offer promise as a vital component in strategic economic and workforce development in a postindustrial society (Jenlink & Eames, 2009).

Academic career pathways, including teacher career pathways, operate in many ways similar to their earlier career and technical education counterparts. They are characterized by a spirit of collaboration, and they operate with a philosophy of shared ownership, described as "What does my institution bring to the table?" (Hull, 2005, p. 171). Within career pathway programs, partnerships are measured pragmatically by their ability to help students progress through the preK–16 educational system and secure productive employment, whether at entry level or in a high-paying, high-demand field. Public school and university administrators and faculty must work across institutions to efficiently seam degree plans that offer smooth transitions across institutions and include financial aid to offset rising tuition costs in postsecondary education (Nourie & Lee, 2006). In teacher career pathway programs, many colleges and universities offer scholarships, tuition discounts, case management, and academic support to support the retention and success of high-performing, underrepresented, and first-generation students who seek to become teachers.

LINKING TEACHER QUALITY WITH WORKFORCE DEVELOPMENT

In the 21st century, the issues of teacher quality, capacity, and licensure must be considered in reforming and redesigning teacher preparation to address the challenges of a declining educational system in America. The issue of teacher quality is paramount in relation to preparing a world-class, globally competitive workforce. Teachers are the link between academic achievement and a strong workforce. If the supply of teachers is underprepared or if there are not enough teachers in a particular academic discipline, this link becomes the weakest one in a chain of interdependent processes necessary to yield a strong workforce that is both competitive and attractive globally. In essence, the nature of teacher preparation is closely linked to economic and workforce development, as the supply and demand in workforce development require a high-quality teacher workforce, one that can prepare highly skilled graduates from secondary and postsecondary educational institutions.

In addition, within the global economy of the 21st century, predictions in workforce trends linked to the supply of teachers in high-demand fields are critical (Harkness, Johnson, Hensley, & Stallworth, 2011). In science, technology, engineering, and mathematics (STEM) fields, persistent shortages of qualified teachers are attributed to an insufficient student enrollment in career fields such health care and technology, where job growth is strongest. Similarly, difficulty in recruiting students to major in a STEM field in college and seek employment in STEM occupations is a factor in perpetuating the critical teaching shortage of STEM teachers (Ingersoll & Perda, 2010).

Thus, in building teacher quality and capacity in the 21st century, numerous questions arise: What does the future portend for determining the supply and demand for teachers the 21st century? What kinds of teachers will be needed? Where will the jobs be? To understand teacher supply and teacher workforce projections in the 21st century, current growth in the teacher workforce and projections for future workforce growth offer an important context.

Trends in Teacher Employment

According to the National Center for Education Statistics (NCES; 2010), the teacher workforce—defined as full-time teachers who are employed in preK–12 classrooms in public and private schools—increased 8% overall, with 3.6 million teachers employed in public and private classrooms in 2007–2008. Although earlier projections forecasted an imminent teacher shortage based on projections of teacher turnover, teacher retirement, and student growth, in reality the growth of teachers from 1999 to 2008 increased faster than did student enrollment (Cochran-Smith, 2004; NCES, 2003; Woullard & Smith, 2004). Projections of significant shortages based on higher-than-usual numbers of teachers retiring—the aging baby boomers in the teacher workforce—and teacher attrition based on low salaries and other factors fell short of the predicted growth needed for teachers in the 21st century (NCES, 2010).

According to the *Digest of Education Statistics* (NCES, 2010), the ratio of male:female teachers in 1999–2000 and 2007–2008 remained fairly constant, at about 1:3. Female-gender dominance in the teacher workforce remained consistent, with a predominantly female workforce of 75% during both periods. Likewise, in 1999–2000 and 2007–2008, the age distribution of teachers remained consistent, with less than 20% of employed teachers under the age of 30 and roughly 25% in each of the three 10-year increments from 30 to 60 years. Fewer than 5% of teachers employed in 1999–2000 and 2007–2008 were over 60 (NCES, 2010). These figures reflect fairly persistent and stable patterns in teacher recruitment, preparation, and retention in the profession, with little change in teacher gender and age (Ingersoll & Perda, 2010).

In the 2010 *Digest of Education Statistics* (NCES, 2010), changes in teacher ethnicity over the past decade reflected little change, with no net changes above 2%. According to the NCES, in 1999–2000 approximately 85% of all teachers were White; 7% were Black; nearly 6% were Hispanic; and fewer than 2% were Asian. (Note: Other ethnicities were not counted.) Nearly 10 years later, in 2007–2008, the NCES reported that 83% of teachers were identified as White. During the same period, Blacks declined slightly, to just fewer than 7%; Hispanic teachers rose slightly, reaching 7%; and Asian teachers declined slightly, representing 1.3% of the teacher workforce. Other ethnicities, including Native American and Alaskan Native, represented less than 2% of the total teacher workforce. From 1999 to 2008, the percentage of White, Black, and Asian teachers declined slightly, while Hispanic teachers rose slightly (NCES, 2010).

Thus, over the past decade, the demographics of the teacher workforce remained relatively constant and continued to be characterized as predominantly White and female, while Hispanic, Blacks, and Asians declined or showed minimal gains in the representation in the teacher workforce. This trend confirms what Futrell (1999) forecast at the close of the 20th century: "As the demographic profile of the U.S. student population is changing and becoming increasingly diverse, the demographics of the teaching profession appear to be moving in the opposite direction" (p. 322).

Trends in Secondary and Postsecondary Education

Today, however, patterns of access and representation in postsecondary education are beginning to shift. With steadily decreasing student dropout rates, record increases in high school graduation rates, and increases in postsecondary enrollment and degree attainment among historically underserved students, it appears that many of the educational reforms designed to close the achievement gap are meeting with success (Kazis, 2004). According to the NCES (2010), from 1989 to 2009, the overall high school student dropout rate decreased from 12.6% to 8.1%, as graduation rates reached a record high of 74.7% nationwide in 2007–2008. During the same time, total enrollment growth in postsecondary education grew 38%, with 14% gains within the traditional college population, defined as students who matriculate to college following high school.

In terms of postsecondary degree attainment, the number of associate degrees earned rose 41%, and bachelor degrees 33%, from 1989 to 2009 (NCES, 2010). Dramatic increases were evidenced among historically underrepresented and underserved populations in postsecondary institutions. The largest increase in enrollment growth was among Hispanic students, which rose 85%, followed by increases of 53% among Black students, 52% among Asian / Pacific Islanders, and 45% among Native Americans and Alaskan Natives.

Despite the dramatic shifts in demographic growth within historically underrepresented and underserved groups in postsecondary education, historical patterns of cultural dominance continue to persist in the demographics of degree attainment (Howell & Tuitt, 2003). According to the NCES (2010), from 1989 to 2009, White students accounted for 71% of bachelor degrees attained, while Black students accounted for 10%. Hispanics accounted for 8% overall degree attainment; Asian / Pacific Islanders accounted for 7%; and Native American students represented 1% of the bachelor degrees attained from 1989 to 2009.

Given the lack of change in the gender and ethnicity of employed teachers, the need clearly exists to increase access and representation and foster successful student transfer, retention, and completion spanning secondary and postsecondary educational settings in teacher preparation (American Association of the Colleges of Teacher Education, 2010). If the future workforce of teachers and educational leaders in America will represent the student demographic it serves in the classroom, educational stakeholders—including school districts, colleges and universities, and policymakers—will need to stay informed of local and regional demographic changes in student dropout rates, graduation rates, and postsecondary enrollment and degree attainment in their regions.

In many areas across the United States, student dropout rates do not mirror the current national trends, and graduation rates and enrollment in postsecondary institutions continue to lag among underrepresented students, most notably among Hispanic students, the fastest-growing student population in the nation (Kazis, 2004). If ignored, issues of social justice and equity will be exacerbated by increasing numbers of students who are ill-prepared beyond high school for the workforce and who will be unable to attain employment at a wage-earning level associated with a postsecondary degree.

TEACHER WORKFORCE SUPPLY AND DEMAND

In considering the historical origins of the teacher career pathways and as we progress in the 21st century, the question arises as to how changing demographics in student populations in schools may be addressed through the teacher career pathway model to ensure a high-quality diverse teacher workforce in America. To answer this question and related ones, it is necessary to link the previous data on student trends with data that forecast student population projections and to relate this information to the forecasted supply and demand for teachers in the nation and in state and regional locales.

Teacher Supply in the 21st Century

How many teachers will America need in the coming decades? In some states, teacher workforce growth over the past decade outdistanced student growth, resulting in lower student:teacher ratios and teacher surpluses. Instead of widespread new hiring practices, the effects of the global economic recession that hit during 2008 and the recent massive cuts in education spending due to a trillion-dollar federal deficit in the United States have caused increased numbers of layoffs, enlarged class sizes, and reductions in support personnel to keep school districts and private schools operating in the black instead of the red. In effect, although careers in education were listed as one of the fastest-growing occupations for the first decade of the millennium, other factors—including slower student population growth and a longer-than-expected economic downtown—have altered the cycle of teacher growth that was originally anticipated (American Association of the Colleges of Teacher Education, 2010; Fuller & Nolen, 2010).

A recent national study on teacher turnover and teacher workforce demand offers insight into teacher attrition. According to Ingersoll and Perda (2010), the majority of teachers who leave the profession are in private schools. More mobile, they represent the smallest sector of the teacher workforce, approximately a half million, as compared to 3.1 million teachers employed in public schools. Ingersoll and Perda report that teachers who leave the profession leave primarily for other jobs and better salaries. The authors maintain that teacher workforce development in the coming decade needs to be aligned with the projections for student growth and enrollment and attend to state and regional demographics, with targeted recruitment for preparing qualified teachers to be successful in hard-to-staff schools—including underresourced schools with disproportionate enrollment of students from low socioeconomic backgrounds, inner-city schools in large urban centers, and geographically isolated schools in rural and remote areas with little access.

Concerning the role of social agency of teacher career pathways, questions arise as to how changing demographics in student populations in schools may be addressed through the career pathways model to ensure a high-quality diverse teacher workforce in America. How may teacher career pathway models increase access and representation in America's teacher workforce to mirror the changing student demographics in schools? In the following section, the data on student population growth and projections for future growth are examined in relation to the forecasted supply and demand for teachers in the nation and in state and regional locales.

Readjusting Earlier Forecasts for Teacher Demand

From 1994 to 2007, a snapshot of student enrollment growth in public and private schools revealed a 10% increase overall in elementary and secondary classrooms, with the strongest growth in secondary classrooms. During the next decade, however, student enrollment growth is projected to slow to a 6% increase from 2007 to 2019. The most dramatic slowing of growth is expected to occur in secondary schools, with a projected 1% increase anticipated in Grades 9–12 from 2007 to 2019. Yet, stronger growth is expected in elementary schools, with a projected 9% increase from 2007 to 2019, as compared to the 5% increase that occurred between 1994 and 2007 (NCES, 2010). Within these demographic projections, it is predicted that student enrollment in schools will increase significantly among Hispanic, Asian/Pacific Islander, and Native American/Alaskan Native students and decline slightly among White and African American populations.

These projections are uneven across states, and it is critical that responsive teacher workforce development take into account the differences in growth within individual states and regions within states. Simply stated, preparing more teachers to build teacher capacity is not the solution (Fuller & Nolen, 2010). According to the NCES, it is anticipated that from 2010 to 2019, some states will continue to project strong increases due to population migration, regional growth, and job development. States such as Texas, with higher densities of Hispanics (the fastest-growing population) predict as high as a 15% overall increase in student growth (NCES, 2010). In states where higher levels of growth are predicted, the demand for teachers will be greater in the coming decade. Likewise, in states where increases in student population growth are expected to significantly slow or decline, the need for teachers will decline.

Concluding Thoughts

Like their predecessors in career and technical education, teacher career pathway programs are designed to respond to local, regional, and state workforce needs. Teacher career pathways recognize the impact of student enrollment created by uneven population growth and its effect on the supply and demand for teachers. Teacher career pathways can serve a role of social agency in effecting change in the demographics of the teacher workforce.

With recruitment among diverse student populations in secondary and postsecondary educational settings, teacher career pathway programs are demonstrating the capacity to transform the demographics of the teacher workforce in America. As students in middle-level and secondary schools are offered opportunities to explore teaching as a career, the exposure to the teaching profession is increased beyond traditional recruitment parameters within today's predominantly White enrollment in 4-year colleges and universities. The growth of career pathways with articulated degree plans that conjoin community colleges with 4-year universities offer additional support in the preparation of a highly qualified, diverse cadre of teachers across secondary and postsecondary educational settings (Gederman, 2001; Locklear, Davis, & Covington, 2009).

Originally designed to address critical teacher shortages and staffing problems, the teacher career pathway model offers a 21st-century solution to address persistent problems of teacher quality, student achievement, workforce development, and social justice and equity. Teacher career pathways represent an idea whose time has come. The maturity of the seeds of educational reform sown in the 20th century has resulted in a model of innovative and entrepreneurial strength, a pipeline for the professional development of a diverse cadre of high-quality teachers whose professional identity development and career path spanned the learning experiences from high school to college to the school classroom.

Linking teacher workforce development with trends in student enrollment growth and general economic development will become increasingly important in the 21st century to produce a sufficient number of teachers to meet the staffing needs in elementary and secondary schools and the needs of students enrolled within (American Association of the Colleges of Teacher Education, 2010; Fuller & Nolen, 2010; Ingersoll & Perda, 2010). For example, projected increased demands in occupations within health care and information technology in the 21st century should correlate with increased attention to recruiting and preparing teachers with strong math and science backgrounds who will be able to foster student interest in occupations where workforce growth will occur and enter careers that will sustain economic security in the future (Harkness et al., 2011).

Teacher career pathways are delivering in their promise to close the gaps by sealing the leaks in educational attainment, bridging the divide of affordability, accessibility, and accountability through shared frameworks of secondary and postsecondary curriculum and degree attainment and increasing access to higher education, making a college degree become an achievable reality for students in America today and in the future.

REFERENCES

American Association of the Colleges of Teacher Education. (2010). *An emerging picture of the teacher preparation pipeline.* Retrieved from http://aacte.org/index.php?/Research-Policy/Research-and-Policy-Statements/an-emerging-picture-of-the-teacher-preparation-pipeline.html

Barlow, M. L. (1976). The coming of age, 1926–1976. *American Vocation Journal, 51*(5), 63–88.

Bragg, D. D. (2007). Teacher pipelines: Career pathways extending from high school to community college to university, *Community College Review, 35*(1), 10–29.

Carnegie Forum on Education and the Economy. (1986). *A nation prepared: Teachers for the 21st century.* New York: Carnegie Corporation.

Cochran-Smith, M. (2004). Taking stock in 2004: Teacher education in dangerous times. *Journal of Teacher Education*, *55*(1), 3–7.

Darling-Hammond, L. (2000). *Solving the dilemmas of teacher supply, demand and standards: How we can ensure a competent, caring, and qualified teacher for every child.* New York: National Commission on Teaching and America's Future.

Fuller, E., & Nolen, A. (2010). *An emerging understanding of the Arkansas teacher pipeline.* Retrieved from http://aacte.org/index.php?/Research-Policy/Recent-Reports-on-Educator-Preparation/an-emerging-understandin-of-the-arkansas-teacher-pipeline.html

Futrell, M. H. (1999). The challenge of the 21st century: Developing a highly qualified cadre of teachers to teach our nation's diverse student population. *Journal of Negro Education*, *68*(3), 318–334.

Gederman, R. D. (2001). The role of community colleges in training tomorrow's school teachers. *Community College Review*, *28*(4), 62–77.

Harkness, S. S., Johnson, I. D., Hensley, B., & Stallworth, J. A. (2011). Apprenticeship of immersion: College access for high school students interested in teaching mathematics or science, *School Science and Mathematics*, *111*(1), 11–19.

Hoffman, N., Vargas, J., Venezia, A., & Miller, M. S. (2007). *Minding the gap: Why integrating high school with college makes sense and how to do it.* Cambridge, MA: Harvard Education Press.

Holland, N. E., & Farmer-Hinton, R. L. (2009). Leave no schools behind: The importance of a college-going culture in urban high schools, *The High School Journal*, *92*(3), 24–42.

Holmes Group. (1986). *Tomorrow's teachers: A report of the Holmes Group.* East Lansing, MI: Author.

Holmes Group. (1995). *Tomorrow's schools of education: A report of the Holmes Group.* East Lansing, MI: Author.

Howell, A., & Tuitt, F. (2003). *Race and higher education: Rethinking pedagogy in diverse college classrooms.* Cambridge, MA: Harvard Educational.

Hull, D. (2005). *Career pathways: Education with a purpose.* Waco, TX: Center for Occupational Research and Development.

Illinois Headstart Association. (n.d.). Retrieved July 9, 2011, from http://ilheadstart.org.

Ingersoll, R. M., & Perda, D. (2010). Is the supply of mathematics and science teachers sufficient? *American Educational Research Journal*, *47*(3), 563–594.

Jenlink, K. E., & Eames, S. (2009, April). *Closing the gaps through an urban teacher career pathway targeting underrepresented high-performing youth.* Paper presented at the American Educational Research Association, San Diego, CA.

Kazis, R. (2004). Introduction. In R. Kazis, J. Vargas, & N. Hoffman (Eds.), *Double the numbers: Increasing postsecondary credentials for underrepresented youth.* Cambridge, MA: Harvard Education Press.

Kazis, R., Vargas, J., & Hoffman, N. (2004). *Double the numbers: Increasing postsecondary credentials for under-represented youth.* Cambridge, MA: Harvard Education Press.

Locklear, C. D., Davis, M. L., & Covington, V. E. (2009). Do university centers produce comparable teacher education candidates? *Community College Review*, *36*(3), 239–260.

National Center for Alternative Certification. (2009). *Number of certificates issued to persons entering teaching through alternative routes, by state: 1985–2009.* Retrieved from http://www.teach-now.org/state_stat.cfm

National Center for Education Statistics. (2003). *Condition of education.* Retrieved from http://nces.ed.gov/pubsearch/pubsinfo.asp?pubid=2003067

National Center for Education Statistics. (2010). *Digest of education statistics.* Retrieved from http://nces.ed.gov/programs/digest/2010menu_tables.asp

National Commission on Excellence in Education. (1983). *A nation at risk: The imperative for educational reform.* Washington, DC: Government Printing Office.

No Child Left Behind Act of 2001, Pub. L. 107-110, 115 Stat. 1425 (2002). Retrieved from http://www2.ed.gov/policy/elsec/leg/esea02/index.html

Nourie, B. L., & Lee, R. E. (2006). The Chicago Teacher Education Pipeline (CTEP): Recruiting future teachers who will return to the city. In National Evaluation Systems (Ed.), *Teacher recruitment and retention* (pp. 66–72). Amherst, MA: National Evaluation Systems.

Office of Vocational and Adult Education. (n.d.). *Tech-prep education.* Retrieved from http://www2.ed.gov/programs/techprep/index.html

O'Keefe, M., & Pelz-Paget, N. (2009). Foreword. In Sid W. Richardson Foundation, *Delivering a high quality teacher workforce for Texas: Reconsidering university-based teacher preparation in Texas, renewing commitments, and improving practice in the twenty-first century*. Fort Worth, TX: Sid W. Richardson Foundation. Retrieved from http://www.sidrichardson.org/SRFEducationReport.pdf

Renaissance Group. (1993). *Educating the new American student*. Cedar Falls, IA: University of Northern Iowa Press.

Threeton, M. D. (2007). The Carl D. Perkins Career and Technical Education (CTE) Act of 2006 and the roles and responsibilities of CTE teachers and faculty members. *Journal of Industrial Teacher Education, 44*(1). Retrieved from http://scholar.lib.vt.edu/ejournals/JITE/v44n1/threeton.html

Woullard, R., & Coats, L. T. (2004). The community college role in preparing future teachers: The impact of a mentoring program for preservice teachers. *Community College Journal of Research and Practice, 28*, 609–624.

II

Addressing Teacher Supply and Demand in the 21st Century

> The ability to flexibly and reflexively respond to the changing social, cultural, economic, and political conditions portrays the necessary element of resiliency as these schools and colleges of teacher preparation continually inquiry, adapt, and redefine their identity in relation to the rapidly changing social contexts of the schools they serve.
> —Jenlink (2005, p. 232)

The epigraph, taken from an earlier text on democratic teacher preparation, is intended as an interpretive frame upon entering part II. Highlighted within this part are five distinguished teacher career pathway programs offering innovative models of teacher preparation. The models are built on collaborative and sustainable preK–16 partnerships among school districts and 2- and 4-year colleges and universities—partnerships that work in concert with nonprofit and state education agencies to strategically address persistent issues of building capacity, diversity, and teacher quality.

These five programs are characterized by a common purpose of preparing and retaining a diverse teacher workforce through the recruitment of historically underserved students who have an interest in becoming teachers. The following chapters elaborate on the start-up of partnerships in "grow your own" approaches for teacher preparation across secondary and postsecondary educational systems and the challenges and mechanisms for ensuring their sustainability. Academic advising, case management and academic support, cohort learning, and mentoring are key structural elements presented within the programs, which have shown a positive difference in enhancing student persistence, success, and completion. Finally, variety in face-to-face, blended, and online program delivery systems demonstrate how these programs meet the instructional challenges of preparing teachers across multiple institutions and in geographically diverse locales through the use of technology, resource sharing, and management.

Modeled after career and technical education and workforce development, teacher career pathways are characterized by carefully articulated curriculum agreements to ensure seamless transition and successful student transfer among secondary and postsecondary educational settings (Bragg, 2007; Locklear, Davis, & Covington, 2009). Unlike postbaccalaureate and other alternative models of educator preparation, teacher career pathways are designed to recruit students in high school or community college who are interested in becoming teachers (Gimbert, Cristol, & Abdou, 2007; Harkness, Johnson, Hensley, & Stallworth, 2011). The five teacher career pathway programs presented here offer models of articulation agreements, program sharing, and successful student transfer within teacher preparation that conjoins high schools, community colleges, and university partners in 2+2 and 2+2+2 teacher career pathways.

Part II focuses on illuminating the diversity of purpose, design, and structure found within teacher career pathway programs. Emerging in response to different local, regional, and state teacher workforce needs, the five teacher career pathway programs featured demonstrate innovation, flexibility, and responsiveness in redesigning educator preparation in partnership with high schools, community colleges, and school districts for the recruitment, preparation, and induction of a stronger, more culturally responsive and resilient teacher workforce.

REFERENCES

Bragg, D. D. (2007). Teacher pipelines: Career pathways extending from high school to community college to university, *Community College Review, 35*(1), 10–29.

Gimbert, B. G., Cristol, D., & Abdou, M. S. (2007). The impact of teacher preparation on student achievement in Algebra in a "hard to staff" urban preK–12 university partnership. *School Effectiveness and Improvement, 18*(3), 245–272.

Harkness, S. S., Johnson, I. D., Hensley, B., & Stallworth, J. A. (2011). Apprenticeship of immersion: College access for high school students interested in teaching mathematics or science. *School Science and Mathematics, 111*(1), 11–19.

Jenlink, K. E. (2005). Reflective and aesthetic inquiry: Seeing the whole. In P. M. Jenlink & K. E. Jenlink (Eds.), *Portraits of teacher preparation: Learning to teach in a changing America* (pp. 221–233). Lanham, MD: Rowman & Littlefield Education.

Locklear, C. D., Davis, M. L., & Covington, V. E. (2009). Do university centers produce comparable teacher education candidates? *Community College Review, 36*(3), 239–260.

Chapter Two

Urban Teacher Enhancement Program: A Promising Career Pathway Model for the Preparation of Teachers in Urban Schools

Deborah Voltz

Teaching in urban schools is both challenging and rewarding. Often, these high-energy settings provide an opportunity for teachers to work with a range of diverse students and to help shape many young lives. The rewards of urban teaching, while not emphasized in the professional literature, are apparent in the careers of the many teachers who do choose to teach in these environments. According to a study of persevering urban teachers, commitment to their students and a sense of satisfaction derived from their work were key factors that contributed to the longevity of their teaching careers (Stanford, 2001). Likewise, factors such as "ability to shape the future" (Nieto, 2003, p. 18), "importance of personal relationships with their students" (Costigan, 2005, p. 138), and "seeing student progress" (Voltz, 2000, p. 47) have been found to contribute to the desire of urban teachers to remain in urban teaching.

Despite these opportunities inherent in urban teaching, high-poverty urban schools are often challenged in recruiting and retaining an adequate supply of highly qualified teachers (Burstein, Czech, Kretschmer, Lombardi, & Smith, 2009; Truscott & Truscott, 2005). Nearly two-thirds of states report that the percentage of core academic classes taught by highly qualified teachers is lower in high-poverty schools than in low-poverty schools (U.S. Department of Education, 2007b). For example, in a comprehensive study of teacher employment patterns in the state of New York, Lankford, Loeb, and Wyckoff (2002) found that "nonwhite, poor, and low performing students, particularly those in urban areas, attend schools with less qualified teachers" (p. 54). These factors underscore the need for recruitment and retention of high-quality teachers for urban schools.

Issues of quantity, however, are not the only concern with respect to the teaching force in high-poverty urban schools. Evidence has suggested that new teachers in high-need urban schools often feel underprepared to teach the diverse range of students with whom they work. For example, a survey of national board–certified teachers indicated that participating teachers felt that "many teachers enter the classroom unprepared to work with high-needs students . . . [and] may not have the knowledge of the community and of the culturally relevant pedagogy that will enable them to teach effectively" (Berry, 2008, p. 768). Likewise, in a comparative observational study of new and experienced teachers in urban and suburban settings, Everhart and Vaugh (2005) concluded that "student teachers are better prepared in a way to teach more comfortably in suburban settings" (p. 228).

The academic underachievement that often is evident in urban schools reflects some of these staffing issues. For example, in the Trial Urban District Assessment Results of the National Assessment of Educational Progress, approximately 90% of the urban districts scored below the national average (U.S. Department of Education, 2007a). On the issue of closing such achievement gaps, Miller, Duffy, Rohr, Gasparello, and Mercier stated,

> Attempts to close the achievement gap for low-income students have often met with limited success. Maybe that's because such efforts have ignored another kind of gap—the gap between the skills that teachers must have to provide high-quality instruction [for students in high-poverty schools] and the preparation that teachers actually receive before they enter the profession. (p. 62)

The Urban Teacher Enhancement Program (UTEP) at the University of Alabama at Birmingham (UAB; 2008) was designed to address the needs in urban educator recruitment and retention. Through federal and local sources, it provides tuition support to individuals at the graduate and undergraduate levels who are interested in teaching careers in urban education. Its goal is to recruit and prepare teachers for high-poverty urban schools who have the knowledge, skills, and dispositions to promote high student achievement and who are committed to remaining in these schools.

UTEP includes a number of critical program elements that support responsive teacher education—specialized recruitment and screening strategies, enhanced program content and delivery mechanisms, and a network of candidate support—each of which is collaboratively planned and implemented by teams of educators from UAB and local high-poverty urban school districts.

This chapter describes how these program elements are applied in the preparation and support of teachers for high-poverty urban schools. Specific strategies are provided as used in the recruitment and selection of candidates, as well as in the design and implementation of the preparation program and induction supports. Outcomes related to each program element are also shared. The following section begins the discussion with an overview of recruitment strategies used in the program.

RECRUITMENT STRATEGIES

The recruitment of an academically strong and diverse pool of applicants was seen as critical to the success of UTEP. While approximately 44% of students in public schools are students of color, teachers of color represent only 17% of the teaching force (U.S. Department of Education, 2008). According to the National Collaborative on Diversity in the Teaching Force (2004), teachers of color "serve as cultural brokers, able not only to help students navigate their school environment and culture, but also to increase the involvement of other teachers and their students' parents" (p. 6). However, an oft challenge is the recruitment and retention of significant numbers of candidates of color in teacher education programs at predominately White institutions of higher education (Villegas & Davis, 2007). Given this, UTEP staff employ a variety of strategies to ensure a strong, diverse pool of applicants. These strategies are briefly outlined as follows.

Networking With a Historically Black College and a Community College

The practice of working in partnership with other institutions of higher education, such as historically Black colleges and universities and community colleges, can boost the number of individuals of color in the applicant pool (Flores, Clark, Clayes, & Villarreal, 2007; Landis, Ferguson, Carballal, Kuhlman, & Squires, 2007; Villegas & Davis, 2007). Additionally, this strategy provides access to a potential pool of applicants who have already completed some basic coursework. In the case of individuals recruited from historically Black colleges and universities, many will already have completed undergraduate degrees in nonteaching fields and are excellent candidates for graduate teacher education programs. According to Villegas and Davis (2007), "people of color who already hold bachelor's degrees in fields other than education comprise another important pool from which to draw new teachers" (p. 143).

UTEP staff network with a local community college and a local historically Black college through staff contacts at each institution who distribute program information to potential applicants and arrange information sessions on their campuses. During the information sessions, UTEP staff present content about the program and share application materials. These information sessions target seniors in noneducation fields at the local historically Black college and individuals near completion of their 2-year program at the local community college. UTEP faculty liaisons then follow up with these information sessions by contacting any individuals who attended and expressed an interest in participating in UTEP. The purpose of these faculty contacts is to provide personal, individualized outreach to potential applicants, answer any questions they may have, and assist them in navigating the process of applying to the desired teacher education program at UAB.

Networking With District and Community Partners

Collaborating with district and community partners has been found to be essential in the recruitment of diverse, high-quality candidates for urban teacher education programs (Ayalon, 2004; Nunez & Fernandez, 2006). According to Burbank and colleagues (2005), "one mechanism for improving teacher recruitment and preparation practices for urban schools is through the creation of venues where multiple stakeholders collaborate" (pp. 54–55). Additionally, evidence suggests that recruiting candidates from within the district (i.e., paraprofessionals, substitute teachers) can lead to enhanced retention rates once these individuals begin teaching (Lau, Dandy, & Hoffman, 2007; Villegas & Davis, 2007).

UTEP staff integrate this strategy by working with district administrators in advertising and implementing informational sessions about the program that are held at the district professional development facility. Information regarding these sessions is sent to district principals who distribute it to any teachers who may not be fully certified, as well as to promising paraprofessionals and substitute teachers working in the school. District central office staff, particularly those in the human resources office, also disseminate program information and encourage promising individuals to attend informational sessions about the program.

In addition to hosting informational sessions as separate events, UTEP staff work as a partner with other district-sponsored events, such as district teacher recruitment fairs, as well as more social events, such as the annual picnic for paraprofessionals and substitute teachers. At such events, UTEP staff have the opportunity to distribute information about the program and interact with potential candidates.

In addition to working with district partners, UTEP staff collaborate with other entities in the education community in the recruitment of potential candidates. For example, UTEP works with the local chapter of Phi Delta Kappa in the dissemination of program information and the recruitment of scholars into the program. Likewise, beyond the education community, UTEP reaches out to local churches for the dissemination of program information. Efforts such as these allow the program to extend its reach into the community to recruit a diverse pool of candidates.

Electronic Dissemination of Program Information

To supplement the face-to-face strategies and to reach out beyond the local community, UTEP staff use social networks through a variety of means to disseminate program information electronically. For example, a UTEP video was developed and is posted on YouTube (http://www.youtube.com/watch?v=l_5FecCMkvY). A website maintained by the UAB School of Education also features the program (http://www.uab.edu/cue/). Additionally, program information is disseminated biannually through UAB's electronic newsletter, which is circulated to the university community both locally and nationally (http://www.vimeo.com/12071576). These strategies allow UTEP staff to reach out to a national audience, as well as to raise the visibility of the program locally.

Recruitment Outcomes

Through its recruitment efforts, UTEP is able to attract a diverse group of candidates, with over 50% of these individuals being individuals of color, whereas the general population of teacher education students within UAB is less than 25% individuals of color. On the application form, individuals are asked how they found out about the program. Figure 2.1 displays their responses.

As is shown, the majority (over 70%) of applicants indicated that they found out about the program through "word of mouth" (Voltz, 2010). Brief follow-up interviews with these applicants revealed that they often found out about the program through conversations with individuals such as school district personnel (i.e., teachers, principals, central office administrators), UAB personnel (i.e., faculty members, departmental chairpersons, staff from the student services office), and other participants already in the program.

Based on this feedback, it appears that strategies that involve human-to-human interaction have the greatest impact in terms of influencing individuals to submit applications. For example, more applicants indicated that they found out about the program by talking with UAB personnel, school district personnel, or others already in the program—in comparison to those

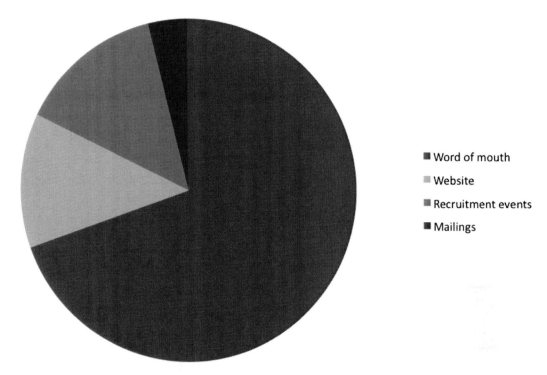

Figure 2.1.   Recruitment Strategies

who indicated that they found out about the program via the website or electronic mailings. One factor that may influence this tendency is that those human-to-human interactions probably often took advantage of preexisting relationships, in that people whom the applicants knew and trusted were encouraging them to participate in the program.

This feedback does not suggest, however, that other strategies should be abandoned. It is very likely that it is through these other strategies that the direct contacts (i.e., district personnel, UAB personnel) were made aware of the program and thus were in a position to pass along the information to others and suggest that they apply. What the feedback does suggest is that strategies such as informational sessions, electronic newsletters, websites, and YouTube videos alone may not be as effective as strategies that take advantage of human-to-human contact and preexisting relationships. This information reinforces the importance of partnering with local school districts and other community agencies for the strategic and targeted recruitment of teachers for urban schools.

SELECTION STRATEGIES

The recruitment of a strong and diverse pool of applicants is an important initial step in identifying program candidates. Once the applicant pool has been developed, the selection process can commence. The importance of the selection process in identifying appropriate candidates for urban teaching has been widely noted. A number of candidate characteristics have been associated with successful urban teaching, such as strong language skills, strong conceptualization skills, strong content knowledge, and facilitating personal characteristics (Caskey, Peterson, & Temple, 2001; Gimbert & Chesley, 2009; Haberman, 2005; Haberman & Post, 1998). The following discussion highlights selection criteria for traditional teacher education programs at UAB, as well as the UTEP-specific strategies used in the selection of candidates. Traditional selection criteria were developed by program faculty across the UAB School of Education; UTEP strategies were developed by faculty associated with the UTEP program.

Selection Criteria

Applicants to the UTEP program are initially screened on the basis of traditional factors, such as grade point average, entrance examination scores, and completion of prerequisite coursework. Graduate candidates are required to have a minimum undergraduate grade point average of 2.5, score at least 388 on the Millers Analogy Test (MAT) or 850 on the Graduate Record Exam (GRE), and have the equivalent of an undergraduate major in the content area in which the individual desires to teach (for secondary applicants) or a minimum of 12 semester hours of credit in each of four core areas—language arts, math, science, and social studies (for elementary and special education applicants). Undergraduate candidates are required to complete specific preteacher education program coursework, have a grade point average of at least 2.5, and complete a minimum of 18 semester hours of content-specific coursework (for secondary applicants) or at minimum of 12 semester hours of credit in each of four core areas—language arts, math, science, and social studies (for elementary and special education applicants). Prior to student teaching, both graduate and undergraduate candidates must obtain the benchmark score on the Praxis II.

It is recognized that a number of traditional requirements (i.e., Praxis, MAT, GRE) have not been found to be strongly correlated with future teaching success in urban schools (Caskey et al., 2001). In fact, such requirements have been noted by many as potential barriers to the recruitment of diverse candidates into teacher education (Bennett et al., 2006; Education Commission of the States, 2003; Strosnider & Blanchett, 2003). Nevertheless, these requirements prevail as admission criteria within UAB, and some are required at the state level; hence, these criteria are required for UTEP candidates.

UTEP-Specific Selection Criteria

Based on the work of authors such as Gimbert and Chesley (2009) and Haberman (2005), criteria critical to successful urban teaching were identified and integrated into the process of selecting UTEP candidates, along with the traditional elements mentioned so far. The factors identified as critical to successful urban teaching include the following:

- *Persistence/commitment/dedication:* the propensity to work with children who present learning and behavioral problems on a daily basis, without giving up on them for the full academic year
- *Organization and planning:* the ability to manage complex classrooms

- *The valuing of student learning:* the degree to which the teacher reflects a willingness to make student learning his or her highest priority
- *Theory to practice/individualized perception:* the ability to connect with and teach students of all backgrounds and levels
- *Ability to survive in a bureaucracy:* the ability to function successfully as a teacher in a large, depersonalized organization
- *Attribution for success:* factors used to determine teacher and student success
- *Fallibility:* how the individual deals with his or her own mistakes

These factors are assessed using (a) letters of recommendation submitted by applicants, (b) a brief written statement submitted by applicants, and (c) in-person interviews. Application materials are reviewed, and interviews are conducted by a selection team consisting of district and university partners.

Interviewing has been found to be a helpful strategy in selecting those who show promise as educators (Clement, 2009; Gimbert & Chesley, 2009; Harrison, McAffee, Smithey, & Weiner, 2006). It provides a means by which interviewers can assess candidate dispositions as well as candidate knowledge and skill levels. Gimbert and Chesley (2009) found candidate interview performance to be correlated with subsequent classroom performance. Given the benefits of interviewing, this strategy is incorporated into the selection of UTEP candidates. Interview questions include the following:

1. Why are you interested in becoming an urban teacher?
2. Describe your previous experiences working with diverse populations in urban settings.
3. What experiences have you had in working with parents and families of urban students?
4. Can you think of a time you faced a difficult challenge? What strategies did you use to overcome this situation?
5. What are your hopes for teaching in an urban setting? What are your fears for teaching in an urban setting?
6. What do you think are characteristics of an effective urban teacher? Which of these characteristics do you think you possess? Which traits do you hope to improve on?
7. Has anyone every pointed out any weaknesses in your academic or professional skills? How did you respond? Provide specific examples.

Selection teams use the rating scale shown in Appendix 2.A to rate interview responses and other application materials. Each team member independently rates applicants using the rating scale shown. Applicants must receive a minimum mean rating of at least 2.25 from each rater on the team.

Admissions

Approximately half the individuals who apply to UTEP are accepted into the program. The majority of these individuals, graduate and undergraduate, have had significant life experiences working with diverse populations, often in school settings. Given the recruitment strategies described so far, this profile is expected.

In terms of general areas of relative strength, successful applicants tended to score higher on items toward the bottom of the scale (experience in multicultural settings, interest/enthusiasm/motivation, perseverance/self-efficacy, and optimism/expectations) (see Appendix 2.B). Preliminary evidence also suggests that individuals who score highest on these items are more likely to begin teaching in high-poverty urban schools and to remain in such schools for 3 or more years (Voltz, 2010).

The majority (approximately 55%) of individuals admitted to the program are graduate career changers, having been employed in nonteaching areas for more than 3 years prior to applying to the program. Many are recent college graduates (approximately 25%), having completed their undergraduate degrees within 3 years of their application to the program. Some are undergraduates (approximately 15%); only a few are paraprofessionals (approximately 5%). Thus far, UTEP has not been as successful as desired in terms of identifying paraprofessionals who meet admissions requirements in terms of MAT or GRE scores. Although the program does offer support such as tutoring and study guides for admissions exams, this support has been minimally effective for paraprofessionals as a group. Once admitted, UTEP candidates are immersed in the program, described as follows.

CANDIDATE PREPARATION

There is significant evidence to suggest that efforts to prepare teachers specifically for urban schools prove beneficial (Andrews, Miller, Evans, & Smith, 2003; Education Commission of the States, 2003; Nelson, 2004; Obidah & Howard, 2005). Many teacher education programs designed for this purpose include a variety of modifications in content, delivery format, fieldwork, and candidate evaluation procedures. Specific elements of UTEP that are aimed toward success in urban schools are discussed as follows.

Program Content: Urban Teaching Competencies

One of the signature components of UTEP is the framework that undergirds researched-based urban teaching competencies (listed in Appendix 2.C). Although portions of the UTEP competencies have been adopted by other teacher education programs, the UTEP competencies were developed by UTEP faculty at UAB in 2004. They are grounded in the research base in urban teaching and have undergone a two-step national validation process involving expert panel review and practitioner interviews (Voltz, Collins, Patterson, & Sims, 2008). These urban teaching competencies are organized in four strands: sociocultural competence, affirming attitude, collaborative skills, and pedagogy for diversity.

Strand 1: Sociocultural competence. The sociocultural competence strand focuses on helping candidates better understand the students and families with whom they will work and the communities in which they will teach. According to Ming and Dukes (2006), it "entails mastering complex awareness and sensitivities, various bodies of knowledge, and a set of skills that, taken together, underline effective cross-cultural teaching" (pp. 42–43). The importance of developing sociocultural competence was underscored in a case study of an urban high school conducted by Patterson, Hale, and Stessman (2007), which illustrated how cultural contradictions contributed to the high school's dropout rate. Similarly, Zenkov, Harmon, Lier, and Tompkins (2009) reported findings from a literacy project that illustrated how urban secondary students' achievement can be enhanced by learning more about their out-of-school activities and using these activities as a gateway to literacy.

The need for cultural understanding also was reflected in a focus group study involving 19 teachers from some of Chicago's hardest-to-staff schools (Fleming, Chou, Ransom, Nishimura, & Burke, 2004). When asked about the challenges faced by teachers and the knowledge base required for urban teaching, these teachers reported a need for deep understanding of cultural knowledge. According to Fleming and colleagues (2004), participating teachers

> often acknowledged challenges in working with children whose backgrounds were very different from their own. . . . Teachers suggested the need for course work that breaks down topics related to race and ethnicity into much more specific discussions and experiences to help students better understand the nuances of particular cultures and school communities. (pp. 106–107)

These nuances included such factors as the impact of poverty on the teaching and learning process, as well as the complexities associated with teaching children who have adult responsibilities.

Strand 2: Affirming attitude. The second UTEP competency strand, affirming attitude, focuses on developing the expectations, optimism, caring, and resilience that are needed to foster high student achievement. This strand includes what Corbett, Wilson, and Williams (2005) described as a "no choice but success" attitude that has been associated with successful urban teachers. A number of research studies support the need for urban teachers to maintain an affirming attitude. For example, a case study of four exemplary urban teachers of African American students revealed that a critical element of their success was their belief in their students' ability to achieve (Howard, 2001). Findings indicated that

> although having a connection to and awareness of the cultural context that students bring from home was important, what seemed to be equally important in the development of these teachers' teaching practices was a belief that their students were capable of being academically successful. Whereas teacher expectations have been associated with student academic performance, student's expectations of their own academic success is often a greater predictor of academic achievement. . . . The teachers in this study believed that it was important to convince their students that they possessed the potential to make a difference in their academic development. (p. 198)

The level of trust that teachers have for their students also has been shown to be an important aspect of developing affirming attitudes. In a study involving 452 urban teachers and 2,536 students in 47 schools, Goddard, Tschannen-Moran, and Hoy (2001) found that "trust was a significant positive predictor of differences among schools in student achievement" (p. 3). Participating teachers were surveyed and asked to indicate the extent to which they agreed with statements such as "Students in this school are reliable," "Teachers in this school trust their students," and "Teachers here believe students are competent learners." The academic achievement of their students was measured by the Metropolitan Achievement Test. Hierarchical linear modeling was used to model teacher trust as a feature varying within and among schools. Results indicated that while the socioeconomic level of the school was shown to be related to the level of teacher trust, once school means were adjusted for socioeconomic status, trust was a significant predictor of differences among schools with respect to achievement. According to the authors, "trust seems to foster a context that supports student achievement, even in the face of poverty" (p. 14).

Strand 3: Collaborative skills. The third strand of UTEP competencies, collaborative skills, focuses on strategies for building effective relationships with the variety of persons with whom urban teachers must work to be effective, including those within schools (e.g., administrators, counselors, other teachers) as well as those external to schools (e.g., parents, social service agencies). For example, Brown (2002) conducted an ethnographic study of an inclusive urban elementary classroom identified as being exemplary by teachers, administrators, parents, and former students. Based on data collected from observations, interviews, and focus groups, several defining elements of classroom practice were noted. Among these elements, teacher–student–parent interaction was shown to be critical. Likewise, in a case study of an urban middle school, Kams (2006) found "collegial planning for students and collaboration of departments contribute to an improved classroom climate, overall school culture and the instructional delivery of all subjects" (p. 22).

Collaborative skills also have been associated with new teacher well-being. Ng and Thomas (2007) examined the practice of new teachers in urban middle and high school settings and found that teachers' ability to "initiate supportive relationships with their colleagues" (p. 16) was one factor that contributed to early success. However, Clark and Holmes (2006) found that such collaboration may be more complex in urban settings. They studied 12 first-year urban middle and high school teachers, using a phenomenological in-depth interview model. Findings indicated that these teachers identified the bureaucratic structure of urban schools and districts as a deterrent to developing ideal collaborative relationships with fellow teachers and administrators. Large school size also was noted as a contributing factor, which these new teachers felt led to a lack of staff collegiality and a sense of isolation for those who were new teachers. These findings underscore the importance of collegial collaboration and the associated challenges that beginning urban teachers must be prepared to address.

Home–school collaboration is another critical area that urban teachers need to be prepared to address. Family involvement has been linked to enhanced student learning outcomes (Fantuzzo, McWayne, Perry, & Childs, 2004; Jeynes, 2005; Musti-Rao & Cartledge, 2004). For example, in a study of 82 urban schools, Sheldon (2003) found that "the degree to which schools were working to overcome challenges to family and community involvement predicted higher percentages of students scoring at or above satisfactory on state achievement tests" (p. 149). However, despite the importance of home–school collaboration, this is an often-cited challenge in urban teaching (Fantuzzo et al., 2004; Lightfoot, 2004), thus emphasizing the importance of developing deeper teacher understanding and competence in this area.

Strand 4: Pedagogy for diversity. The fourth strand, pedagogy for diversity, focuses on strategies for accelerating diverse student achievement, including culturally and linguistically diverse learners as well as students with disabilities. Differentiated instruction and culturally responsive instruction are key elements of this strand. According to Rogers (2008), "a good education . . . is centered upon the interweaving of new understanding and previous experiences" (p. 46). It is widely recognized that learning is a culturally mediated process (McMinn, 2001; Pewewardy, 2002; Richards, Brown, & Forde, 2007; Risko & Walker-Dalhouse, 2007). As stated by Mestre (2009), "as such, cultural adaptations are necessary with diverse learners because students acquire and display knowledge in different ways" (p. 10).

Research in the field supports these ideas. For example, in a large study involving high-poverty urban students in middle schools and high schools, Langer (2001) found that the most successful teachers were able to use a range of instructional strategies that connected learnings and promoted student interaction as a means of developing in-depth understandings. Likewise, in a study involving 251 sixth-grade students, Sternberg (2006) found that those who were taught math via content infused into instruction that reflected the students' culture performed better on math assessments than did those who were taught through a conventional textbook approach. In a similar vein, through a qualitative study, Brooks (2006) found that African American students' reading comprehension improved with the use of cultural knowledge congruent with their own experiences. These findings suggest a need for educators to adapt their pedagogy and teaching strategies from a referent of cultural understanding of their students' culture.

The competencies in the four strands are interwoven throughout UTEP coursework, through the use of course readings, class discussions, videos of exemplary classroom practices, simulations, and case analyses. The following discussion provides an overview of the methods used in delivering program content.

Program and Course Delivery

UTEP scholars complete the program through a modified cohort structure and are required to take four core teacher education courses with their cohort groups. These courses, including Curriculum Methods and Instruction, Classroom Management, and Assessment, are required in the various teacher education programs. This modified cohort structure offers some of the benefits of cohort groups (e.g., building community among students) but reduces the liabilities associated with cohort-based delivery of instruction (e.g., lack of flexibility in scheduling) by allowing some program courses to be taken independent of the cohort structure (Ilmer, Elliott, Snyder, Nahan, & Colombo, 2005; Ross, Stafford, Church-Pupke, & Bondy, 2006).

In delivering these core courses, teams of university faculty and exemplary practitioners from the participating districts coteach the content. Often, these courses are taught on-site at participating schools. Coteaching roles involve collaboratively planning and delivering content, with university and district coteachers present during each class session. Coteachers also work together in assessing student learning outcomes. This collaborative teaching feature provides for the direct involvement of successful educators who are currently practicing in urban schools. Such involvement has been shown to be helpful in providing structured opportunities for aspiring teachers to learn from master teachers in a low-risk setting (Berry et al., 2008; Foster, Lewis, & Onafowora, 2005).

In two of the four core courses, Classroom Management and Assessment, parallel coursework in general and special education has been merged. For example, the Classroom Management course designed for special education majors was merged with the Classroom Management course designed for general education majors, thus producing an integrated Classroom

Management course that better prepared general and special education majors for teaching in inclusive classrooms. The Assessment course was similarly merged. To adequately represent the content in the general and special education versions of the courses, the teaching team for both these courses includes three individuals—a university faculty member from general education, a university faculty member from special education, and an exemplary urban practitioner with expertise in the content being taught.

Through these merged courses, teacher candidates have the opportunity to see collaboration modeled in the coteaching approach used by general and special education teacher educators. Candidates have the opportunity to see teacher educators "practice what they preach." Candidates in general and special education also have the opportunity to work with each other through collaborative assignments. For example, general and special education candidates get to work together as interdisciplinary teams in examining assessment results in case examples during in-class activities. Likewise, these candidates have the opportunity to work together in problem-solving scenarios involving classroom management challenges in inclusive settings. These kinds of activities give candidates practice in the kinds of collaborative roles that will be required of them in inclusive classrooms.

Candidate Preparation Outcomes

Candidate mastery of UTEP competencies is assessed throughout the program by course assignments and performance in the field. Case-based exams, problem-solving scenarios, and other application activities are used to evaluate candidate competency mastery. For example, the following item is a sample taken from the take-home final examination for the Introduction to Special Education course:

> It is the spring of your first year of teaching. You are teaching in a high-poverty school with a high teacher turn-over rate. There are four special education teachers in your school; three of whom are in their first year of teaching. Your principal has announced that the school will move to a more inclusive model of service delivery for students with disabilities next school year. Your principal has asked you to serve on a planning committee with several other teachers charged with helping the school transition smoothly into this new practice. In working with your committee members, what new skills would you suggest that teachers may need to acquire? What kinds of attitudes need to be encouraged in order to facilitate the success of collaborative teaching approaches? What kinds of things can be done to support teachers in developing these skills and attitudes? What would you propose that your committee seek from the principal in support of the move to implement inclusion? Provide a rationale for your responses. Cite at least one reference from the reference list to support your response.

This sample item is one of those designed to assess some of the competencies listed in Appendix 2.C under the collaborative skills strand. In determining the extent to which each candidate has met each competency, responses to items such as this are evaluated using a 4-point rubric: 1 = *not present*, 2 = *emerging*, 3 = *proficient*, and 4 = *distinguished*. Individual rubrics are used for each question to describe the question-specific content required to earn a rating at each of the four levels.

In field settings, an observation protocol instrument grounded in the UTEP competencies is used to evaluate candidate competency mastery. The field observation protocol instrument is divided into six areas of teaching: instructional methods, instructional materials, environment of instruction, content of instruction, educational collaboration, and assessment. The same 4-point rubric that is used in coursework also is used in the field observation protocol. This protocol instrument is designed to reflect instruction that typifies the UTEP competencies. Specific teaching behaviors are identified at each of the four levels for each item within the six areas of teaching. During the culminating student-teaching experience, UTEP candidates are evaluated using this observation protocol for a minimum of six formal observations. Two of these observations are conducted by the cooperating teacher who is hosting the UTEP field candidate. The remaining four are conducted by UTEP faculty.

All program competencies are assessed at least twice during the course of the program, which spans approximately a year and a half for those pursuing the program on a full-time basis. As a requirement of completion, all candidates must demonstrate proficiency (score at least a 3) on each competency at least once, both within the context of coursework and within the context of fieldwork. For the culminating field experience, candidates must receive a rating of at least 3 for each item from each evaluator. In looking at candidate performance across competencies and across coursework and fieldwork settings, several patterns emerge. For example, in the latest UTEP project report (Voltz, 2010), candidates seemed to have found it easier to demonstrate competency mastery in the context of written assignments, such as the sample item shown earlier. However, candidates seemed to struggle more when it came to actually exhibiting these competencies in their classroom performance in field settings. While candidates may have readily achieved a rating of at least 3 on a competency on the first try via a written assignment, these same candidates may have to make several attempts to demonstrate this competency through their performance in the field. Competencies related to infusing multicultural concepts into instruction and differentiating for diverse learning characteristics seem relatively more difficult for candidates to master than do other UTEP competencies, particularly in field settings.

In addition to examining patterns of candidate performance with respect to program competencies, candidates are directly asked to provide feedback regarding their impressions of the program through an exit survey. Using a scale of 1 to 5, ranging from *very poor* to *excellent*, UTEP graduates are asked to rate various elements of the program including UTEP coursework, student teaching, UTEP seminars, and other program supports. The majority of those surveyed indicated all of these items to be *good* or *excellent*, with mean scores ranging from 4.10 to 5.00 (Voltz, 2010).

Open-ended questions are also based on a 5-point scale and used to solicit graduate perceptions with respect to specific components of the program. Some of these comments are included. In terms of program content, one UTEP graduate commented,

> UTEP very thoroughly covered material that was very useful and worked within and even outside the urban setting. I especially enjoyed the workshops in which we were able to share personal stories as well as connect with other professionals who offered insight and suggestions from experience.

Regarding the coteaching component and the semicohort structure of the program, another UTEP graduate commented, "As a UTEP Scholar, I have enjoyed hearing the experiences of veteran and novice teachers. All of this shared peer talk helped deepen my understanding of what it means to become and be a teacher." Likewise, in terms of coteaching, another noted, "Co-teaching proved to be valuable because different teachers have different perspectives on the same issues. Co-teaching in this class worked well because there was good communication between teachers."

Feedback provided by participants is used by program faculty to examine relative strengths and weakness of the program and to refine program content and delivery structures for the enhancement of candidate learning outcomes. The following section describes the kinds of supports that are provided to UTEP participants as they complete program coursework and begin their teaching careers in urban classrooms.

CANDIDATE SUPPORT

To retain and graduate nontraditional teacher education candidates, such as the majority of those in UTEP, teacher education programs must be purposeful in accomplishing this end by implementing specific candidate supports (Haberman, 1999; Kurtts, Cooper, & Boyles, 2007). These supports may include items such as tuition stipends, faculty mentoring, student networks, and social events. According to a case study of a teacher education program populated by nontraditional students, Bernal and Aragon (2004) found that program structures that provided for student networks allowed participants to "find ways to help one another solve or brainstorm solutions to different situations" (p. 208). Likewise, the authors found that faculty mentoring was particularly beneficial to these students because "it may have been a long time since they experienced a college or university setting, and they may feel unsure of their ability to succeed" (p. 209).

During the initial years of teaching, program graduates also need continuing support. First-year teacher turnover rates stand at nearly 30% (Ingersoll & Merrill, 2010). These rates are higher in high-poverty urban schools. Evidence has suggested that up to 50% of new teachers in these settings leave within the first 5 years of teaching. According to Ingersoll and Merrill (2010), "the data show a significant annual shuffling of teachers from poor to wealthier schools, from high-minority to low minority schools, and from urban to suburban schools" (p. 19). Induction supports have been shown to reduce this attrition (Smith & Ingersoll, 2004).

The discussion that follows highlights the support strategies used by UTEP to foster candidate program completion and retention during the initial years of teaching. These strategies include the use of faculty liaisons, the development of a community of learners, and new-teacher mentoring during the initial years of instruction.

Faculty Liaisons

The UTEP network of support begins even before candidates are admitted into the program. Once an individual indicates intent to apply to the program, a UTEP faculty liaison contacts the individual to assist him or her in the application process. This service is particularly helpful since many applicants to the program are unfamiliar with the university application process. Additionally, promising applicants who fail to make requisite scores on admissions examinations (e.g., MAT or GRE) can be assisted by faculty liaisons in connecting to individualized tutoring for these admissions examinations.

Faculty liaisons continue to serve as ombudsmen to candidates after they are admitted to the program, by assisting them in negotiating any challenges, academic or nonacademic, that they may encounter in working toward program completion. Faculty liaisons do not replace traditional program advisors, who primarily advise students regarding coursework to be taken; rather, these liaisons supplement the functions of program advisors. For example, faculty liaisons may assist by helping candidates connect, as needed, to counseling or other support services provided by the university. If additional supports not provided by the university are needed, such as individualized tutoring, faculty liaisons work with UTEP staff to provide these services. Often, though, UTEP candidates rely on a university advocate, an individual who has a personal relationship with them and is invested in their individual success. UTEP faculty liaisons serve in this role.

A Professional Learning Community

According to Slutsky and Allen (2005), developing a community of learners within a teacher education program can facilitate "feeling a sense of belonging, feeling comfortable sharing perspectives, and having a broader understanding of different pedagogies" (p. 278). One aspect of UTEP's approach to this goal is the establishment of the modified cohort course structure. This structure encourages candidates to network with one another and support one another through the completion of the program.

Another aspect of the development of a community of learners is the use of chat rooms and other electronic communication methods embedded in some of the cohort courses. This provides a forum that is always available for the discussion of issues and concerns that emerged within the cohort. UTEP seminars also serve to provide a forum for discussion and contribute to the cohesiveness of the group. These informal, full-day seminars, which are led by district practitioners and UTEP faculty, are typically held one or two Saturdays a semester and are focused on the UTEP competencies.

Aside from strictly academic measures that encourage the development of a community of learners, UTEP also provides social opportunities for candidates to interact with one another in an informal environment. For example, graduation celebrations are held in honor of program graduates. These events, which are hosted by UTEP faculty and district partners, attract students who are currently in the program, as well as those who may have completed the program years earlier. Events such as these further serve to facilitate candidate networking and to strengthen the UTEP family.

Mentoring and Other Induction Support

According to Wood and Stanulis (2009),

a quality induction program enhances teacher learning through a multi-faceted, multi-year system of planned and structured activities that support novice teachers' developmentally-appropriate professional development in their first through third year of teaching. . . . Quality induction provides a bridge between teacher preparation and practice that supports the distinct learning needs of new teachers during their initial years of teaching. (p. 3)

Once UTEP candidates are out in the field teaching in their own classrooms, UTEP staff work with district partners in the induction process. Master teachers from the district serve as mentors to beginning UTEP teachers during their first 3 years of teaching. These mentors are compensated through district and project funds and receive specialized training required by the program with respect to the UTEP competencies. They also are trained in mentoring techniques advanced by the New Teacher Center (Moir, Barlin, Gless, & Miles, 2009). Typically, mentors are master teachers who teach the same subject in the same school where their mentees teach. Mentors spend a minimum of 54 hours per year in working directly with beginning UTEP teachers through activities such as observing and coaching, collaborative planning and problem solving, and sharing resources.

In addition to mentors, beginning UTEP teachers receive other induction services. For example, seminars are held that focus on the developmental needs of beginning teachers. New UTEP teachers also are provided with release time on an as-needed basis to observe master teachers (other than their mentors) who have particular expertise in an area of challenge. For example, if the new UTEP teacher is experiencing difficulty in classroom management, this teacher will have the opportunity to visit the classrooms of several teachers who have exemplary classroom management skills.

Candidate Support Outcomes

Results from the first 5 years of the program indicate that over 90% of the individuals who are accepted into UTEP successfully complete the program. The majority of program graduates (over 70%) teach in high-poverty schools (Voltz, 2010). This outcome is to be expected since teaching in high-needs schools is the focus of the program and about two-thirds of program participants are supported on grants that require them to teach in high-poverty schools upon program completion. Of the individuals teaching in high-poverty schools, more than 80% have remained in such schools for 3 or more years.

When asked to rate the quality of program supports on a scale of 1 to 5, ranging from *very poor* to *excellent*, the majority of UTEP graduates rated these supports as *good* or *excellent*, with mean ratings ranging between 4.10 and 5.00. Graduate write-in comments also supported these ratings. For example, one individual noted, "I like how UTEP gave us continued support. We were able to learn a lot through the seminars and with the help of our liaisons." Likewise, another reported, "I really enjoyed the seminars because it provided me with an opportunity to vent my concerns and voice my victories!"

SOME CHALLENGES

Despite the successes that UTEP has enjoyed, the program faces a number of challenges. These challenges are primarily related to sustainability and operating the program in the context of dwindling resources.

There are a number of threats to UTEP's sustainability. Once of these is related to staffing issues. A core group of faculty and staff within UAB and the partner districts has been the driving force behind UTEP and has worked to conceptualize and implement the program. As these individuals' career paths take them in other directions and, in some cases, as these individuals retire, there will be a continuing need to bring others into leadership roles within the program. Likewise, as district and UAB administrators shift, there is a continuing need to make sure that these changing leaders are supportive of the program. For example, over the last 5 years of the project, the superintendents of all of the partner districts have changed at least once; in our largest partner district, the superintendent has changed three times.

Another threat to UTEP is the challenge of maintaining adequate funding. Since its inception in 2004, UTEP has been supported through a combination of federal, state, and local sources, including private donors. The economic downturn makes the task of institutionalizing UTEP more difficult. While UAB and district partners embrace the project and are committed to its continuation, back-to-back years of proration have reduced financial flexibility within these institutions. For example, it is unclear whether district partners will be able to continue to support mentor stipends. Likewise, private donors have not been able to give as generously as in the past. Given these financial constraints, maintaining program support at current levels will be a challenge.

In addition to UTEP's own funding challenges, the financial challenges of the partner districts have had an impact on our UTEP graduates' ability to maintain continuous employment within these districts. Funding shortfalls in poorer districts with smaller reserve funds, such as those with whom we partner, have prompted teacher layoffs that have adversely affected our recent program graduates who took positions within these districts. Although these districts frequently try to rehire some individuals who have been laid off, these individuals sometimes secure employment elsewhere. Additionally, when districts acquire a reputation of more frequently "pink-slipping" new teachers, prospective teachers are sometimes hesitant to seek employment with these districts. This makes the recruitment process more challenging.

In addressing these challenges, the UTEP team has worked to raise the visibility of the program within the community and has networked with a broad group of program affiliates. For example, UTEP is supported by a diverse advisory board that works to promote the program within the university, the participating districts, and the community at large. This will better position the program to attract new staff as needed and maintain continuity even as UAB and district administrators change. Additionally, UTEP affiliates have explored other funding options to defray some program costs. For example, the Teacher Education Assistance for College and Higher Education program may be helpful in providing tuition support for some UTEP candidates.

CONCLUDING REMARKS

Preparing teachers for high-needs urban schools is an important challenge facing teacher education programs today. By joining forces, university and school district partners can successfully rise to this challenge. UTEP's recruitment and selection strategies allow the program to attract a diverse pool of teacher candidates. These strategies draw heavily on the resources and expertise of the partner districts and tap into the resources of the community. Based on outcomes thus far, it appears that the most powerful asset in this process has been the human-to-human connections that have spawned awareness and interest in the program.

Program content and delivery mechanisms capitalize on the university–school district partnership, in the conceptualization as well as the delivery of the program. Features such as cotaught coursework that allow teams of UAB and school district faculty to work together in planning and teaching courses bring the course content to life for UTEP candidates and situate it in authentic school contexts. The UTEP urban teaching competencies that are infused throughout these courses are grounded in research on successful urban teaching and have been validated by researchers and exemplary practitioners in urban education. Candidate performance with respect to these competencies is tracked in program coursework and field experiences to ensure mastery prior to program completion.

Various supports are integrated throughout the program to enhance candidate success and maximize program completion rates. Program features such as a modified cohort structure, program seminars, and social activities have been included to encourage the kind of student networking that has been found effective in program retention. Faculty mentors also are used to serve as ombudsmen to support and encourage candidates as they matriculate through the program. Finally, as UTEP candidates begin their teaching careers, exemplary teachers within the district serve to mentor them through their first 3 years of teaching.

Evidence thus far has suggested that these program elements have been effective in producing teachers that have the knowledge, skills, and dispositions required to be effective in urban schools and that have a commitment to working in these schools. In the words of one UTEP participant, "the entire program is well developed and organized. I have learned many valuable and life-changing things. Because of this program, I am well able to work in an urban school and fulfill my vision of helping students succeed."

APPENDIX 2.A. APPLICANT RATING SCALE

Please evaluate the applicant in the following areas by marking 3 for above average, 2 average, and 1 below average.

Area to Be Rated	Sources of Information	Rating Scale	Comments
Academic promise	GPA	3 2 1	
Oral communication skills	Interview	3 2 1	
Written communication skills	Application letter	3 2 1	

Professionalism	Interview	3 2 1
	Letters of support	3 2 1
Prior experiences working with children	Interview	3 2 1
	Application letter	3 2 1
Prior experiences in multicultural settings	Interview	3 2 1
	Application letter	3 2 1
	Letters of support	3 2 1
Interest/enthusiasm/motivation	Interview	3 2 1
	Application letter	3 2 1
	Letters of support	3 2 1
Perseverance/self-efficacy: Applicant's belief in his or her ability to work effectively with urban students	Interview	3 2 1
	Application letter	3 2 1
	Letters of support	3 2 1
Optimism/expectations: Applicant's belief in ability of urban students to achieve at high levels	Interview	3 2 1
	Application letter	3 2 1
	Letters of support	3 2 1

General Comments

APPENDIX 2.B. SCORING GUIDE FOR APPLICANT RATING SCALE

	1	2	3
Academic Promise	GPA below 2.75	2.75 – 3.0 GPA	GPA above 3.0
Oral Communication Skills	• Inappropriate volume / rate / articulation / vocabulary • Poor grammar • Disorganized response / does not address question	• Appropriate volume / rate / articulation / vocabulary / grammar / organization • Response addresses question	• Masterful use of spoken language to convey ideas • Response addresses question
Written Communication Skills	• Many mechanical errors • Poor organization • Did not respond to the prompt	• Few mechanical errors • Adequate organization • Responded to the prompt	• Masterful use of written language to convey ideas • Responded to the prompt
Professionalism	• Late • Inappropriately dressed • Inappropriate behaviors / speech • Little evidence of professionalism in letters of support	• Timely / appropriate dress • Some evidence of professionalism in letters of support	• Timely / appropriate dress • Strong evidence of professionalism in letters of support
Prior Experiences Working With Children	• Little or no experiences working with children in any setting	• Some experiences working with children in at least one setting	• Many experiences working with children in multiple settings

Prior Experiences in Multicultural Settings	• Little or no experiences in culturally diverse settings • Sees differences as deficits	• Some experiences in culturally diverse settings	• Many experiences in culturally diverse settings • Sees differences, not deficits
Interest / Enthusiasm / Motivation	• Demonstrates little or no interest in urban teaching	• States interest in urban teaching • Some supporting evidence in prior experiences and other application materials.	• Excited about urban teaching • Much supporting evidence in prior experiences and other application materials.
Perseverance / Self-Efficacy	• Not able to describe any significant challenge that was successfully overcome • No evidence in other application materials	• Able to describe a significant challenge that was successfully overcome • No additional evidence in application materials	• Able to describe a significant challenge that was successfully overcome • Additional evidence in application materials
Optimism / Expectations	• Expresses low expectations for urban students • Holds negative, stereotypical beliefs about urban schools.	• Does not address issue of expectations • Does not express belief in ability to make a difference	• Expresses high expectations for urban students, and a positive view of urban schools • Expresses belief in ability to make a difference

APPENDIX 2.C: COMPETENCIES

Sociocultural Competence

- *SC1:* Understands the influences of culture on learning and behavior, as well as how culture influences teaching.
- *SC2:* Is knowledgeable about the local community in which he or she teaches, and is aware of the educational assets of that community (e.g., schools, parks, speakers on specific topics, neighborhood leaders, social service agencies, students' families).
- *SC3:* Understands that education includes the intellectual, social-emotional, physical, and ethical development of students; and occurs both inside and outside of schools (e.g., neighborhoods, families, and peer groups).
- *SC4:* Recognizes that the context of schooling is complex and reflects historical, political, social, and economic influences; and that teachers must consider these issues in their teaching.

Affirming Attitude

- *AA1:* Exhibits a strong belief in the capacity of urban students to achieve at high levels and communicates this belief to students.
- *AA2:* Demonstrates and engages in systematic and continuous inquiry that promotes teacher reflection, especially in regard to teacher attitudes and beliefs.
- *AA3:* Exhibits resiliency and a sense of self-efficacy with respect to educational challenges, and promotes similar resiliency and self-efficacy in his or her students.
- *AA4:* Exhibits and encourages respect for students' home community, language, and culture.
- *AA5:* Models and demonstrates the ability to teach conflict resolution skills.
- *AA6:* Is a reflective, responsive teacher-leader who recognizes and addresses inequities in education related to aspects of student diversity such as race, class, disability, gender, linguistic difference, and sexual orientation.

Collaborative Skills

- *CS1:* Demonstrates the ability to plan and problem-solve with other education and social service professionals in order to promote student success.
- *CS2:* Engages in collaborative efforts/activities with other teachers that promote mutual respect and high student achievement.
- *CS3:* Demonstrates ability to work effectively with diverse parents and families in order to promote the educational success of students.
- *CS4:* Demonstrates knowledge of effective ways to send and receive information to students in order to foster inquiry, collaboration, and engagement in learning environments.
- *CS5:* Recognizes the importance of being a student advocate and works effectively with others within and outside of school environments.
- *CS6:* Promotes personal and professional resiliency in self and other colleagues.

Pedagogy for Diversity

- *PD1:* Plans and implements a variety of developmentally appropriate and culturally responsive instructional strategies that respond to diverse learning styles.
- *PD2:* Demonstrates competence in universal design, and accommodation/modification strategies for students with special needs and students receiving ELL services.
- *PD3:* Uses classroom management strategies that respect cultural differences and establish a classroom climate that promotes positive social interaction, active engagement in learning, and self-motivation.
- *PD4:* Demonstrates competence in the use of community resources to meet the needs of diverse students.
- *PD5:* Demonstrates competence in alternative assessment strategies that can help identify diverse student strengths as well as ways of learning.
- *PD6:* Demonstrates competence in incorporating students' experiences, cultures, and community resources into instruction.

- *PD7:* Demonstrates competence in his or her teaching field, including the ability to present multiple perspectives in the discussion of subject matter.

REFERENCES

Andrews, L., Miller, N., Evans, S., & Smith, S. D. (2003). An internship model to recruit, train, and retain special educators for culturally diverse urban classrooms: A program description. *Teacher Education and Special Education, 26,* 74–78.

Ayalon, A. (2004). A model for the recruitment and retention of minority students to teaching: Lessons from a school/university partnership. *Teacher Education Quarterly, 31*(3), 7–23.

Bennett, C. I., McWhorter, L. M., & Kuykendall, J. A. (2006). Will I ever teach? Latino and African American students' perspectives on Praxis I. *American Educational Research Journal, 43,* 531–575.

Bernal, C., & Aragon, L. (2004). Critical factors affecting the success of paraprofessionals in the first two years of career ladder projects in Colorado. *Remedial and Special Education, 25,* 205–213.

Berry, B. (2008). Staffing high-needs schools: Insights from the nation's best teachers. *Phi Delta Kappan, 89,* 766–771.

Berry, B., Montgomery, D., Curtis, R., Hernandez, M., Wurtzel, J., & Snyder, J. (2008). *Creating and sustaining urban teacher residencies: A new way to recruit, prepare, and retain effective teachers in high-needs districts.* Carrboro, NC: Center for Teaching Quality.

Brooks, W. (2006). Reading representations of themselves: Urban youth use culture and African American textual features to develop literary understandings. *Reading Research Quarterly, 41,* 372–392.

Brown, E. L. (2002). Mrs. Boyd's fifth-grade inclusive classroom: A study of multicultural teaching strategies. *Urban Education, 37,* 126–141.

Burbank, M. D., Bertagnole, H., Carl, S., Longhurst, T., Powell, K., & Dynak, J. (2005). University–district partnerships and the recruitment of tomorrow's teachers: A grassroots effort for preparing quality educators through a teaching academy. *The Teacher Educator, 41*(1), 54–67.

Burstein, N., Czech, M., Kretschmer, D., Lombardi, J., & Smith, C. (2009). Providing qualified teachers for urban schools: The effectiveness of the accelerated collaborative teacher preparation program in recruiting, preparing, and retaining teachers. *Action in Teacher Education, 31,* 24–36.

Caskey, M. M., Peterson, K. D., & Temple, J. B. (2001). Complex admission selection procedures for a graduate preservice teacher education program. *Teacher Education Quarterly, 28*(4), 7–21.

Clark, S. R., & Holmes, G. (2006). Demystifying urban teaching: New lessons from the field. In J. Kincheloe & K. Hayes (Eds.), *Metropedagogy: Power, justice and the urban classroom* (pp. 195–208). Rotterdam, Netherlands: Sense.

Clement, M. C. (2009). Hiring highly qualified teachers begins with quality interviews. *Phi Delta Kappan, 91*(2), 22–24.

Corbett, D., Wilson, B., & Williams, B. (2005). No choice but success. *Educational Leadership, 62*(6), 8–13.

Costigan, A. T. (2005). Choosing to stay, choosing to leave: New York City teaching fellows after two years. *Teacher Education Quarterly, 32,* 125–142.

Education Commission of the States. (2003). *Eight questions on teacher preparation: What does the research say?* Denver, CO: Author.

Everhart, B., & Vaugh, M. (2005). A comparison of teaching patterns of student teachers and experienced teachers in three distinct settings: Implications for preparing teachers for all settings. *Education, 126,* 221–239.

Fantuzzo, J., McWayne, C., Perry, M. A., & Childs, S. (2004). Multiple dimensions of family involvement and their relations to behavioral and learning competencies for urban, low-income children. *School Psychology Review, 33,* 467–480.

Fleming, J., Chou, V., Ransom, S., Nishimura, M., & Burke, K. (2004). Putting literacy in context: What practicing teachers say about the realities of teaching in urban schools. In D. Lapp, C. Block, E. Cooper, J. Flood, N. Roser, & J. Tinajero (Eds.), *Teaching all the children: Strategies for developing literacy in an urban setting* (pp. 103–121). New York: Guilford Press.

Flores, B. B., Clark, E. R., Clayes, L., & Villarreal, A. (2007). Academy for teacher excellence: Recruiting, preparing, and retaining Latino teachers through learning communities. *Teacher Education Quarterly, 34*(4), 53–69.

Foster, M., Lewis, J., & Onafowora, L. (2005). Grooming great urban teachers. *Educational Leadership, 62*(6), 28–32.

Gimbert, B. G., & Chesley, D. (2009). Predicting teacher success using teacher selection practices and classroom performance assessment. *Journal of School Leadership, 19*(1), 49–80.

Goddard, R. D., Tschannen-Moran, M., & Hoy, W. K. (2001). A multilevel examination of the distribution and effects of teacher trust in students and parents in urban elementary schools. *Elementary School Journal, 102*, 3–17.

Haberman, M. (1999). Increasing the number of high-quality African American teachers in urban schools. *Journal of Instructional Psychology, 26*, 208–212.

Haberman, M. (2005). Selecting "star" teachers for children and youth in urban poverty. In D. Kauchak, P. Eggen, & M. Burbank (Eds.), *Charting a professional course: Issues and controversies in education* (pp. 251–256). Upper Saddle River, NJ: Merrill.

Haberman, M., & Post, L. (1998). Teachers for multicultural schools: The power of selection. *Theory Into Practice, 37*(2), 96–104.

Harrison, J., McAffee, H., Smithey, G., & Weiner, C. (2006). Assessing candidate disposition for admission into teacher education: Can just anyone teach? *Action in Teacher Education, 27*(4), 72–80.

Howard, T. C. (2001). Powerful pedagogy for African American students: A case of four teachers. *Urban Education, 36*, 179–203.

Ilmer, S., Elliott, S., Snyder, J., Nahan, N., & Colombo, M. (2005). Analysis of urban teachers' 1st year experiences in an alternative certification program. *Action in Teacher Education, 27*, 3–14.

Ingersoll, R., & Merrill, L. (2010). Who's teaching our children? *Educational Leadership, 67*(8), 15–20.

Jeynes, W. H. (2005). A meta-analysis of the relation of parental involvement to urban elementary school student academic achievement. *Urban Education, 40*, 237–269.

Kams, M. S. (2006). A new kind of middle school. *Leadership, 35*(5), 20–23.

Kurtts, S. A., Cooper, J. E., & Boyles, C. (2007). Project RESTART: Preparing nontraditional adult teacher education candidates to become special education teachers. *Teacher Education and Special Education, 30*, 233–236.

Landis, M., Ferguson, A., Carballal, A., Kuhlman, W., & Squires, S. (2007). Analyzing an urban university's diversity dilemma. *Teacher Education Quarterly, 34*(4), 121–136.

Langer, J. A. (2001). Beating the odds: Teaching middle and high school students to read and write well. *American Educational Research Journal, 38*, 837–880.

Lankford, H., Loeb, S., & Wyckoff, J. (2002). Teacher sorting and the plight of urban schools: A descriptive analysis. *Educational Evaluation and Policy Analysis, 24*(1), 37–62.

Lau, K. F., Dandy, E. B., & Hoffman, L. (2007). The pathways program: A model for increasing the number of teachers of color. *Teacher Education Quarterly, 34*(4), 27–40.

Lightfoot, D. (2004). "Some parents just don't care": Decoding the meanings of parental involvement in urban schools. *Urban Education, 39*, 91–107.

McMinn, M. P. (2001). Preparing the way for student cognitive development. *Multicultural Education, 9*(1), 13–15.

Mestre, L. (2009). Culturally responsive instruction for teacher-librarians. *Teacher Librarian, 36*(3), 8–12.

Miller, S., Duffy, G. G., Rohr, J., Gasparello, R., & Mercier, S. (2005). Preparing teachers for high-poverty schools. *Educational Leadership, 62*(8), 62–65.

Ming, K., & Dukes, C. (2006). Fostering cultural competence through school-based routines. *Multicultural Education, 14*(1), 42–48.

Moir, E., Barlin, D., Gless, J., & Miles, J. (2009). *New teacher mentoring: Hopes and promises for improving teacher effectiveness*. Cambridge, MA: Harvard Education Press.

Musti-Rao, S., & Cartledge, G. (2004). Making home an advantage in the prevention of reading failure: Strategies for collaborating with parents in urban schools. *Preventing School Failure, 48*(4), 15–21.

National Collaborative on Diversity in the Teaching Force. (2004). *Assessment of diversity in America's teaching force: A call to action*. Washington, DC: Author.

Nelson, C. (2004). Reclaiming teacher preparation for success in high-needs schools. *Education, 124*, 475–480.

Ng, J., & Thomas, K. (2007). Cultivating the cream of the crop: A case study of urban teachers from an alternative teacher education program. *Action in Teacher Education, 29*(1), 3–19.

Nieto, S. (2003). What keeps teachers going? *Educational Leadership, 60*(8), 15–18.

Nunez, M., & Fernandez, M. R. (2006). Collaborative recruitment of diverse teachers for the long haul—TEAMS: Teacher education for the advancement of a multicultural society. *Multicultural Education, 14*(2), 50–56.

Obidah, J. E., & Howard, T. C. (2005). Preparing teachers for "Monday morning" in the urban school classroom: Reflecting on our pedagogies and practices as effective teacher educators. *Journal of Teacher Education, 56*, 248–255.

Patterson, J. A., Hale, D., & Stessman, M. (2007). Cultural contradictions and school leaving: A case study of an urban high school. *High School Journal, 91*(2), 1–15.

Pewewardy, C. (2002). Learning styles of American Indian/Alaska Native students: A review of the literature and implications for practice. *Journal of American Indian Education, 41*(3), 22–56.

Richards, H. V., Brown, A. F., & Forde, T. B. (2007). Addressing diversity in schools: Culturally responsive pedagogy. *Teaching Exceptional Children, 39*(3), 64–68.

Risko, V. J., & Walker-Dalhouse, D. (2007). Tapping students' cultural funds of knowledge to address the achievement gap. *The Reading Teacher, 61*(1), 98–100.

Rogers, C. (2008). Confronting coyote: Culturally responsive pedagogy in an era of standardization. *Democracy and Education, 17*(3), 46–49.

Ross, D. D., Stafford, L., Church-Pupke, P., & Bondy, E. (2006). Practicing collaboration: What we learn from a cohort that functions well. *Teacher Education and Special Education, 29*, 32–43.

Sheldon, S. B. (2003). Linking school–family–community partnerships in urban elementary schools to student achievement on state tests. *The Urban Review, 35*, 149–165.

Slutsky, R., & Allen, A. (2005). A time for change: Implementation of a community of learners model. *The Teacher Educator, 40*, 278–298.

Smith, T. M., & Ingersoll, R. M. (2004). What are the effects of induction and mentoring on beginning teacher turnover? *American Educational Research Journal, 41*, 681–714.

Stanford, B. H. (2001). Reflections of resilient, persevering urban teachers. *Teacher Education Quarterly, 28*(3), 75–87.

Sternberg, R. J. (2006). Recognizing neglected strengths. *Educational Leadership, 64*(1), 8–15.

Strosnider, R., & Blanchett, W. J. (2003). A closer look at assessment and entrance requirements: Implications for recruitment and retention of African American special educators. *Teacher Education and Special Education, 26*, 304–314.

Truscott, D. M., & Truscott, S. (2005). Differing circumstances, shared challenges: Finding common ground between urban and rural schools. *Phi Delta Kappan, 87*, 123–130.

University of Alabama at Birmingham. (2008, October 7). *Urban Teacher Enhancement Program*. Retrieved from http://www.youtube.com/watch?v=l_5FecCMkvY

U.S. Department of Education. (2007a). *The nation's report card reading 2007: Trial urban district assessment results at grades 4 and 8*. Washington, DC: Author.

U.S. Department of Education. (2007b). *State and local implementation of the No Child Left Behind Act*. Washington, DC: Author.

U.S. Department of Education. (2008). *Mini-digest of education statistics 2008*. Washington, DC: Author.

Villegas, A. M., & Davis, D. E. (2007). Approaches to diversifying the teaching force: Attending to issues of recruitment, preparation, and retention. *Teacher Education Quarterly, 34*, 137–147.

Voltz, D. L. (2000). Challenges and choices in urban teaching: The perspectives of general and special educators. *Multiple Voices for Ethnically Diverse Exceptional Learners, 4*(1), 41–53.

Voltz, D. L. (2010). *Urban teacher enhancement program*. Unpublished project report.

Voltz, D. L., Collins, L., Patterson, J., & Sims, M. (2008). Preparing urban educators for the twenty-first century: What the research suggests. In C. J. Craig & L. Deretchin (Eds.), *Teacher education yearbook XVI: Imagining a renaissance in teacher education* (pp. 25–40). Lanham, MD: Rowman & Littlefield Education.

Wood, A. L., & Stanulis, R. N. (2009). Quality teacher induction: "Fourth-wave" (1997–2006) induction programs. *The New Educator, 5*(1), 1–23.

Zenkov, K., Harmon, J., Lier, P., & Tompkins, E. (2009). Through students' eyes: Seeing city youths' perspectives on the social nature of literacy. *Journal of Reading Education, 34*(3), 15–22.

Chapter Three

Infect Your Own: Delaware's ASPIRE— Academic Support Program Inspiring Renaissance Educators

Melva L. Ware

Recruitment is an inadequate objective. In a recent study that sought recommendations for recruiting students of color into teaching, teacher informants rather poignantly redefined the objective. How, they questioned, can students be recruited for careers that require 4 years of college, when so few graduate from high school or graduate with profiles that allow them to pursue 4-year college degrees (Gordon, 2000)? For teacher education degree programs, recruitment of students of color and others who face challenges in preparing for postsecondary degree opportunities must begin as precollegiate academic and enrichment support. Improving the academic performance and increasing the achievement motivation of vulnerable students in middle school and high school are accurately defined as key issues in preparing a more diverse teaching workforce.

The emerging teacher preparation "pipeline" efforts at the University of Delaware are designed to build early awareness and readiness for undergraduate study. The vision for this work includes capturing the attention of cohorts of underrepresented students and working with them and their families from middle school through high school graduation to track course-taking behavior. It also includes providing guidance and tutoring while facilitating access to extra-time acceleration and enrichment activities that highlight career opportunities as well as the social value and personal rewards of teaching. This vision is moderated by available resources, although there is a continuing discussion at the University of Delaware about the value of improving campus diversity of longitudinal process models. Current targeted teacher education recruitment activities have achieved some success in expanding the scope and scale of a program that was created to recruit high school seniors and support their admission to and retention in teacher education degree programs.

HISTORY: INCREASING OPPORTUNITY TO PURSUE TEACHING CAREERS

The Academic Support Program Inspiring Renaissance Educators (ASPIRE) was developed in 1991 with funding from the Pew Charitable Trusts to address the inadequate representation of students of color enrolled in the University of Delaware's teacher education programs. Responding to local school districts' needs for teachers of color to employ in Delaware public schools with increasingly diverse student populations, the program was designed to circumvent some admissions-sorting mechanisms and enroll students of color who expressed a desire to teach and the desire to get a college education. According to program records and the oral history of the program provided by the program's first coordinator, the earliest ASPIRE participants were exclusively low-income, first-generation, ethnic minority college students who were recruited from the Delaware public school population. [1]

Delaware's public school population reflects the demographics of mid-Atlantic suburban communities, with an overall enrollment that is 44.6% African American and Latino (48.5% all ethnic minorities) and 51.5% White. [2] The largest school districts in the state serve a vocal African American urban community in northern Delaware, the city of Wilmington. In 2000, within a resurrected National Urban League framework, the Metropolitan Wilmington Urban League organized an effort to advocate for equity and access in education and other public policy domains. Subsequently, in partnership with the University of Delaware's Louis L. Redding Chair Leland Ware, the Metropolitan Wilmington Urban League supported a broad-based civil rights discussion. During the Louis L. Redding Civil Rights Symposium, researchers documented the disparate schooling outcomes of low-income and minority students and tied these to the issue of inadequately prepared, unresponsive, and culturally different teachers (Scott, 2002; Sims-Peterson & Ware, 2002). For more than two decades, minority teachers in Delaware have constituted only 13% of the teacher workforce (Rys, 1993; Van Dornick, 1999).

In 1991, the first year of ASPIRE, there were 16 minority students enrolled in the College of Education out of 713 students who were pursuing elementary and special education degrees: 2 of the students were Latino, 14 were African American, and there were no males in the group (Rys, 1993). The enrollment in the College of Education's 1991 freshman class included 1 African American student, 2 Latino students, and 196 Caucasian students. By 1993, responding to the explosive growth of the Latino community statewide, ASPIRE's mission expanded to include the recruitment and support of students from all underrepresented demographic groups. With a clear emphasis on supporting African American and Latino students, by 1995 ASPIRE succeeded in increasing the enrollment of students of color in teacher education to 10% of entering freshmen majors. While this increase in enrollment represents growth, it lags behind the 15% enrollment rate for ethnic minority groups at the University of Delaware. [3]

According to data maintained by the Delaware Center for Teacher Education, from 2008 to 2010 the enrollment of ethnic minority students among entering freshmen education majors averaged 12%, and the freshman-through-senior enrollment hovered above 11%. In fall 2010, education students were equally represented among elementary and secondary education majors. [4]

Teacher education accrediting standards require that institutions provide opportunities for all teacher education candidates to interact within a diverse community of peers during their training, and meeting this standard reinforces concerns about ethnic minority enrollment. The University of Delaware's programs are accredited by the National Council for the Accreditation of Teacher Education.

HISTORY, CULTURE, AND ADMISSIONS REQUIREMENTS DEPRESS THE ENROLLMENT OF ETHNIC MINORITY STUDENTS IN TEACHER EDUCATION PROGRAMS AT THE UNIVERSITY OF DELAWARE

Opened in the mid-1700s, the shaping influences of University of Delaware's traditions and cultural features are reflected in the historical record that is accessed from the History link on the university's website (http://www.udel.edu/aboutus/history.html). The third and fourth photographs feature a picture of the all-white-male 1901 football squad and the all-white group of students who were the first to travel abroad in what the university terms its invention of travel-abroad experiences. Despite the fact that the memberships of similar groups today display the range of ethnic diversity that is visible on the campus, many ethnic minority students approach their daily interactions with the apprehension and caution of travelers in a foreign land who are viewed with curiosity by the natives and lack access to insider knowledge of social and academic traditions. The institution's history of exclusion and resistance to desegregation predictably continues to influence the racial climate on campus (Hurtado, 1992; Peterson et al., 1978).

A 2009 report on the status of campus diversity at the University of Delaware was commissioned by the Office of the President. The report found that the top two issues that require campuswide attention are (1) building and nurturing a welcoming campus climate and (2) ensuring equity, inclusion, and representation (Andersen & Debessay, 2009). The report acknowledges a fairly widespread perception of "outsider status" held by ethnic minority, international, and gay and lesbian students. The authors of the report offer "programmatic and symbolic actions" that might signal the institution's intentions to transform the culture (Andersen & Debessay, 2009).

The University of Delaware is classified as a "research university with very high research activity" by the Carnegie Foundation for the Advancement of Teaching. Fewer than 100 academic institutions in the United States have achieved this designation.[5] Efforts are underway to enhance the research profile of the institution to position the University of Delaware among the most productive national institutions.[6] The campus culture is shaped by an academically competitive, suburban, largely White (78.5%) undergraduate student population. African American and American Latino students compose only 12% of the community, and this factor continues to pose interesting challenges to recruitment and retention of students from these population groups. Given the university's rigorous admission requirements, the pool of eligible African American and Latino students is fairly shallow, and the most competitive of these students have many institutional and degree options, representing career pathways that offer better growth opportunities and more lucrative compensation than does teaching (Goldhaber & Hannaway, 2009).

Economists explain that young people, particularly those who are positioned to select from many career options, choose occupations by weighing the return on skill across occupations, essentially determining whether their preparatory cost and effort will result in desired levels of personal satisfaction and financial reward. They also consider whether the conditions and terms of work offer opportunities to structure advancement plans that once executed increase rewards (Goldhaber & Hannaway, 2009). Given such considerations, education is often not an attractive career option among competitive students across the socioeconomic spectrum, from those who are making their way into the middle class on one end to those in the opposite position who are second- or third-generation professionals.

The University of Delaware competes for the attention of the most accomplished ethnic minority high school graduates with the range of prestigious regional and national universities. To improve the attraction of these students to the University of Delaware, the institution is challenged to distinguish itself in ways that matter to selective students and their parents. These include programs with influential faculty as well as visible and highly accomplished alumni. The most competitive students may certainly elect membership in environments that have inherited or consciously shaped perceptions of campus climates that value diversity and where student interactions are more collegial. The University of Delaware has only recently begun to address these issues, and as documented in the 2009 report, much of the effort is symbolic (Andersen & Debessay, 2009).

Affirmative Efforts Confer Outsider Status

ASPIRE was created to serve as an advocacy effort designed to go the extra mile to enroll high-potential students who require support to succeed in the university's curriculum (Rys, 1993). Initially, the program scheduled ASPIRE elementary education majors to selected sections of core courses and provided weekly support to help students work within the program community to develop study skills and coping strategies (Rys, 1993). Students received full tuition scholarships and were required to participate in the supplementary guidance and instructional support activities. By 1998, the program expanded to support a secondary education major and added an undergraduate internship requirement, the student organization, and professional development workshops conducted by the program coordinator (Van Dornick, 1999). While the frequency of interactions and relationships between staff and students affirmed positive attachment of the students to the program, at its inception and through much of its history, the program was largely perceived as an affirmative action effort designed to facilitate the enrollment of underprepared students, a deadly perception that served to foster outsider status for and among ASPIRE members (Rys, 1993).

The education faculty at the University of Delaware includes several nationally recognized scholars who critically examine and question the value of affirmative efforts that increase access for underrepresented groups to higher education enrollment, specifically in rigorous and prestigious programs. One of these faculty members is active in the study and use of "IQ tests to help understand why the differences they measure have practical value in virtually all arenas of social life, but especially education and work."[7] The original ASPIRE program design might also have made participating students an identifiable target for faculty who hold such views and who may resent the work of administrators to give "extra attention" to ethnic minority students by supporting them in identifying ways to earn required credits in specific sections of courses or at other institutions that are judged to provide better opportunities for some students to succeed.

Tensions among faculty and administration exist as selected faculty may feel that these administrators utilize unwarranted power to shape the composition of the student body and even to evaluate the instructional effectiveness of the faculty. The outcome, particularly among elementary education majors, resulted in punitive actions directed at individual students, intended to lower the student's academic standing and cast doubt on the importance of seeking advice from administrators and inevitably increasing perceptions of the climate as hostile.[8] Perceptions of hostility among students spread to the larger community and pose a significant barrier to attracting ethnic minority students into some education majors at the University of Delaware. More perniciously, the unwelcoming climate undermines some students' efficacy perceptions, serving ultimately to reproduce expectations that ethnic minority students are not capable and therefore not entitled to participate (Bennett, Cole, & Thompson, 2000; Powell, 1998; Turner, 1994). Institutional climate and features are empirically linked to student persistence and success (Pascarella et al., 1996; Pascarella, Smart, Ethington, & Nettles, 1987).

Researchers have identified the potential positive effects of minority recruitment and campus support programs on the college access and adjustment of ethnic minority students, but they also caution that such efforts should consciously avoid segregating or placing ethnic minority students at the margins of campus life. While increasing the representation of ethnic minority students is the most sought-after mechanism to support successful integration into campus life, this structural change alone does not substantively improve the campus racial climate. Increasing the number of ethnic minority students without accompanying shifts to "student-centered" teaching and learning approaches by faculty (Hurtado, 1992) and opportunities for normalized communications and cross-racial interactions (Chang, Witt-Sandis, & Hakuta, 1999) has been noted to increase racial tension and exacerbate perceptions of outsiderness on campuses (Hurtado & Carter, 1997).

Moving Beyond Race and Ethnicity to Achieve Equity and Access

Consistent with federal concerns about the achievement gaps, Delaware's political leaders encourage preK–12 education reform that will improve the opportunities of ethnic minority and low-income students to effectively prepare for postsecondary admission leading to the range of career opportunities. Delaware, like other states, has evidence of achievement gaps for low-income and ethnic minority citizens across the spectrum of opportunities, including access to the education workforce. Delaware's recent national achievement as recipient of the first Race to the Top funding from the U.S. Department of Education does not appear to have replaced concerns about teacher workforce diversity with the newly elevated emphasis on

teacher qualifications and effectiveness. The state's education website provides easily accessible data tables on the racial ethnic composition of students and staff at state, district, and
school building levels.[9]

Shift in the ASPIRE Program's Ideological Orientation Continues to Emphasize Diversity and Yields Distinguishing Program Features

Mindful of emerging political shifts in national and state priorities for constituting the education workforce, the university's teacher education community is informed by well-established
research that documents the value added when teaching and learning occur in environments
characterized by high levels of diversity (Banks & Banks, 2004; Bell, 2002; Cochran-Smith,
2004). Until there is an evidence base linking student achievement in Delaware and beyond to
the emerging priorities of teacher qualifications and yet-to-be-defined attributes of effectiveness, it is more responsible to continue to consciously work toward an adequate or representa-
tional enrollment of ethnic minority students in teacher education degree programs. As noted
by Jason Irizarry (2007),

> the most meaningful learning happens among students rather than through transmission from
> teacher to student. Institutions of higher education that do not actively recruit and retain students of
> color [in teacher education programs] are potentially compromising the personal and professional
> development of their students. (p. 99)

Recognizing that most competitive students will go where they feel welcomed and valued, the
within-institution challenge then is to fashion developmental experiences that attract admis-
sible students—specifically students who are first-generation college going and from ethnic
minority backgrounds—to valued membership in the university and in teacher education
programs. At research-engaged institutions, perceptions of value and insider status accrue to
students who participate in research and associate through that enterprise with faculty and
majority students (Braxton, 2000). At the University of Delaware, engaging undergraduate
students from diverse backgrounds in opportunities to conduct research requires actively
seeking the support of social justice–minded faculty who are willing to share cultural capital
by building inquiry-focused student communities. These faculty foster inclusion of students
who are traditionally underrepresented among the institution's most valued and promising
members.

In 2008, the University's Council on Teacher Education authorized work that consciously
shifts the program's emphasis from facilitating student adjustment within a segregated and
somewhat remedial framework to assertive engagement within an emerging set of activities
designed to foster engagement with faculty. The more engaged approach is conducted within
campus programs that support undergraduate student research as well as the development of
strategic relationships with the external community (Van Dornick, 2008).

Today, ASPIRE continues to function as a recruitment and support agent, but it seeks a
much further reach into the larger university community. Students representing the full range
of racial, ethnic, and sociocultural backgrounds are encouraged to belong. While some academic support activities have been retained, they relate primarily to preprofessional develop-

ment, such as preparation for the Praxis I examination. The mission of the program has shifted from providing segregated developmental experiences to community building and achievement visibility.

The primary staff role too has shifted, placing the director, who holds a terminal degree in education and has held faculty status in other institutions, into the most visible leadership role. In the original program design—and consistent with retention strategies that are implicated in the first edition of Vincent Tinto's work *Leaving College: Rethinking the Causes and Cures of Student Attrition* (1987)—the primary staff person monitored individual student behavior, reminding students to attend class, sit in the front of the class, and study in groups.[10] The ASPIRE director now acts as a facilitator, assisting ASPIRE students to refine their outreach activities, identify internships, faculty research mentors, and campus leadership opportunities that serve to attach the ASPIRE students to the academic and cultural life of the institution in ways that confer status.[11]

The emerging program retains the program's freshman cohort approach that invites all first-generation and students of color who are education majors into a support structure that augments faculty advisement and consists of early year guidance designed to assist the students in navigating advisement, registration, campus memberships, leadership development opportunities, and other resource identification. The cohort development feature of this work is designed to establish key activities identified by a Teacher Education Advocacy Center model enrollment and retention program, including early support, community building, connections to the larger community, and strategic faculty interactions that position faculty and professional staff as partners in the student support effort (Lucas & Robinson, 2002).

ASPIRE HAS THREE ANCHORING COMPONENTS

The ASPIRE support structure has three components that engage students beginning in the freshman year and continuing through the senior year: (1) scholarship support and guidance; (2) leadership development within a student-led organization, with guidance and problem-solving expertise as cultural capital; and (3) access to research opportunities with faculty and community partners.

Scholarship Support and Guidance

During the initial months of the academic year, ASPIRE guidance sessions include only education majors. The group enlarges during the year to include roommates of education majors, undeclared students, and others who are searching for supportive relationships within the university community.[12] Annually, as many as 30 students receive academic scholarships and book awards. At the freshman level, each scholarship recipient is required to attend a fall orientation meeting and a spring update session with the ASPIRE director. The sessions are held for groups and individual students. The sessions focus on planning and problem solving, based on each student's program of study. General guidance includes a review of the registration process, including encouragement to meet early and often with the academic advisor assigned by the student's college, guidance for preparing for the meeting with the advisor, and the use of the online catalogue. Problem-solving discussions help students understand the importance of developing the right study-and-college-life balance, including the crucial issue of protecting the grade point average by planning strategically to take compatible general and major area requirements. Protecting one's grade point average is very important to education majors across the five colleges. All programs require that students achieve average grades of 2.6 or higher to achieve upper-division status. Several programs require that general grades average 2.75 or higher and that grades in the major area (e.g., English) average 3.0. or higher.

Leadership Development, Recruitment, and the ASPIRE Student Organization

Well-established research indicates that peer groups play a significant role in shaping members' expectations for social and academic achievement (Chickering, 1969). Consistent, achievement-focused interactions also build community efficacy, which is described as central to the creation of access platforms that can support systemic change (Tierney & Venegas, 2006). Building community and "fictive kin" relationships yields the additional benefit of attracting students who come to college undecided about a career pathway, especially those who believe that engagement and action within a community that shares critical perspective will result in positive societal change and affirm relational ties.

Relationships with community partners afford opportunities for ASPIRE students and noneducation majors who join the ASPIRE student organization to take actions that they believe can help to close achievement gaps. This community engagement also confers status on the university students who return to their communities to encourage younger students with similar profiles to consciously prepare for college and, specifically, to prepare for membership in the University of Delaware community.[13]

Characterized by high energy, visible service to the university, and engaged leadership, the student-led organization is very effective in attracting students to teacher education as a major. Since 2008, the group that actively participates in ASPIRE community activities has increased significantly, with as many as 40 students attending regular monthly meetings, compared to fewer than 10 who regularly attended 2 years ago.[14]

Thinking Forward: Aspiring to Grow a Community of Educators

A primary focus of the ASPIRE student-led organization is the outreach to help students who face challenges in preparing for college build an information base that supports college access, with some emphasis on encouraging precollege students to plan for careers as teachers and educators. This outreach has some potential to develop into a system of services, community engagement, and formal dual-enrollment opportunities for precollege students, as it aligns well with "grow your own" initiatives in the country, specifically the work that is underway within the Urban Teacher Academy Program in Broward County, Florida.[15] These approaches are partially rooted in the critical race thinking of African American and Latino scholars who, in examining the relative increases in enrollment of students of color in higher education in the last 10 years, find onerous the static racial/ethnic composition of teacher education programs (Harvey, 2002; Irizarry, 2007).

Culturally conscious scholars favor a "home growing," or talent development, approach in teacher education that recruits teacher candidates through explicit uplift messages that tap into the service and community development passion of students who want to improve the communities in which they are raised and educated (Irizarry, 2007). Consistent with the advocacy of Sonia Nieto (2000) and Jacqueline Jordan Irvine (2003), the emerging Delaware approach supports a vertically integrated recruitment and retention structure comprising education faculty, graduate, undergraduate, and high school students, which serves as an additional opportunity structure by supporting college awareness and preparation "spanning [the period] from the pre-pre-application process through the induction years in the profession" (Irizarry, 2007, p. 88).

Confident and committed to diversity, ASPIRE students conduct campus- and school-based outreach programs to help urban and rural middle school students plan for college. If brought to scale, this work might provide a solid "career corridor into teaching" (Haselkorn, 2000). Conceivably, students inspired in middle school to undertake the rigor and achieve grades required for admission to the University of Delaware will earn seats as high school juniors and seniors in the Aspiring Teacher Internship experience, which encourages competitive students to select the University of Delaware. Interns learn about the major from ASPIRE members, who share personal experiences that sell the campus community and build relationships to assist in yielding students into subsequent freshmen classes as teacher education majors.

While these emerging recruitment strategies are designed to encourage students from all backgrounds to prepare for teaching careers, the work is specifically responsive to challenges noted by researchers as barriers that inhibit the participation of people of color in teaching. The research suggests that negative school experiences and lack of encouragement from teachers, along with the poor image of teaching as a profession, constitute major factors that prevent an interest in teaching among students of color, specifically those with the academic profiles that support access to and success in competitive teacher preparation programs (Gordon, 2000; Smith, Mack, & Akyea, 2004; Wakefield, 2007). The outreach conducted by undergraduates is designed to create community and to position ASPIRE students as information sources and achievement models, building "social capital" within a defined relational construct (Maroulis & Gomez, 2008).

ASPIRE Fosters Development of Critical Social Capital Within the Institution and Community

ASPIRE students also plan and host monthly professional development workshops that allow teacher education majors and interested other undergraduates to interact with faculty and local education leaders, with whom they engage in discussion of issues relevant to success as classroom teachers, socioeconomic and political factors that influence student success, as well as a range of topics related to career opportunities pursued by education professionals. Scholars speculate that students' academic status and expectations at the university level are shaped by the interaction between students' habits and experiences with faculty who are subject to the same biases as K–12 educators who view and interact differently with students with different levels of cultural capital (Astin, 1993). Appearing as guest lecturers in sessions developed, convened, and facilitated through the inquiry-focused voluntary activities of ASPIRE undergraduate students increases faculty perceptions of the cultural capital of the students.

Access to Research Opportunities

With support from the university's Office of Undergraduate Research and selected faculty, ASPIRE has succeeded in constructing a vertically integrated system of interactions that supports graduate, undergraduate, high school, and middle school students in forming a summer research-centered community, with research teams that are led by graduate and undergraduate students and that include high school student interns. The teams work with middle school learners to reinforce academic and social skills. With support from faculty, relevant research problems or topics of inquiry are identified, and the work with community sites is defined. The work includes researching and developing the review of the literature, the development of treatments or activities, data collection, analysis, and reporting.

While these scholarly activities reinforce existing relationships with university faculty and strengthen the attachment of ASPIRE students to the valued research habitude of the institution, they also strengthen community bonds as they support development of a social network. Once introduced to one another, the network of students establishes its own life in cyberspace as well as in real-time encounters within the community with the powerful connecting message continuing to affirm the potential of the youngest students to pursue higher education, influenced by positive relationships with near peers who are preparing to teach. Emerging studies seem to indicate that social relations play a role in determining student performance and aspirations, leveling family and other characteristics (Maroulis & Gomez, 2008).

This work began in 2008, when the first ASPIRE student research project supported a literature review to define strategies that might be developed to encourage middle and high school students who face challenges in preparing for college because of social and academic factors. In 2009, a second project was built from the literature base: a set of strategies developed as workshops for middle and high school students to provide college awareness. Operation CARE (College Awareness Reaching Everyone) was launched by the ASPIRE community during a university admissions–sponsored weekend, which historically has attracted very few low-income and ethnic minority families. ASPIRE members networked with local middle and high school teachers who are involved in school-based college awareness activities to increase the college-going rate of ethnic minority and low-income students. Inviting these teachers to bring their students to campus on a "Blue and Golden Saturday," the ASPIRE members generated attendance of more than 100 low-income and ethnic minority students for their workshops, which were held in collaboration with the university's regularly featured campus awareness activities in October 2009.[16]

The "coloring up" of the community on that Saturday resulted in a request from the admissions office for ASPIRE to support a dedicated middle school Saturday for families, which would not be held in tandem with regular campus awareness events for prospective students. The first of the dedicated programs was held in March 2010, and it was also attended by as many as 100 families.[17]

In summer 2010, a third set of research and applied research activities was conducted as part of a 5-week program established by a partnership between ASPIRE and a local middle school. This program model was designed to provide literacy and numeracy academic enrichment to as many as 30 middle school students who attend school in the city of Wilmington, in a community with one of the state's highest free and reduced-priced lunch rates. The ASPIRE undergraduate students worked within an integrated community of researchers that included faculty and high school students. Two teams of ASPIRE undergraduates worked on distinct projects. A literacy team guided development of digital stories or multimedia autobiographies that engaged the younger students in telling their own life and community stories, using the range of media presentations done in moviemaker or similar programs. Telling Our Stories is designed to help students express their hopes and dreams as well as the challenges they plan to surmount in pursuit of them.

Additionally, the undergraduates conducted a qualitative study, working with a College of Education faculty member to investigate "identity formation and school attachment of African American girls and Latinas." The second study, conducted with an additional group of middle school students at this site, allowed an undergraduate and high school team to facilitate Measuring Up for Leadership, a problem-based course that builds confidence for mathematics problem solving and leadership. Pre- and post-course mathematics assessments, school attitude, and career interest surveys provide data for a descriptive study that investigates the "effects of high engagement literacy and numeracy activities on the academic performance, school attachment, and interest in teaching of urban middle school students."

Through these interactions, the preservice teacher education students gain status and campus visibility among the most accomplished undergraduates. The ASPIRE students select, and are selected by, faculty mentors who attach the students to their research and support them in constructing questions and defining research agendas. This proximity to faculty confers status as a contributing member within the academy. In 2008 and 2009, only 1 African American student was among the 25 undergraduate student researchers. In 2010, ASPIRE students achieved 6 undergraduate student research scholarships and fellowships, signaling conscious attachment of these students to core values of the institution.

CHALLENGE AND PROMISE

The shift in emphasis of the program has produced very desirable results on two fronts: first, resetting the conceptual framework for a program that has strong ties to the minority community, moving from remediation centered to achievement centered as a primary program characteristic; second, expanding the reach of the program to create a community-anchored pipeline into teacher education, thereby fostering interactions and proximity that researchers associate with joining behavior and the enablement of a culture of success (Christakis & Fowler, 2009; Tierney & Venegas, 2006).

This teacher pipeline places University of Delaware students from the range of backgrounds into interactive relationships with target community students. The University of Delaware ASPIRE student leader role models are racially and culturally connected to the target student community, and there is visible comfort and fluidity in relationships developed among members functioning at multiple levels of the ASPIRE and Aspiring Teacher community, from faculty to undergraduates to prospective undergraduates (Irvine, 2003).

In their Operation CARE, ASPIRE students focus on helping urban and rural middle school students plan for high school enrollment in rigorous courses and participation in summer and after-school programs that provide the prerequisite preparation for admission to the University of Delaware, with particular interest in providing this information to Delaware students.[18] Operation CARE and related outreach activities consciously associate middle school, high school, and undergraduate students. Given the hierarchal developmental stages of the students, their network is less dense and associated with more autonomous, opportunity-expanding behavior based on the effective use of information that supports establishing new and more positive norms (Maroulis & Gomez, 2008). A longitudinal study of the academic achievement, postsecondary access, and career pursuits of students who are involved at each stage of this process seems warranted.

The emerging work also uses peer relationships in the final stages of the recruitment process by encouraging qualified students to elect membership in ASPIRE and to enroll at the University of Delaware as teacher education as a majors. ASPIRE students serve as facilitators of summer internship experiences for selected high school juniors and seniors who spend 20–30 hours as instructional assistants in a selected track (early childhood, elementary, or secondary school). During the 3- to 6-week internship opportunities, the ASPIRE students actively engage the high school students in their preprofessional community, providing the high school interns opportunities for career pathway discussions as well as an orientation to campus academic support and student leadership opportunities. By integrating high school interns into research teams and informational sessions with undergraduates who describe their own experiences as resident assistants, service learning scholars, and Freshman Year Experience and student life leaders, ASPIRE students sell the campus community and build relationships that assist in yielding students into seats as education majors.

While still rooted in a history of enabling African American, Latino, and ethnically diverse students to succeed at the University of Delaware, ASPIRE today serves as a model connected community. A growing body of literature describes how social networks shape behavior and build social capital. A long-term benefit of nurturing purposeful networks might well lead to the emergence of new identity movements (Christakis & Fowler, 2009; Maroulis & Gomez, 2008). In the case of teacher education, early and sustained participation in community with others who are defined by positive attributes makes membership (becoming a teacher) desirable. The challenge to attract more and diverse applicants to teacher education programs might well include creating conditions that support a more contagious, or peer-to-peer, spread of interest in the field.

In July 2010, the high school internship program, which in Years 1 and 2 focused only on Delaware students, concluded a third summer of operation and enrolled several students from Philadelphia Boys' Latin high school. Approximately 50% of ASPIRE's high school interns go on to pursue education degrees at the University of Delaware. The yield of Delaware students of color into the university's teacher education program increased from 53% in 2007 to 74% in 2009 (Van Dornick, 2009), but the overall enrollment of students of color within the university continues to hover just above 10%. While there are no specific numerical targets, the university, through the Delaware Center for Teacher Education, supports the internship program and related outreach as efforts that constitute conscious work to include ethnic minority students in teacher education degree programs.

A 2009 report by a Teacher Effectiveness Task Group appointed by governor Jack Markell included a broad recommendation for development of a Delaware teacher career ladder that builds a pipeline into the profession, beginning in the high school grades.[19] Given Delaware's enhanced funding through the Race to the Top initiative, there is a mandate to target additional academic and career preparatory support to students who face the greatest challenges in preparing for postsecondary opportunities, particularly those from ethnic minority backgrounds. ASPIRE's programmatic features—the summer internship, the engaged campus community outreach, the achievement-focused and very diverse core group of teacher education majors—position ASPIRE to serve as a model to support the state in realizing its goals to achieve a more diverse and highly effective teaching workforce. The primary challenge to testing the efficacy of the model to yield a substantially more diverse and effective teacher education workforce lies, perhaps, in development of a full-scale K–16 integrated program with a stable funding stream and appropriate institutional support.

NOTES

1. The interview responses and commentary of James Shaw, ASPIRE coordinator from 1992 to 1999, are featured in a videotape documentary that chronicles the history and development of the program, produced by Serviam Media, Wilmington, Delaware, 2009.

2. The website of the Delaware Department of Education provides demographic data on statewide enrollment of students (http://www.doe.k12.de.us/infosuites/schools/default.shtml; see profiles.doe.k12.de.us/).

3. The website of the University of Delaware provides data on the ethnicity of enrolled students by time status (http://www.udel.edu/aboutus; see "Facts and Figures").

4. Courses required for the elementary teacher education major at the University of Delaware are outlined on the School of Education's webpage (http://www.udel.edu/education/ete/index.html; see "Program Information").

5. The University of Delaware's Office of Research is led by Mark A. Barteau. The website outlines the university's competitive research agenda (http://www.udel.edu/research/about/facts.html).

6. The University of Delaware's strategic plan emphasizes growth in research as an important achievement milestone. Go to http://www.udel.edu/prominence/.

7. See L. S. Gottfredson for a list of authored publications on IQ and intelligence as a factor in academic achievement and vocational decisions (http://www.udel.edu/educ/gottfredson/reprints/pubtopics.htm#gfactor). The website for FairTest (National Center for Fair and Open Testing) makes the following assessment of Gottredson's work: "Another researcher who has argued that IQ tests prove genetically-based racial inferiority, Linda Gottfredson, released a survey a few years ago noting that most "intelligence researchers" agree with her position. (Ironically, this came at a time when evolutionary biologists have reached wide agreement on the meaninglessness of race as a genetic concept.)." See http://www.fairtest.org/racism-eugenics-and-testing-again.

8. Comments made by James Shaw off camera described his efforts to help students achieve required grade point averages to continue as teacher education majors. These efforts often included referring students to the local community college to take courses that the students failed multiple times.

9. The website of the Delaware Department of Education provides demographic data on statewide enrollment of students (http://www.doe.k12.de.us/infosuites/schools/default.shtml; see profiles.doe.k12.de.us/). The information on teachers accessible from the site provides the "highly qualified" status rating by content area (http://profiles.doe.k12.de.us/SchoolProfiles/State/Default.aspx). Go to a selected school profile and to the staff page for data on the ethnic composition of that staff.

10. Additional comments made by James Shaw on and off camera describe his efforts to recruit first-generation and low-income students for the teacher education degree program at the University of Delaware. These comments include explanations of key supportive features of the program, including close monitoring by staff, study skills development sessions, and group study sessions.

11. *Report of Activities and Accomplishments Related to the Path to Prominence: Strategic Plan for the University of Delaware Submitted to the Interim Dean of the College of Education and Human Development*, by Carol Vukelich, director of the Delaware Center for Teacher Education, June 2010.

12. *ASPIRE: Summary of 2009–2010 Program Activities*, by Melva Ware, revised February 4, 2010. Submitted to the University Council on Teacher Education, February 2010.

13. See video clip of Operation CARE at http://www.aspire.udel.edu.

14. See membership records for 2008–2009 and 2009–2010. ASPIRE student organization membership in 2009 was 20 students, and membership information was collected on 58 undergraduates in 2010.

15. See Robert D. Parks, "Urban Teacher Academy Project: Growing Our Own Teachers," *Teachers College Record*, May 16, 2005, at http://www.tcrecord.org (No. 11975). The Urban Teacher Academy Program prepares high school students for careers in urban education. It was initiated in Broward County, Florida, and it provides scholarships to support urban students in training to teach. The program includes career growth stages for which specific support is provided to prospective, novice, and veteran teachers.

16. See "ASPIRE Program Encourages High School Students," at http://www.udel.edu/udaily/2010/jul/aspire071309.html/.

17. See "Southern Delaware Middle School Students Learn About College Life," at http://www.udel.edu/udaily/2010/may/Middleschoolvisit050610.html.

18. The University of Delaware's Commitment to Delawareans is an academic roadmap that shows Delaware students the courses and grades that are required to achieve admission to the Newark campus of the university. See http://www.udel.edu/commitment.

19. The Enhancing Teacher Effectiveness Committee was created as a component of the work of governor Jack Markell's Government Efficiency Project during the spring of 2009. The committee met a total of six times over a period of 3 months to develop a definition of teacher effectiveness, and the committee considered relevant issues of preservice preparation and recruitment. The preliminary recommendations of the Enhancing Teacher Effectiveness Committee were issued in June 2009.

REFERENCES

Andersen, M., & Debessay, A. (2009, February). *The path to prominence through diversity: University of Delaware diversity task force final report*. Newark, DE: University of Delaware Office of the Provost.
Astin, A. W. (1993). *What matters in college: Four critical years revisited*. San Francisco: Jossey-Bass.
Banks, J. A., & Banks, C. M. (2004). *Handbook of research in multicultural education*. 2nd ed. San Francisco: Jossey-Bass.
Bell, L. A. (2002). Sincere fictions: The pedagogical challenges of preparing White teachers for multicultural classrooms. *Equity and Excellence in Education, 35*(3), 236–244.
Bennett, C., Cole, D., & Thompson, J. (2000). Preparing teachers of color at a predominantly White university: A case study of project TEAM. *Teaching and Teacher Education, 16*(4), 445–464.
Braxton, J. (Ed.). (2000). *Reworking the student departure puzzle*. Nashville, TN: Vanderbilt University Press.
Chang, M. J., Witt-Sandis, D., & Hakuta, K. (1999). The dynamics of race in higher education: An examination of the evidence. *Equity and Excellence in Education, 32*(2), 12–16.
Chickering, A. W. (1969). *Education and identity*. San Francisco: Jossey-Bass.
Christakis, N., & Fowler, J. (2009). *Connected the surprising power of social networks and how they shape our lives*. New York: Little, Brown.
Cochran-Smith, M. (2004). *Walking the road: Race, diversity, and social justice in teacher education*. New York: Teachers College Press.
Goldhaber, D., & Hannaway, J. (Eds.). (2009). *Creating a new teaching profession*. Washington, DC: Urban Institute Press.
Gordon, J. (2000). *The color of teaching*. New York: Routledge/Falmer Press.

Harvey, W. B. (2002). *Minorities in higher education 2001–2002: 19th annual status report.* Washington, DC: American Council on Education.

Haselkorn, D. (2000, September). *Recruitment and retention of quality teachers.* Washington, DC: U.S. House of Representatives.

Hurtado, S. (1992). The campus racial climate: Contexts for conflict. *Journal of Higher Education, 63*(5), 539–569.

Hurtado, S., & Carter, D. (1997). Effects of college transition and perceptions of the campus racial climate on Latino college students' sense of belonging. *Sociology of Education, 70*(4), 324–345.

Irizarry, J. G. (2007). Home-growing teachers of color: Lessons learned from a town-gown partnership. *Teacher Education Quarterly, 34*(4), 87–102.

Irvine, J. J. (2003). *Educating teachers for diversity: Seeing with a cultural eye.* New York: Teachers College Press.

Lucas, T., & Robinson, J. (2002). Promoting the retention of prospective teachers through a cohort of college freshmen. *The High School Journal, 86*(1), 3–14.

Maroulis, S., & Gomez, L. M. (2008). Does "connectedness" matter? Evidence from a social network analysis within a small-school reform. *Teachers College Record, 110*(9), 1901–1929.

Nieto, S. (2000). Placing equity front and center: Some thoughts on transforming teacher education for a new century. *Journal of Teacher Education, 51*(3), 180–188.

Pascarella, E. T., Smart, J. C., Ethington, C., & Nettles, M. (1987). The influence of college on self-concept: A consideration of race and gender differences. *American Educational Research Journal, 24*, 49–77.

Pascarella, E. T., Whitt, E. J., Nora, A., Edison, M., Hagedorn, L. S., & Terenzini, P. T. (1996). What have we learned from the first year of the national study of student learning? *Journal of College Student Development, 37*(2), 182–192.

Peterson, M. W., Blackburn, R. T., Gamson, Z. F., Arce, C. H., Davenport, R. W., & Mingle, J. R. (1978). *Black students on White campuses: The impacts of increased Black enrollments.* Ann Arbor: University of Michigan, Institute for Social Research.

Powell, M. (1998). Campus climate and students of color. In L. Calverde & L. Castenell (Eds.), *The multicultural campus: Strategies for transforming higher education* (pp. 95–118). Walnut Creek, CA: AltaMira Press.

Rys, G. (1993). *Funding application submitted to the U.S. Department of Education: Programs to encourage minority students to become teachers for support of the Aspire to Teach Partnerships Program.* Newark, DE: University of Delaware, College of Education.

Scott, W. B. (2002). The miseducation of White America. *Widener Law Symposium Journal, 9*(1), 73–37.

Sims-Peterson, M., & Ware, M. (2002). From risk to promise: Changing the education contract for poor children and children of color. *Widener Law Symposium Journal, 9*(1), 121–127.

Smith, V. G., Mack, F., & Akyea, S. G. (2004, spring). African-American make honor students' view of teaching as a career choice. *Teachers Education Quarterly*, pp. 75–88.

Tierney, W., & Venegas, K. (2006). Fictive kin and social capital: The role of peer groups in applying and paying for college. *American Behavioral Scientist, 49*(12), 1687–1702.

Tinto, V. (1987). *Leaving college: Rethinking the causes and cures of student attrition.* Chicago: University of Chicago Press.

Turner, C. (1994). Guests in someone else's house: Students of color. *Review of Higher Education, 17*(4), 355–370.

Van Dornick, B. (1999). *Application for funding of the Delaware teacher recruitment program. Submitted to the U.S. Department of Education, Teacher Quality Enhancement Program. Delaware Center for Teacher Education.* Newark, DE: University of Delaware, College of Human Resources, Education and Public Policy.

Van Dornick, B. (2009). *Report of enrollment data for teacher education majors to the University Council on Teacher Education.* Newark, DE: University of Delaware, College of Education and Public Policy.

Wakefield, D. (2007). NCLB keeps some great teaching candidates out forever. *Education Digest*, 51–57.

Chapter Four

Grow Your Own Illinois: Taking Action in Chicago Neighborhood Schools

Anne C. Hallett

In 2004, the Illinois General Assembly passed the nation's first Grow Your Own Teachers law. Five of Chicago's most experienced community organizing groups proposed, wrote, and advocated passage of the law, which was modeled on an initiative that one of the organizations and its university partner had developed. The following year, the community organizations returned to the state capitol to advocate, successfully, for the first year of what is now 6 years of hard-won state funding. Grow Your Own (GYO) was developed as a strategy for developing a pipeline of teachers of color, for reducing teacher turnover in high-poverty schools, and for preparing teachers for hard-to-fill positions who share the culture, language, and community of the students.

The initiative creates access for people of color to attend college, and it is designed to ensure their success as well. In Illinois, over the past decade, the number of teachers of color has decreased from 14% to 13%, while during the same period, students of color increased from 35% to 40%. The current pipeline for teachers is not solving this problem, and GYO was developed as one solution. One GYO candidate commented on the importance of having teachers of color: "Children of color are now having the opportunity to see someone who looks like them, which is encouraging and motivational."

This chapter describes how community organizers developed Grow Your Own Teachers as a community-based solution to high rates of teacher turnover. The GYO organizers wanted highly effective teachers for their own neighborhood schools: teachers who look like the students. Therefore, they decided to invest in people who pass the "zip code test"—who already live in the low-income communities where they plan to teach. To achieve this, they developed relationships with colleges of education, organized school districts, and identified other interested community groups. Together, they began the steady work of developing a robust, equitable, and innovative teacher preparation program that now has candidates in 16 locations in Illinois: 8 in Chicago and 8 in other high-need communities.

HISTORICAL BACKGROUND

Project Nueva Generación

In the late 1990s, Chicago's Logan Square Neighborhood Association (Warren, 2005) created a parent leadership program called Parent Mentors. Parents were trained as leaders, and they worked for 100 hours in a classroom, being mentored by a teacher. By the end of their training, participants—often, formerly shy and stay-at-home mothers—had become active leaders in the schools and in the community. Mentor graduates realized that they loved working with children whose language and culture they shared. Some knew that they would love to be teachers but could not afford college.

Joanna Brown, the education organizer at Logan Square, found Dr. Maria Teresa Garreton, a higher education faculty member in the bilingual education program at Chicago State University who understood the Parent Mentors population and its dreams very well. Dr. Garreton successfully wrote a 5-year federal grant proposal that would cover the students' college costs. Then, Logan Square and Chicago State together established an innovative community-based model for teacher preparation for this group of mentors, called Project Nueva Generación. This initiative had been underway for 2 years when the Logan Square Neighborhood Association joined with another community organization, Action Now, in a campaign to improve teacher quality.

Action Now, formerly Illinois ACORN, worked in North Lawndale, a low-income African American neighborhood in Chicago. Action Now knew that its schools faced serious problems attracting highly effective teachers. To address its teacher recruitment problem, Action Now trained its members to help interview potential teachers. It organized summer institutes to introduce newly recruited teachers—young, inexperienced, and suburban—to North Lawndale, taking them on bus tours and introducing them to neighbors so they would feel more comfortable in the schools. They influenced Chicago Public Schools to fill all vacancies at its schools at the start of the school year. But North Lawndale schools were still a revolving door for teachers.

Action Now realized that the problem was not recruitment. The new teachers, no matter their credentials, were not "highly qualified" to teach in the low-income North Lawndale schools, because they did not plan to (nor did they) stay in their schools more than a year, maybe two. In 2003, Action Now conducted research on 64 of its neighborhood schools and was alarmed to find that up to 40% of new teachers leave their schools every year (Frost, 2003). As is true of 85% of all teachers who end up teaching within 40 miles of where they grew up (Boyd, Lankford, Loeb, & Wyckoff, 2005), the new teachers went home to teach, and "home" was not North Lawndale. The problem in North Lawndale was teacher retention, not teacher recruitment.

Madeline Talbott, lead organizer of Action Now, realized that solving teacher quality issues required additional organizing strength. She convened a coalition of organizing groups, named the Chicago Learning Campaign, with the Logan Square Neighborhood Association as the first member. The groups made an early decision to learn more about one another's education organizing work. Logan Square invited Action Now's members to visit and observe its Project Nueva Generación. The Action Now leaders loved the project. Because the project was investing in local residents and helping them to become teachers, the Action Now leaders realized right away that this was a potential solution to the high rates of teacher turnover they were wrestling with in North Lawndale. They had inadvertently discovered the organizing–higher education partnership program that was to become the model for Grow Your Own Teachers. Soon afterward, three other community organizations—Kenwood Oakland Community Organization, Southwest Organizing Project, and TARGET Area Development Corporation—were invited to join the Chicago Learning Campaign.

The community solution represented by Project Nueva Generación struck a chord with all of them. The community groups realized that by organizing and by growing their own teachers from parents, community leaders, and paraprofessionals (their members), they could create a pipeline of highly qualified teachers of color who live in their neighborhood; who understand and respect the students, their families, and their culture; and who would stay in the schools, once hired, since they were already home. This strategy would also support family and community economic development in their low-income neighborhoods. The community groups decided to put the Project Nueva Generación concept into state law to gain greater legitimacy and to tap a source of financial support.

Passing the Illinois Grow Your Own Teacher Education Act (2004)

The organizers were not deterred by the fact that none of them had ever written or advocated a bill into law. The groups figured out each of the steps. They drafted a bill; they found a sponsor and got it introduced; they met with their legislators and encouraged them to sponsor the bill as well; they met with the governor's staff and other allies; and they tracked their bill through committees and onto the house and senate floors. They worked hard advocating for this community-based concept of preparing teachers for low-income schools. Their efforts paid off in the 2004 passage of the Grow Your Own Teachers law.

The 2004 Grow Your Own Teachers Education Act turned into law the elements of Project Nueva Generación, the Logan Square–Chicago State initiative. The law mandates that a community organization, a 4-year higher education institution, and a school district or group of schools form a consortium to create a GYO initiative. Community colleges are usually involved, and unions and other groups may be involved as well. The GYO Teachers law also identified elements that each initiative should include:

- Experience of the community organization in organizing parents and community leaders to achieve school improvement and a strong relational school culture
- Previous experience of higher education in preparing candidates for hard-to-staff schools and from nontraditional backgrounds
- The relevance of the curriculum to the needs of low-income schools
- College classes that are accessible to candidates in terms of both time and location
- Articulation agreements between the community college and the 4-year institution
- Availability of support services, such as counseling, child care, and tutoring
- Inclusion of community-organizing strategies in the teacher preparation program

Today, the target population for GYO candidates identified in the law are adults—parents, community members, and paraprofessionals—people who are already active in their local schools. With a median age of 40, they are nontraditional candidates, and they must have a high school diploma or a GED but may not yet have a bachelor's degree.

The law describes the supports that the GYO candidates are to receive, important to their success since most of them have been out of school for years. A key support is the forgivable loan that covers the cost of tuition, books, and fees directly connected to college attendance, funds that are available after the candidate's federal financial aid is used. The loan will be forgiven after the candidates graduate as teachers and teach for 5 years in an eligible, low-income school, most likely in the community where they live. The law also calls for classes to be held in the community at a time and place convenient for the candidates, recognizing that most work full-time. GYO grant funds may cover tutoring, child care, and laptop computers.

These supports are very important, but the most important source of support is the GYO cohort coordinator. The coordinator (or coordinators)—either one full-time or two part-time people, one at the community organization and one at the university or school district—tracks and supports the candidates as they progress through the program. The coordinator plays multiple roles, helping the candidates negotiate the bureaucracy of the higher education institution, ensuring that the candidates get to know and support one another, tracking their academic progress, arranging for tutoring, if needed, and arranging for workshops that help candidates prepare for and pass the Basic Skills test, passage of which is a requirement to enroll in the college of education. The coordinators support the candidates to develop roles as active community leaders at the same time that their college coursework is preparing them to be teacher leaders.

In summary, the Grow Your Own Teachers law incorporates key elements of effective education of adult learners: good screening; strong academic instruction; a cohort model for mutual support; a full-time coordinator to provide support and help to keep candidates on track academically; strong community connections; and important supports, such as tutoring, child care, and transportation, as well as classes in the community (Berry & Young, 2007). These supports are wise investments that will produce highly effective teachers of color, but they do cost money.

Advocating for GYO Funding

The law passed in 2004 only after the groups agreed to remove the appropriation that had been attached since the legislature was hesitant initially to fund it. But key legislative allies knew that the organizers would be seeking funds, and, in fact, the Chicago Learning Campaign was back the following year advocating for funding for the new law.

In 2005 (and every year since), the organizations prepared a GYO appropriations bill that specified the funds needed for the coming fiscal year. They lined up legislative sponsors to introduce the bill in both the senate and the house of representatives. Since approved appropriations are included as part of the overall fiscal year state budget, the groups knew that an individual appropriations bill of this kind served primarily as an organizing tool. The organizing groups asked legislators to cosponsor their appropriations bill as an indication of their support for GYO. When the appropriations bill was heard in committee, the groups, candidates, and their supporters testified about the importance of the program, making the case for funding and raising the visibility of the initiative.

In 2005, the General Assembly approved a planning grant of $1.5 million. These funds were available both to support a contractor to help implement the law and to provide emerging consortia with small planning grants. Following the appropriation, the Illinois State Board of Education, the administering agency, issued a competitive request for proposal for a contract to help implement GYO statewide. The Chicago Learning Campaign competed for and won this implementation contract against two other bidders. It wanted to ensure that the initiative stayed true to its vision and to organize the initiative around the state.

Grow Your Own Illinois

The Chicago Learning Campaign won the contract in the fall of 2005 (renewed five times since then). After winning the state contract, the Chicago community organizations (originally five, now seven) that had worked as the Chicago Learning Campaign officially changed their name to Grow Your Own Illinois (GYO IL). Since the initiative was state law and would be implemented statewide, they needed a name more descriptive of the work and one that reflected the statewide focus, not simply Chicago. The GYO IL coalition was made up of the executive director plus one or two other staff members from each organization. Their first task was to figure out how to organize statewide.

Going to Scale in Illinois

GYO IL's initial work under the contract was conducting research to identify high-need areas, looking for school districts that had high rates of teacher turnover, large numbers of hard-to-staff schools or positions, high percentages of low-income schools, and significant disparities between the numbers of students of color and teachers of color. Representatives of GYO IL then used any contacts they had to identify someone in these areas to host a meeting for them. Sometimes they first conducted a scouting trip to the area, seeking a community organization who might agree to be the lead organization or meeting with a higher education collegiate. To each introductory meeting, they invited representatives of the partners who would be needed to form a GYO consortium—a community organization, the school district, the nearest 4-year university or college, and usually a community college.

After the initial meeting, if there was interest, GYO IL representatives would follow up to support the formation of a GYO consortium in that community. They prepared and shared how-to documents that described the steps needed to develop a GYO initiative, such as how to develop a consortium and strategies for recruiting a cohort of candidates. They also encouraged the interested groups to apply for a $40,000 planning grant from the state. The planning grants were used by each emerging consortium to further develop the relationships among consortium members, to recruit candidates, and to prepare a proposal for an implementation grant.

Forming Consortia

Each of the five Chicago community organizations formed its own GYO consortium and each recruited 35 to 45 candidates. Logan Square, whose Project Nueva Generaciòn was the original cohort, formed a second cohort. By the end of the planning year in June 2006, 11 emerging consortia—6 in Chicago and 5 in other Illinois high-need communities—had received planning grants, formed their consortia, and recruited almost 400 candidates. Project Nueva Generaciòn also received state funds, since its federal grant had ended, bringing the total to 12 GYO consortia.

The following year, 4 more consortia were formed, resulting in the current 16 GYO consortia, 8 in Chicago and 8 in other high-need areas in Illinois. Of the 16, 3 were formed by school districts to create a pipeline of teachers of color for their districts. As of spring 2011, the 16 GYO consortia in Illinois include 16 community organizations, 8 of Illinois's 12 public universities, 3 private colleges or universities, 11 community colleges, 23 school districts, and 2 unions.

Implementing GYO

All consortia include at least three partners—a community organization, a 4-year degree-granting higher education institution, and a school district or group of schools. In theory, the community organization would take the lead role in recruiting and supporting candidates; the higher education institution would prepare the candidates as teachers; and the school district would support the candidates and hire the new teachers. These partnerships were not tension-free. A challenge was blending the distinctly different cultures, especially those of higher education and community organizations. Community organizations have small staffs, make decisions collaboratively and rapidly, and tend to be nonhierarchical. University faculty work in large institutions with layers of bureaucracy and a great deal of hierarchy. Decisions are made slowly and may have to go through several departments. Whereas an executive director of a community organization can sign needed paperwork at once, getting a university president's signature may require an appointment made a week in advance. And there are other issues.

Consortia had to get used to shared decision making—develop a budget together, for example. Sometimes the university, as fiscal agent, developed the budget, and the community organization saw it only the day before it was due. In one case, without consulting its community partners whose cohort coordinators were being paid only a stipend, the higher education partner returned a large sum of GYO grant money to the state.

In addition to these cultural differences, the community organizations made some false starts in developing their relationships with higher education partners. For example, the law calls for the "inclusion (in teacher preparation) of strategies derived from community organizing that will help candidates develop tools for working with parents and community members." The community organizations wanted to create an organizing curriculum that higher education would offer. They presented this idea to higher education rather than discussing the concept with it.

To remedy this, GYO IL and higher education jointly formed the Grow Your Own Partners Council in 2009, with representatives from 2- and 4-year higher education institutions and school districts, both from Chicago and from other parts of Illinois.

Since the program design is in state law, the 16 consortia that have developed GYO initiatives are roughly similar. But each also reflects particular local conditions and local partners. For example, one consortium is rural, and transportation is a much more important issue than it is in Chicago, where public transportation is available. In another case, the candidates live in Chicago, but the university is located in another city. The consortium's community college partner allows the 4-year university to hold its GYO classes on its campus in Chicago, not an ideal solution since candidates do not receive a full college experience. The three consortia that were developed by school districts have very close working relationships with the district, making human resource decisions and mentoring easy, while the school district relationships in other consortia are often less well developed since candidates will not graduate and be hired as teachers for several years.

Recruiting Candidates

Consortia recruit potential candidates from paraprofessionals and other school employees. The community organizations advertise the opportunity of GYO widely within their organizations. They tap parents active in the schools, their members, and other community leaders. Consortia members encourage the principals of schools in their neighborhoods to encourage paraprofessionals and other school employees to get involved. Once a potential candidate has shown interest, a serious discussion takes place with them so they realize the two-way commitment that is both offered and expected. To be eligible, potential candidates need to have at least a high school diploma or a GED but possibly not a bachelor's degree. Since candidates will need to apply for federal financial aid—funds that are used for tuition before the GYO forgivable loan—they also had to be either a citizen or a legal immigrant.

Interested candidates bring their transcripts for review; they are interviewed; and their academic readiness assessed by members of the consortium. As often as possible, different consortia members participate in the interviews since they bring different lenses to what constitutes a candidate who would be successful. For example, a university partner may look for academic readiness, and the community partner might look for other assets, such as the record of leadership and commitment. Candidates who enter the program sign a contract that stipulates what they will receive and what they will be expected to contribute in return. They are then placed in classes at their level of readiness, taking classes as often as possible as a cohort, together with other GYO candidates.

GYO Candidate Profiles

Teacher candidates are the heart of the GYO initiative. With a particular interest in increasing the numbers of teachers of color, GYO recruits as candidates people who have deep ties to the neighborhoods and the schools in which they will teach. They are often members of the community organization. Since many are people who have always wanted to be teachers, they have a track record of working with children and in the schools as teacher aides, janitors, security guards, secretaries, or parent volunteers (Berry & Young, 2007).

Most of the candidates work full-time, are older, and have dependent children. (One faculty member called them "nontraditional nontraditional candidates.") As most of them have been out of school for 10 to 15 years, becoming students again is daunting. They form their own most important supporters—giving one another academic, social, and emotional support as they faced their shared challenges of juggling full-time work, families, and college. Whenever possible, they took classes together (initially held in the community), studied together, celebrated together, and built strong friendships. Candidates typically say that their cohort became "like family."

In 2011, the profile on the GYO teacher candidates revealed the following:

- Over 350 GYO candidates are in college studying to become teachers;
- 84% are people of color (51% African American, 33% Hispanic);
- 73% work full-time in addition to attending college;
- 67% are between the ages of 30 and 50 years old;
- 81% are women;
- 38% have passed the Basic Skills test, required to enter the college of education;
- 41% are preparing for hard-to-fill positions, such as bilingual and special education; and
- 45 GYO teachers have graduated or will graduate in 2011.

By 2011, graduating seemed a long way off when most GYO candidates began the program in 2006. A long academic road ahead has been traveled.

Attending College as a GYO Student

GYO is not an alternative certification program. GYO candidates go through the same teacher preparation program as any student in Illinois who wants to be a teacher. Since GYO candidates have often been out of school for years, some of them need developmental coursework, especially math, to refresh their academic skills. These courses are not credit granting, however, and candidates do not like to spend too much time taking them. They usually take their initial courses at community colleges because the needed courses are offered there and are less expensive.

Once they complete their community college courses, a Basic Skills test is required for admittance to a college of education. This test was always a barrier and, as is discussed later, is now much more of a barrier since the cut scores have been dramatically increased. Many candidates do not take tests well, especially if English is not their first language. Some experience strong test anxiety. This test is one that can make or break their plans to become teachers. As of this writing, approximately 65% of GYO candidates have taken the Basic Skills test, and of those who have taken the test, about 50% have passed.

After they pass the Basic Skills test and can enter the college of education, most begin taking classes on the campus of the 4-year institution. This is sometimes difficult for the candidates. At least some of them have been taking GYO college classes in their own communities in the evening, with child care provided. The university campuses are often far away (or seemed so), large, and impersonal. Rather than being in classes with their GYO cohort members, they are likely to be taking classes with other students, most of whom are much younger. This makes the faculty members' understanding of GYO candidates especially important.

Higher education deans discovered that some faculty members work very well with GYO candidates—the ones who "got" their strengths, assets, and academic backgrounds. The college courses are most successful when they are taught by carefully selected faculty members. These faculty members respect the candidates and the multiple life skills they bring to the class. They are skilled at helping to connect the curriculum to the cultural references of the GYO candidates. They understand how to use the experiences of the GYO candidates to help them and other students in the classroom master academic content and pedagogy and how to use their community connections and wisdom.

In addition to learning content and teaching skills, the GYO candidates know that they are becoming teachers who can help build important bridges between the school and the community. Their college professors prepare them to be teacher leaders, and their cohort coordinators and community organizations encourage them to play active roles in the community, helping them to develop as community leaders as well. One candidate noted, "This isn't just about changing lives in the classroom, but about changing the community." Another said, "I would hate for people to go through a program like this, and then realize that they just wanted the education piece." A cohort coordinator reflected that if candidates are not actively involved in community activities, "then they're kind of producing the same teachers we have in our communities a lot of the time." This community base of the GYO initiative reflects its community history and sets it apart from other teacher preparation programs.

The Community Base of GYO

Community organizers (Gold, Simon, & Brown, 2002) developed GYO as an innovative teacher preparation solution for the persistent problems they were encountering in the low-income neighborhood schools where they worked. Since education policymakers never consult community organizers when they are considering methods for preparing teachers for high-poverty urban schools, solutions tend to require technical and professional expertise—hiring more recruiters, paying incentives to teachers, or reducing class sizes. But organizers know that without political will and powerful constituencies, such solutions are not likely to improve teaching in low-income schools. Organizers and their vocal constituencies ensure that the low-income schools in their neighborhoods will benefit and so will the students of color who attend them and who rely most heavily on public education (Oakes & Rogers, 2006).

Candidates and Community

GYO is preparing highly effective teachers who live in the low-income communities where they will teach. The candidates understand the community's assets and challenges since they live there. Jeff Bartow, who directs the Southwest Organizing Project, reflects on the candidates with whom his community organization works:

Most GYO candidates were active with a member institution or in the organization's activities before becoming candidates. Some teacher candidates have remained active on community issues in addition to attending college. As organizers, however, we first encourage them to pursue excellence in their studies as they prepare to become teachers.

But we also believe there are analogies between learning to become teachers and many of the skills learned through participation in public life: specifically, relational skills that require the development of trust and accountability and diagnostic skills related to breaking a problem down into actionable solutions. So we encourage candidate participation in the organization's actions, where these public life skills can be learned.

Beyond skill building, we believe it is important for teacher candidates to have a genuine understanding of the challenges families of their future students face and resources these families bring on their own behalf. Although the candidates are themselves of the community, there is no substitute for real interaction with others in our community to complement teacher classroom preparation.

GYO teacher candidates are part of an extraordinary and bold statewide action, an action aimed at transforming schools and communities by bringing teacher candidates from those communities into the classroom as agents of change—rooted in community power represented most concretely by the mutual support and accountability strengthened among candidates through regular participation in their monthly cohort meetings. Community actions should be in the service of their growth as future teachers, unless it's for the sheer joy and transformative impact of being part of a powerful collective action! (personal communication, 2009)

Another powerful rationale for building bridges to the community: research has demonstrated that the social capital represented by such community connections improves student achievement (Woolley et al., 2008). Identifying and using research related to GYO is one of the roles that GYO IL plays under contract, in support of all consortia.

GYO IL's Contract Work

GYO IL has had a state contract since 2005 to help with implementation of GYO, working with consortia as supporters, troubleshooters, and the communication center. GYO IL coordinates informational activities with policymakers, carries out strategic communications, and presents GYO at conferences locally and nationally. With a committee of consortia representatives, GYO IL organizes an annual conference—the Statewide Learning Network meeting, which brings together representatives of all consortia to share experiences with one another—and hosts an annual planning retreat. GYO IL provides support for the independent GYO evaluation called for in the law. The GYO website functions as a source of information.

GYO IL has also established GYO partnerships between two consortia so they can build relationships, thus getting to know each other's staff and candidates. Together, they visit each other, meet, enjoy meals together, and share training on community organizing and other topics. They commiserate and exchange promising solutions to shared problems. The candidates always enjoy meeting candidates from another community.

GYO Challenges

Funding. There are several significant challenges that GYO faces. One challenge is maintaining state funding. In Illinois, the state budget must be approved annually. Fighting for the funds for GYO is time-consuming and especially difficult since Illinois has an enormous fiscal deficit, one of the nation's largest. The state is far behind in paying its bills. (At this writing, 9 months into the fiscal year, the 16 GYO consortia have received no payments at all from their fiscal year grants).

GYO IL holds an annual Rally Day, which brings candidates from all over the state to the state capitol. They hold an energetic rally in the middle of the rotunda. Candidates tell their own stories about their challenges in returning to college, the importance of GYO support, and what a difference their becoming teachers is making to their children and families. Many legislators stop by to speak and offer their support.

Because of the strong relationships that the community organizers and candidates have developed with legislators and the staff in the governor's office and because an enormous effort is made every year, GYO has maintained most of its funding.

Every year since 2006, GYO has unsuccessfully requested an appropriation of $4.5 million that would allow it to expand into new high-need communities, to actively recruit new teacher candidates, to pay candidates for student teaching, and to provide mentoring. The annual financial uncertainty takes a large financial toll on the consortia and a large psychological toll on the candidates, who have made major commitments to attend college and are unsure every year whether funds will be forthcoming. It is small compensation that GYO teachers will be well schooled in state fiscal policy.

Basic Skills test. In September 2010, the Illinois State Board of Education dramatically increased the cut scores on the test that all potential teachers in Illinois must pass to get accepted into the college of education. In addition to the increased cut scores, test takers can take the test only five times, although they can "bank" the subtests they have passed. Before the test scores were increased, there was already a significant disparity in pass rates among Caucasians (92% passed), African Americans (59% passed), and Latinos (70% passed). Since the cut scores were raised—an increase that was 2 standard errors of measurement above what an expert panel had recommended—very few are passing.

The combined results of the six tests for which results are available in spring 2011 show that only 22% of all test takers statewide have passed. Among Caucasians, 27% have passed; among African Americans, only 6%; among Latinos, only 9.5%. These results are terrible across the board and are particularly devastating for potential teachers of color, which include GYO candidates. GYO IL has mounted a Basic Skills campaign, in partnership with colleges of education, to try to find a solution to this enormous problem.

They are cutting their budgets and laying off teachers. A new and unexpected challenge is that, like other new hires, some GYO new teachers are being temporarily laid off due to district-wide reduction in force, also referred to as "RIFing."

GYO Successes

Community engagement. GYO has generated national interest as a community-based model that is preparing a pipeline of teachers of color. Representatives from five states have visited GYO representatives in Illinois to learn more. Interest in GYO stems from its ability to prepare community members to be highly qualified teachers. The success of GYO provides a strong platform for community organizations to work on related educational issues in their low-income neighborhood schools. For example, community organizations are now learning about and advocating for strong induction and mentoring programs at their schools so that GYO teachers, when hired, will be well supported. They are working with local school principals and teachers to engage them with GYO candidates on issues of effective teaching. They are examining measures of teacher effectiveness and nontraditional assessments of teaching quality. As the foundation of all this work, the groups continue to build strong grassroots leadership and develop the powerful relationships that have helped to create the GYO victories to date.

The partnerships between community organizations and higher education are becoming increasingly rich and beneficial to both partners. For example, two community organizations have hosted their university partner on field trips to their neighborhoods. Fifteen faculty members have attended all-day sessions that involve school visits, a neighborhood tour, conversations with candidates, discussion with organizers working on issues of foreclosures and immigration as well as education, and meetings with other community groups. This has been eye-opening; many of the faculty members had not actually been in a low-income urban school or neighborhood for many years. The community organizations then attended a faculty retreat at the university. The dean of the college of education is now institutionalizing this approach in her college and raising funds to support this kind of community–faculty exchange.

Underserved student success. At a time when the number of students of color in Illinois public schools is increasing, the number of teachers of color from Illinois universities is decreasing. GYO creates a critical pipeline of color for parents, teachers aides, and community leaders from low-income communities to become teachers. They are to be teachers who understand the culture and the community of the students they are teaching—students who are "their children," certainly figuratively and often literally. This alone is a powerful rationale for a GYO initiative.

In the 6 years since the GYO law was passed, the retention rate of candidates remains high. Almost half of candidates have family incomes of under $30,000, which means that they are living at the margins. If a husband loses his job or if a child or parent or the candidate herself gets sick, the family can be thrown into crisis. Over half the candidates are still in the program, even though they are juggling many responsibilities, and since they work full-time, they can attend college only part-time, which makes the pace of their progress through college sometimes frustratingly slow. Consortia have been stretched financially since funding has been shaved for the past few years. However, most consortia feel the need to recruit anew, both to add new candidates and to fill shortages.

Katelyn Johnson, the North Lawndale cohort coordinator, has developed a new recruiting strategy that recognizes fiscal constraints and the importance of identifying candidates who will fit the GYO model and be academically successful. She has created a Pre-GYO cohort.

Pre-GYO candidates make a commitment to be actively engaged with the GYO program and with other candidates, but they use their federal financial aid, not GYO funds, to pay for selected college courses. When they have shown that they can successfully complete one or two math courses and have been active with GYO, they are then invited to be full GYO candidates.

CONCLUSION

Overall, the good news far outweighs the bad. The inspirational GYO teachers to be; the unusual and innovative community, school, and university partnerships; and the goals now being attained have won GYO a growing national reputation. Recent baseline data from observations and assessments of the first cohort of GYO teachers indicate that the GYO hypothesis—that teachers grown from the community will be highly effective—is proving true. A first-year report on new GYO teachers showed that they demonstrated excellent results on content knowledge, classroom management, and engaging students and parents. GYO is confident that the creative career pathway that GYO candidates and the new GYO teachers are traveling will bring excellent teaching skills and high expectations to the students in their low-income neighborhood schools who need them the most.

REFERENCES

Berry, J., & Young, V. C. (2007). *Grow Your Own Illinois: An innovative approach to providing high quality teaching in low-income communities*. Independence, OH: Center for Collaboration and the Future of Schooling.

Boyd, D., Lankford, H., Loeb, S., & Wyckoff, J. (2005). The draw of home: How teachers' preferences for proximity disadvantage urban school. *Journal of Policy Analysis and Management, 24*(1), 113–132.

Frost, S. (2003). *Here one year, gone the next: Summarizing the teacher turnover data for 64 ACORN neighborhood schools, 2002–2003 to 2003–2004*. Chicago: ACORN.

Gold, E., Simon, E., & Brown, C. (2002). *Strong neighborhoods, strong schools; The indicators project on education organizing*. Chicago: Cross City Campaign for Urban School Reform.

Oakes, J., & Rogers, J.(2006). *Learning power: Organizing for education and justice*. Los Angeles: UCLA.

Warren, M. (2005). Communities and schools: A new view of urban education reform. *Harvard Educational Review, 75*(2), 133–173.

Woolley, M. E., Grogan-Kaylor, A., Gilster, M. E., Karb, R. A., Gant, L. M., & Reischl, T. (2008). Neighborhood social support, poor physical conditions, and academic achievement. *Children & Schools, 30*, 133–145.

Chapter Five

The Online Completer Program: A Regional Teacher Pipeline With 22 Community Colleges in Rural East Texas

Dawn Michelle Williams and Paula Griffin

Consider the following scenario:

> A nondegreed person works as a paraprofessional in a classroom. She would like to finish a teaching degree but cannot afford to be without the income that her job provides while doing so. Furthermore, there is not an accredited university within driving distance of her residence. Combine these things with family responsibilities, gas prices, and the funds needed to pay for college.

The Stephen F. Austin State University (SFASU) Online Completer Program provides an avenue for such a person to fulfill the dream of becoming a teacher.

Teacher recruitment and retention are of great concern to school administrators (Kaplan & Owings, 2002; Rotherham & Mead, 2003). This is particularly true because of the requirement to provide highly qualified teachers as defined by No Child Left Behind (2002; U.S. Department of Education, 2002). One solution to the problem of teacher recruitment and retention is to "grow your own" (Clement, 2006)—that is, to educate and train people already working in education in some capacity. Paraprofessionals already working with students in our schools provide a large pool of potential teachers (Forbush & Morgan, 2004; Kaplan, 1977). These are individuals who have already proven their ability to work with students but are unable to complete their degree due to a variety of challenges, including distance from the university, work schedules, financial issues, and parenting responsibilities (White, 2004).

The goal of the Online Completer Program at SFASU is to provide an avenue for nontraditional students who are enrolled in community colleges to complete their bachelor's degrees and obtain their teaching certificates without having to travel to campus for coursework. The Texas Education Agency (Ramsey, 2011a) reports that the first-year teacher attrition rate is particularly high in rural school districts. Ramsey (2011a) states that first-year attrition at districts under 1,000 students averages approximately 20%. Data from Texas Education Agency (Ramsey, 2011b) shows that the demand for teachers has decreased somewhat since 2006, but indicates that a large percentage (30%) of those teaching math, science, English/language arts, and social studies at the middle level are teaching outside their certification area (Ramsey, 2011c). The online program provides an avenue for administrators in these districts to "grow their own" teachers within the community, individuals who live there and plan to stay there.

HISTORICAL OVERVIEW

Hussar (1999) predicted that the nation's school districts would need to hire between 1.7 million and 2.7 million teachers between 1998–1999 and 2008–2009. Wayne's (2000) analysis produced similar results. Likewise, in Texas the demand for public school teachers continues to increase. Fuller (2002) reported a 47% increase from 1996 to 2002. In Texas the demand for public school teachers continues in specific teaching fields. Data from the Texas Education Agency (Ramsey, 2011) show that the demand for teachers has decreased somewhat since 2006 but that a large percentage (30%) of those teaching math, science, English/language arts, and social studies at the middle level are teaching outside their certification areas. While the percentage of teachers who are not certified is decreasing, 6.9% at the middle level and 3.9% at the elementary level in Texas are not certified to teach.

With an increased need for qualified teachers in Texas, the Department of Elementary Education at SFASU began the EC-6 (early childhood through sixth grade) Online Completer Program in January 2005. This program was a cooperative effort among the university, area schools, and 22 Texas community colleges offering the associate of arts in teaching degree for those students interested in pursuing a 4-year degree and teaching certification. SFASU's elementary education department has over 1,200 majors and is recognized for its outstanding teacher education program. The James I. Perkins College of Education's 2005–2006 annual report cites a 98% overall pass rate on the TExES certification exams. One hundred percent of EC-6 students and Grade 4–8 students (detailed later) passed the certification exams prior to student teaching. This rate has been consistent throughout the past 10 years. Online courses were developed by elementary education faculty to closely mirror the content delivered in the face-to-face program, as it was crucial to SFASU that the integrity and reputation of the teacher preparation program be kept intact. Seventeen teacher candidates, 11 of which were paraprofessionals, made up the initial cohort. The EC-6 program has grown to include two 25-member cohorts, which begin each fall and spring semester.

FUNDS FOR THE IMPROVEMENT OF POSTSECONDARY EDUCATION GRANT

In October 2006, the SFASU Department of Elementary Education was awarded a federal grant from the U.S. Department of Education: Funds for the Improvement of Postsecondary Education. Totaling approximately $600,000 over 3 years, this grant directly benefited the online completer programs. A portion of the grant funds was allocated for improvement of online courses and to assess the effectiveness of utilizing webcam technology to observe online teacher candidates real-time during field experiences. As a result of the grant, which ended in September 2010, each EC-6 online course received revisions, and new online courses were created to facilitate teacher candidates' success in online educational studies, including a virtual lab for online students' initial education course pertaining to the psychosocial development of children. Webcam implementation began in 2007 and is available and successfully used each semester of the online program with particular focus on the two internship semesters prior to student teaching.

Since its inception in the spring of 2005, more than 300 students have graduated from the EC-6 program, with 83% being Caucasian, 11% being Hispanic, and 6% being African American. Additionally, 99% of the graduates were female. Seventy-one percent of those graduates were paraprofessionals, and 93% were hired and retained to teach in the district in which they were already working. SFASU has maintained a 99% pass rate on the teacher certification exams for both the face-to-face program and the online program. School administrators recognized the success of the EC-6 online completer program and requested that an online program be developed to prepare teachers to teach in Grades 4–8. As a result, the Middle Level Grades (MLG) Online Completer Program was developed and initiated in January 2009 with 23 students participating in the first cohort. This first group of 22 teacher candidates graduated during the 2010–2011 school year. All of these teacher candidates passed the required Texas certification exams prior to graduation.

THE PROGRAM

Overview

The Online Completer Program is designed for students who have completed an associate of arts degree in teaching or at least 45 hours at a Texas Community College. Interested students must apply for admission and meet at least one of the following criteria: live 60 or more miles from campus, be employed full-time in a school as a paraprofessional, have other full-time employment, or be unable to attend classes on campus due to other extenuating circumstances. Other requirements include a grade point average of 3.0 or higher, commitment to come to campus 2 or 3 days each semester, prior experience with online courses, access to the necessary technology, and prior experience with children. The online completer student may choose to specialize in EC-6 generalist, MLG English/language arts, MLG mathematics, MLG social studies, or MLG generalist, which allows the candidate to teach any of the four core subjects in Grades 4–8. Teacher candidates complete 47 to 48 credit hours of core curriculum (at the community college), approximately 42 to 46 hours in their academic major, 12 preprofessional hours, and 18 professional teacher education hours, totaling 120 to 124 credit hours to graduate with a degree in interdisciplinary studies.

The online completer program is fully accredited through the National Council of Accreditation of Teacher Education, the Southern Association for Colleges and Schools, and the State Board for Educator Certification. Entrance standards to the program are purposefully high because research shows that programs with stringent requirements are more successful (Denton et al., 2009; Rotherham & Mead, 2003; Schweizer, Hayslett, & Chaplock, 2008). Both Denton and colleagues (2009) and Schmeizer and colleagues (2008) studied online programs for postbaccalaureate teacher candidates and describe the importance of testing for content knowledge prior to entry into the program. The SFASU program requires a 3.0 grade point average for core coursework completed at the community college to ensure success as the teacher candidates prepare for the content exams.

SFASU online completer teacher candidates complete the same program as those who attend classes on campus. The online program therefore provides the same training and experience as the face-to face program. Teacher candidates complete approximately 48 hours of university core curriculum coursework, most of which is completed at a regional community college. They then complete the remainder of the teacher certification program online with 9 hours of preprofessional hours, 42 to 46 hours in their major area, and 18 hours of professional teacher education. One of the major differences between the online program and the face-to-face program is that the online completer teacher candidates are organized into cohort groups and progress through the entire program as a group. For this reason there is a set sequence of courses that the students must complete together each semester. There are currently 220 students involved in the EC-6 program and 130 students in the MLG program. The first 22 MLG teacher candidates graduated during the 2010–2011 school year.

On-Campus Learning Activities

The SFASU Online Completer Program requires some activities on campus. Teacher candidates are required to come to campus for a 2- or 3-day class meeting each semester. Students are made aware of this requirement prior to acceptance into the program. The 2-day agenda includes advising, test preparation, and observation in SFASU's charter school and local middle schools. These face-to-face meetings provide concentrated opportunities for developing a sense of community among cohort members within the learning environment. During this time on campus, teacher candidates meet with university faculty and engage in activities designed to enhance online content. Time is provided for students to file degree plans and take practice versions of state-mandated pedagogy and content area tests prior to the actual exams. Teacher candidates are also issued webcams for observations and trained in the protocol for use in field experiences.

EC-6 teacher candidates spend 3 days on campus each semester and are provided focused opportunities to interact with elementary students in SFASU's charter school for students in Grades K–5. Founded in 1998, the charter school is housed with the Department of Elementary Education in the Early Childhood Research Center, a $38-million state-of-the-art facility on the SFASU campus, which opened during the fall of 2009.

The charter school is rated exemplary according the Texas Education Agency accreditation standards. Additionally, EC-6 cohort members observe developmentally appropriate practices implemented in the classrooms of SFASU's Early Childhood Lab School. The lab school is housed in the same building as the charter school and includes state-of-the-art classrooms for infants, toddlers, and prekindergarten students. University faculty facilitate guided observations focusing on literacy development and guided reading strategies utilizing the charter school observation booths during the third-semester campus visit of the online program. The following semester, Intern II online students observe teaching and learning in the areas of math, science, and social studies, followed by debriefing and explanation with university instructors. During the campus visits, teacher candidates have the opportunity to observe and make connections between the implementation of developmentally appropriate practice and theories taught in online courses.

Similarly, MLG teacher candidates spend 2 days each semester on campus. These visits include observations in both the SFASU charter school and local middle schools. During the first semester of the program, MLG cohort members take a block of courses that includes early literacy development. Therefore, time is included during the face-to-face meeting to observe young children (kindergarteners and first graders) learning to read, as well as fourth and fifth graders reading. Teacher candidates spend approximately 8 hours each week during Intern I and 16 hours per week during Intern II in local middle schools to learn about appropriate middle school practice and to focus on content area specialization. Teacher candidates observe effective classroom procedures and management techniques and developmentally appropriate middle school practice in fourth- and fifth-grade classrooms at the charter school and in sixth-, seventh-, and eighth-grade classes at local middle schools. Time is also designated for MLG cohort members to meet with their professors, take certification practice tests, participate in training for webcam observations, and complete necessary paperwork for student teaching, degree plans, and so on. With changes in Texas legislation, all teacher candidates are required to student-teach during their final semester in the program. Prior to 2011, educational aides (paraprofessionals) were able to waive student teaching due to their experience in the classroom.

Internships

Two internships are completed in the school in which the candidate is employed. Teacher candidates shadow a mentor teacher in the classroom to complete field experience activities. Using webcams, SFASU professors observe and conference with the candidates as they teach the required field lessons. Teacher candidates who do not work in a school (either as a paraprofessional or as a regular substitute) must secure a classroom in a public school to complete the two internships, and they are required to complete the student-teaching semester. Currently, there are 134 (94 EC-6 and 40 MLG) students in the program who are paraprofessionals or substitutes who will be exempt from student teaching and 170 (145 EC-6 and 25 MLG) who are not working in a school and will be required to student-teach. Previously, student teaching was waived for those who had been a paraprofessional for at least 2 years and had passed all certification exams prior to the student-teaching semester. Teacher candidates in the program are now required to make arrangements to student-teach full-time in a classroom during the last semester for 13 weeks.

EC-6 internships. EC-6 teacher candidates participate in two internships. During the Intern I semester, teacher preparation classes are focused in and around literacy development of the elementary student. Teacher candidates work with the classroom teacher to select a small group of students of similar literacy abilities in Grades 1–6 to complete a semester-long literacy project. The project involves assessment of each student's reading, comprehension, and fluency levels. From these assessments, the teacher candidate creates meaningful guided reading lessons, vocabulary study, and literacy activities designed to facilitate the improvement of individual students' reading abilities. Student progress and data are recorded and analyzed after each lesson to direct the focus for subsequent small group lessons. Teacher candidates are involved in communicating with the families of these students throughout the semester under the supervision of both the classroom teacher and the college instructor. Webcam technology is utilized by the college instructor to observe at least two and sometimes more of these small group lessons. Teacher candidates and college instructors conference via webcam immediately following each transmission to discuss the literacy lesson.

The second internship semester is patterned after the first internship. Expectations are similar, but the teacher education classes are focused on the content areas of math, science, and social studies rather than literacy. Teacher candidates are learning the theory and practice of teaching in those areas through the online courses with an emphasis on constructivist learning and practices. They create lesson and activity plans, including active hands-on learning, informal and formal assessments for lesson objectives, strategies for integrating English-language learners, and extensions for students to connect learning with the world about them. The candidates implement these lessons with a small group of students. College instructors observe at least three of these lessons via webcam, followed by a conference with the observing instructor.

MLG internships. Likewise, MLG teacher candidates complete two internships. Intern I focuses on classroom management, lesson planning, middle-level concept, response-to-intervention, and school law. Intern II reinforces those concepts and focuses on the content area methods. Teacher candidates are responsible for securing a classroom to complete their internship activities. Internships must be conducted in a classroom in Grades 4–8, and it must be in their area of specialty if they are specialists. Candidates seeking MLG generalist certification may choose an internship placement in a classroom in any of the four core subject areas. MLG teacher candidates must participate in a 10–credit hour block of courses that include the lab or field experience. Throughout the internship, teacher candidates participate in online discussions, chats, and journal entries concerning their classroom experiences and the course content. University faculty observe the teacher candidates as they teach lessons in their assigned classrooms and conference with them immediately following the observation, through the use of webcams and the Eluminate program.

For many of the online completer students (both MLG and EC-6), the second internship is their final semester before graduation from the program and the university. Immediate feedback and discussions after each lesson to debrief and dissect the teaching and learning are essential to the candidates' understanding and proficiency in teaching. During the final internship, teacher candidates complete the final assessments of the program, including a work sample project that illustrates their ability to plan, teach, and assess a lesson. They also prepare for, take, and pass their content certification test during the second internship. SFASU professors continually give support and feedback to ensure that online teacher candidates are prepared and ready for their first teaching position.

Financial Assistance

Not only do the online programs provide high-quality academic support, but a number of financial aid opportunities are available to the online teacher candidates as well. In Texas, students with at least 1 year as an instructional aide who also meet income eligibility are eligible to receive the Educational Aide Tuition Exemption. There is also a Community College Transfer Scholarship, which is awarded to those students who transfer from a community college with a grade point average of 3.0 or better. Students are automatically eligible to receive the Community College Transfer Scholarship. Candidates in the online program often qualify for Pell Grants, and some qualify for the TEACH Grant, which provides up to $4,000 per year which the student is not required to pay back as long as he or she teaches in a high-needs school district for 4 years after graduation. This grant is available only to those teacher candidates specializing in a subject area in which there is a great demand for teachers. Only those MLG teacher candidates who are generalists or specializing in English/language arts or mathematics are eligible for the TEACH grant. This grant is based, not on financial need, but on area of specialty.

In the past, teacher candidates in Texas with at least 1 year as an instructional aide who also met income eligibility were eligible to receive the Educational Aide Tuition Exemption, which covered the cost of tuition. With recent state budget cuts, this is no longer an option for these students. The future of this option is unclear at this time.

Successes and Challenges

Today online educator preparation programs continue to increase in number and often are criticized and labeled as degree mills (Sawchuk, 2009). Huss (2007) noted the apprehension of some principals about online teacher candidates concerning the dispositions and interactions of teachers trained online. However, Schweizer and colleagues (2008) acknowledged that the quality of online education is equal to, and may actually surpass, on-campus instruction. Nontraditional students face a number of obstacles in attending face-to-face classes in college: distance from campus, work schedules, family obligations, low socioeconomic status, the role of a single parent or head of household, and so on (Schweizer et al., 2008; White, 2004). Thus, online programs provide the flexibility and support that many nontraditional students need to complete their college degree and become certified to teach.

Schweizer and colleagues (2008) reported eight qualities that potential students considered when choosing a teacher education program: flexibility and convenience, time for family, flexibility for work, quality and reputation, instructional format, distance from home, time involved in completion of the degree, and price. Although there is concern that online students may lack the experience and interactions necessary to develop as quality teachers, several studies suggest that online courses provide as much, if not more, interaction than do face-to-face courses (Sawchuk, 2009; Smith Canter, Voytecki, & Rodriquez, 2007). Smith Canter et al. (2007) stressed the importance of learner-to-learner, learner-to-instructor, and learner-to-content interaction within the online course.

To ensure quality online teaching, SFASU provides an intensive web design course to all faculty members interested in developing web-based courses and teaching online. In the MLG online program, quality student–teacher interaction is provided through video conferencing, discussion boards, chats, e-mail, and instant messaging. Pena and Almaguer (2007) also acknowledged the benefits of using WebCT to provide online mentoring and interaction with student teachers in the field. Teacher candidates in the MLG Online Completer Program are able to interact with one another and their professors in a variety of ways. Student success is measured through work samples, field experiences, dispositional surveys, diagnostic exams, teaching philosophy papers, and certification exams. Webcams are checked out to students prior to their internships and used in classroom observations and video conference before and after the lessons are taught.

In a survey concerning the effectiveness of using webcams to observe and conference, 88% of EC-6 teacher candidates participating in Intern II were satisfied in the support and effectiveness of the internship supervision using the webcam technology. Similarly, 88% of mentor teachers felt that the internship was effective using the webcams. However, 25% of the mentors reported some difficulty with the technology. SFASU continues to make adjustments in the program to better support the teacher candidates and their mentors throughout the internship.

Sustainability. Online teacher candidates have been successful in passing all required state certification exams prior to student teaching. The pass rate is nearly 100%. Evaluations by mentor teachers and university supervisors in regard to lesson planning, teaching, and professional dispositions are completed with 98% rated *acceptable* or *exemplary*. Districts have shown confidence in the SFASU teacher candidates, as 93% have obtained teaching jobs in their home districts.

Recruitment and retention. Program coordinators work closely with community college partners and Texas public schools to recruit potential students. However, the best recruiters are the online teacher candidates themselves as they talk with other paraprofessionals about the program. These individuals who have already proven their ability to work with students are often unable to complete their degree due to a variety of challenges, including distance from the university, work schedules, financial issues, and parenting responsibilities (White, 2004). The online completer programs at SFASU provide an avenue for these individuals to complete their bachelor degrees and obtain their teaching certification while continuing to work in their current positions.

SFASU EC-6 Online Completer Program students have been successful in obtaining teaching positions in their local school districts. Ninety-three percent of the online teacher candidates working as paraprofessionals have secured teaching positions in their local district after completing the program. In a postgraduation survey of EC-6 teaching candidates, 95% agreed that they felt confident in their pedagogical and content knowledge and that the EC-6 Online Completer Program had been successful in giving them the knowledge, skills, and support needed to teach.

Although not all teacher candidates complete the program at the same rate, approximately 90% of teacher candidates who begin the online program complete the certification program and graduate with a bachelor's degree. According to a 2001 longitudinal study conducted by the National Center for Education Statistics (2001), approximately 20% of all bachelor degree graduates, or 200,000 students, completed their degree having transferred from a 2-year community college program. Students are required to pass an Elementary Admissions Exam early in the program, meet teacher education requirements (successful completion of 60 credit hours; maintain a 2.5 grade point average; earn acceptable test scores in math, reading, and writing) before they are allowed to register for internships and pass the certification exams prior to student teaching. These requirements ensure that SFASU teacher candidates have the knowledge, skills, and professional dispositions necessary to be competent teachers.

DISCUSSION

Online teacher education programs are becoming more popular and, as a consequence, are expanding opportunities for individuals who otherwise would not be able to complete a degree (Sawchuk, 2009). The SFASU Online Completer Program is designed to support paraprofessionals who are already working in the schools, as well as other nontraditional students who might not otherwise complete their degrees. For many participants, the online program is the only option for completing a teaching degree.

The students in this program have strong ties to, and want to stay in, their communities. This online program allows school districts the opportunity to grow their own (Clement, 2006; White, 2004). SFASU remains committed to preparing teacher candidates who are prepared for the responsibilities and challenges involved in teaching while meeting the needs of these nontraditional students through quality online courses combined with practical and relevant experience. The program currently functions without the assistance of external funds. This program enables paraprofessionals to realize their dreams of becoming teachers.

Candidate Voices

SFASU Online Completer Program teacher candidates voice satisfaction with their experiences in the program. Here is what one student said about the program:

> I am thankful that online courses are available. It makes it possible for single mothers like me to further their education. Without online courses I would not be able to attend college because I must hold down a full time job and care for my child. I appreciate this online program.

Other students similarly commented: "I have learned so much in this program. —— always made herself available to help me and answer anything I needed. I feel more prepared and more informed about my next step as a teacher." "The online program is such a blessing and —— made it even better. This class has changed my perspective of teaching in a very positive way."

Conclusion

As the demand for highly qualified teachers continues to grow, one alternative is to "grow your own" (Clement, 2006) by training paraprofessionals already working in our schools (Forbush & Morgan, 2004; Kaplan, 1977). These individuals, who have already proven their ability to work with students, are often unable to complete their degrees due to a variety of challenges, including distance from the university, work schedules, financial issues, and parenting responsibilities (White, 2004). The SFASU Online Completer Program provides an avenue for these individuals to complete their bachelor degrees and obtain their teaching certifications while continuing to work in their current positions. At the same time, it provides schools across Texas with a pool of highly qualified teachers who will remain in their communities and teach.

REFERENCES

Clement, M. C. (2006). My mother's teaching career: What it can tell us about teachers who are not fully certified. *Phi Delta Kappan, 87*(10), 772–776.

Denton, J. J., Davis, T. J., Capraro, R. M., Smith, B. L., Beason, L., Graham, B. D., et al. (2009). Examining applicants for admission and completion of an online teacher certification program. *Educational Technology & Society, 12*(1), 214–229.

Forbush, D. E. & Morgan, R. L. (2004) Instructional team training: Delivering live, internet courses to teachers and paraprofessionals in Utah, Idaho, and Pennsylvania. *Rural Special Education Quarterly, 23*(2), 9–17.

Fuller, E. (2002). Elements of the demand for Texas public school teachers. *State Board for Educator Certification Issue Brief.*

Huss, J. A. (2007). Perceptions of secondary principals toward online teacher preparation. *Journal of Ethnography and Qualitative Research, 2*(1), 23–31.

Hussar, W. J. (1999). *Predicting the need for newly hired teacher in the United States to 2008–09.* Washington, DC: US Department of Education, National Center for Education Statistics.

Kaplan, G. (1977). *From aide to teacher: The story of the career opportunities program.* HEW Publication No. OE 76–12010. Washington, D.C.: U. S. Department of Education.

Kaplan, L., & Owings, W. A. (2002). The politics of teacher quality: Implications for principals. *National Association of Secondary School Principals Bulletin, 86*(631), 16–31.

National Center for Education Statistics (2001). 2001 Baccalaureate and beyond longitudinal study. Retrieved August 29, 2011, from http://nces.ed.gov/das/epubs/showTable2004.asp?tableID=140&rt=bb

No Child Left Behind Act of 2001, H. Res. 1, 107th Cong., 110 (2002) (enacted).

Pena, C. M., & Almaguer, I. (2007). Asking the right questions: Online mentoring of student teachers. *International Journal of Instructional Media, 34*(1), 105–13.

Ramsey, M. C. (2011a). *One year attrition by district size 2008–2010. SBEC: Who is teaching by district data.* Retrieved from http://www.tea.state.tx.us

Ramsey, M. C. (2011b). *Out of field teacher credentials 2008–2010. SBEC: Who is teaching by district data.* Retrieved from http://www.tea.state.tx.us

Ramsey, M. C. (2011c). *Uncertified teachers 2006–2010. SBEC: Who is teaching by district data.* Retrieved from http://www.tea.state.tx.us

Rotherham, A. J., & Mead, S. (2003). Teacher quality beyond no child left behind: A response to Kaplan and Owings (2002). *National Association of Secondary Principals Bulletin, 87*(635), 65–76.

Sawchuk, S. (2009). Teacher training goes in virtual directions. *Education Week, 28*(26), 22–24.

Schweizer, H., Hayslett, C., & Chaplock, S. (2008). Student satisfaction and performance in an online teaching certification program. *Journal of Continuing Higher Education, 56*(2), 12–15.

Smith Canter, L. L., Voytecki, K. S., & Rodriquez, D. (2007). Increasing online interaction in rural special education teacher preparation programs. *Rural Special Education, 26*(1), 23–27.

U.S. Department of Education. (2002). *Meeting the highly-qualified teacher challenge: The secretary's annual report on teacher quality.* Washington, DC: Office of Postsecondary Education, Office of Policy Planning and Innovation.

Wayne, A. J. (2000). Teacher supply and demand: Surprises from primary research. *Education Policy Analysis Archive, 8*(47). Retrieved from http://epaa.asu.edu/epaa/v8n47.html

White, R. (2004). The recruitment of para educators into the special education profession: A review of progress, select evaluation outcomes, and new initiatives. *Remedial and Special Education, 25*(4), 214–218.

Chapter Six

CERRA: A Statewide Pipeline for Teacher Recruitment, Preparation, and Induction in South Carolina

Gayle Sawyer

A close look at the Center for Recruitment, Retention, and Advancement (CERRA) of South Carolina detects a unique example of statewide programming and collaboration among stakeholders that strategically addresses both the need for and the needs of educators. CERRA's (2010b) mission is

> to provide leadership in identifying, attracting, placing and retaining well-qualified individuals for the teaching profession in our state. In doing so, CERRA will respond to changing needs for teachers from underrepresented populations, in critical subject fields and in under-served geographical areas in South Carolina. The Center will work cooperatively with other organizations to promote the education profession.

The center, the brainchild of a consortium of South Carolina teacher education institutions, was borne to improve the recruitment and quality of teacher education candidates in response to growing concerns for the quality of teaching and learning (National Commission on Excellence in Education, 1983) and for a teacher shortage predicted by educators such as Linda Darling-Hammond (1984). Its continuing intentional impact is to increase the number of qualified, caring, competent teachers working in public school classrooms across South Carolina.

Innovative elements and flexibility distinguish the center from other educator initiatives. First of all, CERRA, neither a part of the South Carolina Department of Education (SCDE) nor a part of a college of education, functions statewide, partnering with 24 public and private teacher education institutions and 199 high schools and middle schools. Similarly, CERRA serves all 85 South Carolina school districts, as well as a number of special schools.

CERRA's strongest element is the continuity of targeted recruitment and retention initiatives through a continuum of resources, beginning in middle schools and culminating with practicing, accomplished teacher leaders. Through CERRA, South Carolina's "grow your own" initiatives begin at the precollegiate level, with ProTeam at the middle school level and with Teacher Cadets at the high school level, the standards and curricula for which have been approved as career cluster courses in South Carolina and endorsed by national organizations. Teacher Cadets, South Carolina's flagship recruitment program among high school students, is an honors-level, dual-credit course enriched by collaboration with South Carolina colleges and used in 34 additional states.

At the preservice level, CERRA's teacher recruitment services include South Carolina's Teaching Fellows Program, the Job Bank, the State Online Educator Employment and Certification Application, and the Expo Educator Recruitment Fair. In addition, CERRA has partnered successfully with the South Carolina Diverse Pathways to attract high school students to 2+2 teacher preparation programs (Center for Teacher Quality, 2009). Finally, at the in-service level, the continuum extends to the development of teacher expertise, through innovative retention models of teacher leadership, National Board Certification loans and support, and comprehensive mentoring and induction training, as well as to research, including the annual South Carolina educator supply-and-demand survey.

CERRA continually assesses programmatic changes and growth to better serve the needs of South Carolina educators facing the strategic challenges of the global economic crisis, loss of educator positions, increases in diverse student populations, impending retirement of many baby boomer educators, and pressure to increase teacher effectiveness and student achievement. More teachers are needed in critical-needs subjects and underperforming geographical areas, and classroom teachers need more support and training to help them adapt to rapid changes in student populations, economic conditions, and instructional expectations.

WHEN THE STARS ALIGNED

The idea of a center to manage a coordinated statewide teacher recruitment initiative originated in 1984 with a group of educators and state leaders who were concerned that 54% of South Carolina's teachers came from out of state, that diversity in the teaching profession was declining, that a shortage of teachers was imminent, and that no marketing campaign or pipeline for attracting South Carolinians to the education profession existed. The South Carolina Center for Teacher Recruitment became a reality when "the stars aligned" three times (Graham, 2009).

The first alignment occurred when a university-based consortium of a majority of South Carolina's colleges of education identified the core issues and brought to the attention of the education community that (1) no single teacher education program could solve these core issues and (2) resolving these concerns required a statewide collaboration of business, preK–12 education, higher education, policymakers, and education agencies. The consortium of state leaders became the South Carolina Educator Recruitment Task Force, a team of dedicated visionaries.

Star players in the development of the center were the second alignment. In the governor's office was a strong proponent of education, governor Richard W. Riley, who would later become U.S. secretary of education. Other leading players were Dr. Terry Peterson, Governor

Riley's senior education advisor; Dr. Phil Lader, president of Winthrop College and later U.S. ambassador to Great Britain; and Dr. Jim Rex, dean of the School of Education at Winthrop College, who was elected state superintendent of education in 2007.

The final alignment of stars provided funding and a home for the center. The South Carolina General Assembly authorized the Commission on Higher Education to award grants to public or private colleges to improve the recruitment of teacher education candidates, allocating $236,000 from the newly passed Education Improvement Act of 1984 for this purpose. The South Carolina Recruitment Task Force submitted a proposal to establish the center, which was approved by the commission and has been funded annually since fiscal year 1985–1986.

Winthrop College, now Winthrop University, was selected as the location of the center for several reasons. First, Drs. Lader and Rex, two influential supporters, were employed with Winthrop. Second, the college had a history of excellence in teacher education, was committed to the development of the Teacher Cadets program, offered to function as the fiscal agent for the center, provided gratis housing for the start-up, and invested additional funds from an existing grant, the Winthrop Initiative for the Improvement of Teaching (Graham, 2009). Although the center is not considered a part of the university, the university serves as CERRA's fiscal agent and houses the center in the Stewart House, on the campus across from the Richard W. Riley College of Education.

In 2003, the name of the South Carolina Center for Teacher Recruitment was changed by request to the South Carolina Legislature to CERRA, pronounced "Sarah," to reflect the expanding mission of the organization to meet the need for teacher retention, a rising interest in maintaining a strong, experienced teaching workforce (Ingersoll, 2001; National Commission on Teaching and America's Future, 2003). The name change reflected growth in the interpretation of the original mission of recruitment based on the added programs for retention—mentoring initiatives, management of the state's national board certification loan application process, and teacher leadership.

A CONNECTED CONTINUUM OF PROGRAMS AND SERVICES

The cohesive nature of the center's mission focuses on targeted recruitment and retention initiatives through a continuum of resources, beginning in middle schools and culminating with practicing, accomplished teacher leaders. The levels of engagement through the continuum are *precollegiate* (middle level and high school), *preservice* (teacher education programs and teachers seeking employment in South Carolina), and *service* (in-service teacher retention and leadership) (see Appendix 6.A for the continuum of programs and services). The following section explains the differences among these categories.

Precollegiate Recruitment Programs and Resources

The precollegiate category encompasses three programs: ProTeam, Teacher Cadets, and Teacher Educators. ProTeam is a middle-level teacher recruitment program designed to target male and minority students in the top 40% of their class. The curriculum, *Dreamquest*, currently in its eighth edition, was developed by the center in 1990. *Dreamquest* encourages seventh and eighth graders to consider college as an option and teaching as a career choice. The course standards are aligned with those of the comprehensive school reform model Making Middle Grades Work, from the Southern Regional Education Board. Interest in ProTeam in South Carolina has surged with the passage of the Education and Economic Development Act of 2005, which requires initial career planning in middle school. ProTeam is part of the Education and Training career cluster of the act. More than 13,000 students have participated in ProTeam since its inception (CERRA, 2010b).

The second precollegiate program for teacher recruitment is Teacher Cadets, which is closely aligned with the third precollegiate division, Teacher Educators. The Teacher Cadets program is designed for high school juniors and seniors and has as its primary goal the recruitment of the academically talented students with exemplary interpersonal and leadership skills to teaching as a career choice. The secondary goal of the Teacher Cadets course is to encourage these talented students to become advocates for education by providing them with insights about schools and the teaching profession (even if they decide not to become teachers) in the hopes of recruiting some to a career in teaching. "Teacher Educators" refers to representatives of the 24 South Carolina teacher education institutions, called College Partners, who collaborate with the Teacher Cadets and ProTeam classes.

The Teacher Cadets program includes a daily one-period class for two semesters or an equivalent. This intense course receives honors credit from the high school and receives up to 3 hours of dual credit from its College Partner. Each Teacher Cadets program offers its high school and the local district the opportunity to "grow your own" by identifying and recruiting talented potential teacher candidates from its own population. In addition, College Partners who host activities on their campuses for Teacher Cadets benefit by the opportunity to recruit the "brightest and best" for their programs. Teacher education institutions compete among themselves to attract Teacher Cadets classes to their partnerships, often offering incentives such as college ID cards, no application fees, free admission to sports activities, T-shirts, workshops, library privileges, and access to other campus activities. The College Partner also collaborates with the Teacher Cadets instructor and bolsters the rigor of the program.

The Teacher Cadets program *is* rigorous in its requirements, which is the reason why College Partners agree to offer college credit. Criteria for admission to Teacher Cadets are a minimum of a B grade point average, enrollment in college preparatory courses, and teacher recommendations. High schools also may opt to require either an essay, in which the student discusses why he or she desires to participate in the course, or an interview with a selection panel (or both).

In its 10th edition, *Experiencing Education*, the Teacher Cadets curriculum, is aligned with the standards established by the Interstate New Teacher Assessment and Support Consortium, the National Council for Accreditation of Teacher Education, the Association of Teacher Educators, and the National Board for Professional Teaching Standards. Furthermore, the standards for Teacher Cadets have been endorsed by Phi Delta Kappa International as the national standards for its Future Educator Association (FEA). Since the program began in 1986, the curriculum has been used in 34 states from coast to coast, reinforcing the importance of national standards.

Using the nationally recognized curriculum, the Teacher Cadets instructor leads students in hands-on activities through all phases of the profession. The curriculum is shaped around four sections: "Experiencing the Learner," "Experiencing the Profession," "Experiencing the Classroom," and "Experiencing Education."

In "Experiencing the Learner," Teacher Cadets explore personal values, the role of self-esteem, personality and learning styles, human growth and development from birth to adolescence, and special needs students. As part of their experience, cadets observe students at various developmental stages in area schools. In "Experiencing the Profession," they study the history of schools, the governance of schools, the roles of school personnel, the roles of parents and the public in the school environment, and the organization and management of schools. In the third section, "Experiencing the Classroom," cadets explore the process of becoming a teacher, the characteristics of today's teachers, teachers' responsibilities, variables that contribute to effective teaching, classroom culture, and careers in education. At the conclusion of this section, cadets work with master classroom teachers in an extended field experience at the early childhood, elementary, middle, or high school level. In the final section, "Experiencing Education," cadets are provided with an opportunity to reflect on the totality of their Teacher Cadets experiences. They weigh the pros and cons of the profession and provide feedback regarding program strengths and weaknesses (CERRA, 2010d). Through analysis and reflection on their field experiences, the students engage in developing a personal philosophy of education and therein examine their role as teachers.

As described earlier, the Teacher Cadets program began in 1986 with classes in 24 high schools, and it expanded to approximately 170 high schools in South Carolina (75% of all public in-state high schools), in addition to numerous high schools in 34 other states. In South Carolina, roughly 190 classes of Teacher Cadets are offered each year. Some high schools offer more than one course, while others offer a 2-year Teacher Cadets program containing extended field service opportunities for the students. In addition, in 2010–2011, several high schools piloted unique Teacher Cadets classes, including single-gender (all-male) cadets and "coaches in training." These strategies were employed to attract more males to the profession who want to coach as well as teach. From 2004 to 2009, CERRA participated in Diverse Pathways in Teacher Preparation, a U.S. Department of Education Teacher Quality Partnership Grant designed to foster collaboration among 2- and 4-year colleges. The purpose of the project was to support the development of a highly qualified teaching force that reflected the diversity of the state's population. All partners agreed to provide learning community support and services to students from 2-year colleges who intended to transfer to 4-year institutions through articulated transfer agreements. Statewide partners included the University of South Carolina, Orangeburg-Calhoun Technical College, Midlands Technical College, the College of Charleston, and Trident Technical College. Serving on the Advisory Committee, CERRA collaborated with grant partners, offering recruitment opportunities through Teacher Cadets and ProTeam for the 2-year institutions, providing professional development for students and technical college faculty, hosting statewide student conferences, and establishing FEA chapters at the technical colleges.

In the fall of 2009, the Teacher Cadets program was granted a Career and Technology Education course code, thus making it a Career and Technology Education completer course in South Carolina and continuing the connection with ProTeam in the Education and Training career cluster. Similarly, CERRA's Teacher Cadets data and multistate connections assisted Phi Delta Kappa International and FEA to earn status as a career and technology student organization. Through such status, Perkins IV funds are available to local education agencies using state-approved Career and Technical Education programs of study that are affiliated with FEA as the cocurricular student organization (FEA, 2009). Because of the relationship between the goals of CERRA and FEA, CERRA has become the South Carolina hub for FEA, assisting in the establishment of 29 FEA chapters in the state.

Not only does CERRA provide a curriculum for Teacher Cadets, but the center also administers other forms of support. It offers financial support through site grants to the Teacher Cadets classrooms and to the College Partner institutions. In addition, CERRA trains the Teacher Cadets instructors in the curriculum and provides for them during the school year professional development to which ProTeam instructors and Teacher Educators are invited. Further support consists of a network of Teacher Cadets instructor liaisons, exemplary cadet instructors who are able to offer regional assistance, including mentoring new cadet instructors and maintaining communication among the instructors. The center also provides the *College Financial Newsletter* to students, guidance counselors, and teachers in all South Carolina high schools. The newsletter, which is available online, guides students in finding scholarship information for college, with an emphasis on promoting scholarship and loan opportunities for students interested in pursuing a teaching degree.

The newest form of support for South Carolina's Teacher Cadets programs, as well as programs around the nation, is the Teacher Cadets Interactive Technology Hub (http://www.teachercadets.com), launched in the summer of 2010. The purpose of the hub is to enhance communication among cadet classes and to augment the Teacher Cadets curriculum with access to information and resources supplementing the cadet curriculum. These resources include demonstration lessons, educational videos, current education research and trends, best practices, contact information and links to webpages for College Partners and Teacher Cadets schools, an interactive message board, podcasts, and a photo gallery.

The fact that the Teacher Cadets program has grown from 24 high schools to 170 high schools and expanded into web-based support is one indication of the program's growth. Other indications of success are noted in efficacy data for the program. In the past 5 years, an average of 2,400 students each year has completed the program. Of those students, 19% are males, and 29% are students of color; in 2009–2010, the percentages of those students were the highest recorded, at 22% and 34%, respectively. Also, in the past 5 years, the percentage of students who indicated in their end-of-year online survey that they plan to teach has risen from 37% to 48% (CERRA, 2009). In 2009–2010, nearly one out of every four Teacher Cadets who were undecided about teaching or were considering another profession changed his or her mind as a result of the class and chose teaching; as many as 94% of students have indicated that the class was either effective or very effective in helping them formulate a positive perception of the teaching profession; and 65% of all students completing the class submitted an application for the South Carolina Teaching Fellows Program (CERRA, 2009, 2010b). Of the completers whom the center was able to identify since 1986–1987, a total of 4,043 Teacher Cadets (an estimated 11% of South Carolina's in-state trained teachers) were employed in South Carolina classrooms during the 2008–2009 school year, and one out of every five program completers achieved South Carolina teacher certification (CERRA, 2009). South Carolina is currently developing a comprehensive data system that will assist CERRA with more accurate identification of students who have completed recruitment programs and entered the profession in South Carolina.

Combining the efforts of ProTeam and Teacher Cadets, the precollegiate division of CERRA's continuum utilizes an intertwined programmatic infrastructure for hometown recruitment and for encouragement of middle and high school students to enter the education profession. The infrastructure is enriched by the network of Teacher Educators from the teacher preparation institutions that partner with the programs. The next division of the continuum focuses on preservice recruitment and retention for teacher candidates and certified teachers.

Preservice Recruitment and Retention Programs and Services

The second level of the continuum, preservice, encompasses a variety of recruitment services: the South Carolina Teaching Fellows Program, the South Carolina Teacher Job Bank, the Online Employment and Certification Application System, and the South Carolina Educator Expo Job Fair.

South Carolina's prestigious statewide collegiate recruitment program is the Teaching Fellows Program. Established in 1999 by the General Assembly and modeled after North Carolina's Teaching Fellows program, the mission of the Teaching Fellows is to recruit high school seniors into the profession who have exhibited high academic achievement, a history of service and leadership in the school and community, and a desire to teach. The program awards up to $6,000 a year for up to 4 years. Funded from sales tax monies, the fellowship is considered a loan from the state that is forgivable by service in a South Carolina public school. The program in 2010–2011 was funded for 523 teacher candidates and, until the recent economic crisis, served an average of 607 per year.

The rigorous selection process for Teaching Fellows consists of an online application and an in-person interview. The application takes into account the student's grade point average, class rank, college entrance test scores, community service, leadership, and references and recommendations. From as many as 1,100 applications, up to 450 top-ranked students are invited to interview with teams of educators in one of five locations in the state.

Students who are awarded fellowships must be accepted to 1 of the 11 public and private Teaching Fellows institutions in the state, who were awarded Teaching Fellows programs based on approved proposals and funding: Anderson University, Charleston Southern University, Lander University, Furman University, University of South Carolina–Columbia, University of South Carolina–Upstate, College of Charleston, South Carolina State University, Columbia College, Newberry College, and Winthrop University.

Each institution provides internal funding and a campus director who supervises the Teaching Fellows cohort. Each institution also ensures that every fellow is provided diverse experiences and enrichment opportunities within his or her teacher education program. Some of these experiences include participating in advanced professional development in Teaching

Fellows seminars, working with business and community partners, assisting university faculty with research projects, providing community service, and observing and working in local public school classrooms as early as the freshman year of college.

Longitudinal data indicate that South Carolina Teaching Fellows is an effective, efficient, and relevant recruitment and new teacher retention effort. Since the initial cohort of fellows in 2000, the program has achieved a program completion rate of 76% and a teacher retention rate of 75%. In the 2009–2010 school year, 591 fellows were employed in 70 of South Carolina's 85 public school districts and special schools; of those teachers, 371 (54%) teach in critical-need schools, which meet one or more of three criteria: a report card rating of "at risk" or "below average," a teacher turnover rate of 20% or higher, or a minimum poverty index of 70%. Although the percentage of underserved populations in the program continues to rise (program average for males, 15%; for minorities, 14%), challenges remain to increase the number of students from underserved populations and in critical-need content areas, such as special education, math, and science (CERRA, 2010b).

The Teaching Fellows program focuses on expanding South Carolina's in-state recruitment efforts to ensure that a pool of talented high school graduates are offered the opportunity and college financial support to become highly effective classroom teachers. Although Teaching Fellows participation is available only to South Carolina students, other strategies and services for preservice recruitment are available for all teacher education graduates and for certified teachers from around the world. Working with the Personnel Division of the South Carolina Association of School Administrators, CERRA maintains the South Carolina Teacher Job Bank. District personnel officers notify CERRA of current and pending vacancies, which are posted online and thus available to teachers seeking positions using CERRA's website.

Similarly, CERRA, in collaboration with the SCDE, maintains the statewide Online Employment and Certification System, which allows teachers to apply for both a teaching position and a South Carolina teaching license at the same time. Through a user agreement for confidentiality, districts are able to access the system 24 hours a day. Since its inception in 1999, the South Carolina Online Employment and Certification System has handled more than 128,000 applications. During the 2009–2010 hiring season, more than 13,000 new applications were created, and more than 19,000 existing applications were modified (CERRA, 2010a).

Another strategy in South Carolina to match districts with vacancies to new teachers, career changers, and experienced educators seeking positions is the South Carolina Expo for Teacher Recruitment. The Expo, first held in 1988 and annually held in early June, is another partnership with the South Carolina Association of School Administrators. Historically, Expo participation has included as much as 80% of the state's public school districts and as many as 1,200 participants. Under the challenging conditions of the recession in 2010, the Expo was held in a virtual format that allowed a small number of districts to introduce participants to the vacancies that were available and the SCDE to promote its Program for Alternative Certification for Educators. Both CERRA and the SCDE reserved telephone lines for questions concerning the application and certification processes.

CERRA conceivably operates as a full-service partner with teacher education colleges and universities, school districts, and other state organizations. It provides a full range of employment assistance to in-state teaching candidates and teachers desiring to relocate to South Carolina.

Service: Retention and Advancement Trainings and Resources

The third category of CERRA's continuum kicks in for teacher retention and advancement once an educator has been hired by a South Carolina public school, but it also affects the recruitment of teachers in South Carolina. The service component is designed to support teacher growth from induction to accomplished levels, utilizing experienced teachers who wish to remain in the classroom in leadership roles to support their peers, to promote the profession, and to increase student achievement through application of professional development. These services incorporate several related categories: research, teacher leaders, National Board for Professional Teaching Standards support, and mentor training. Although the national board is an important component of teacher advancement and retention and although research drives decision making at the center, for the purposes of this discussion, commentary on the service category of the continuum focuses mainly on mentoring and teacher leadership.

First of all, CERRA is charged by the State Board of Education to deliver mentoring training to experienced teachers and administrators, enabling them to have the knowledge and skills essential for the support of beginning teachers. The *Code of Laws of South Carolina* stipulates that the SCDE develop guidelines for teacher induction to include long-term coaching and assistance. The guidelines must include criteria for the selection and training of teachers to serve as mentors.

In 2006, the South Carolina induction and mentoring program's implementation guidelines were approved as part of the state's teacher evaluation process, in alignment with the performance dimensions of that system: ADEPT (Assisting, Developing, and Evaluating Professional Teaching). The guidelines state,

> Under these legislative mandates, South Carolina's induction and mentoring initiative exists as a collaborative effort among the state's school districts, the teacher education programs in the state's colleges and universities, the SCDE's Division of Educator Quality and Leadership (DEQL), and the Center for Educator Recruitment, Retention, and Advancement (CERRA) of South Carolina. Implemented by the individual school districts statewide, these induction and mentoring programs have one overriding objective: to inform, encourage, and support beginning teachers for the purpose of improving the quality of teaching in the state, raising the level of student achievement, and reducing the rate of attrition among our newest teachers. (SCDE, 2006, p. 2)

The guidelines and the associated professional training—developed in collaboration with the New Teacher Center, then at the University of California–Santa Cruz—are based on nationally recognized, research-based mentoring models. Unfortunately, the South Carolina mandate for the mentoring components of the teacher induction program is unfunded; however, school districts use local, other state, or appropriate federal funds to support their mentoring initiatives.

The initial professional development training for mentors, Foundations in Mentoring, is a 3-day interactive workshop that reviews the components of ADEPT, the roles of mentors, and the characteristics and needs of beginning teachers and provides strategies and tools for mentoring them. Teachers who successfully complete Foundations in Mentoring receive certification as a mentor and are qualified by the SCDE to mentor beginning teachers in their district.

Although increasing student achievement through teacher retention is the main goal of the program, a secondary goal is to build capacity and leadership within districts—especially in targeted high-needs, hard-to-staff schools. Capacity is created by increasing the number of trained mentors available but also by enabling districts to train their own mentors. Certified, experienced mentors may be recommended by their districts to complete the 2-day Train the Trainer workshop. After successfully cotraining with a CERRA trainer, the teacher can be certified as a Foundations in Mentoring trainer.

As of June 2010, the state's mentor database has tracked more than 5,700 certified mentors dispersed through all of the state's public school districts, several institutions of higher education, and a number of special schools. More than 170 of these certified mentors also have become certified trainers.

In addition to the initial Foundations in Mentoring and Train the Trainer workshops, CERRA—in collaboration with the SCDE's Office of Exceptional Children—in 2008 developed customized training for mentors of beginning special education teachers, which was implemented in 2009–2010. A review of the literature on special education teacher attrition, as well as in-state research by CERRA, indicates that special education teachers were more likely than other teachers to move from their schools or leave the teaching profession and that mentoring has a positive impact on the retention of special education teachers. "Given the diverse needs of special education teachers and their students, carefully-designed and organized induction support is needed, including a trained mentor who fully understands the needs of a new special educator" (CERRA, 2010c, p. 3). As of June 2010, more than 160 experienced mentors have completed the specialized training for mentors of special education teachers.

Similarly, in response to feedback from school district personnel administrators and the SCDE, CERRA is developing an advanced mentor training for teachers who mentor alternatively certified teachers, focusing on the needs of those new teachers. This work is in collaboration with Newberry College through a grant from the South Carolina Commission on Higher Education.

CERRA's vision for the future of mentoring in South Carolina is to continue to collaborate with teacher education institutions, districts, and the SCDE in collecting data on teacher retention to support the effectiveness of the training and implementation of the guidelines. CERRA continues to provide leadership in statewide efforts for professional development of aspiring and experienced mentors, designed to build capacity and collegiality and improve teaching quality and retention for the purpose of increased student achievement.

The second category of the service portion of the continuum is teacher leaders. This leadership initiative has had a national effect sparked by the concept of a statewide Teacher Forum, a network of current and past district and state teachers of the year.

The purpose of the Teacher Forum is to develop confidence and leadership skills among these accomplished teachers, to help them utilize their leadership voice in the policymaking arena, and to affect the professional development of teachers in their districts. The Teacher Forum is led by the South Carolina state teacher of the year, who takes a sabbatical from the classroom to serve as a teacher in residence at CERRA. The Teacher Forum is expanded by the district teacher on the local level as an organization of the school-level teachers of the year, and it engages these teachers in supporting recruitment through local scholarships, sponsoring teacher recognition and professional development, involving the community to affect educational issues, organizing local legislative delegation meetings, and working closely with district leaders in an advisory capacity.

To promote teacher leadership through professional development, CERRA offers teacher leaders regional and state workshops through the Teacher Forum. The South Carolina state teacher of the year in 1985, Terry Dozier, who became national teacher of the year, spearheaded the forum initiative statewide. Subsequently, as a special advisor on teaching for U.S. Secretary of Education Riley, Dozier became the driving force for the national model.

A significant aspect of the teacher leader component is the CERRA Advisory Board, the members of which are elected from categories representative of CERRA's network: district teachers of the year, national board–certified teachers, Teacher Cadets or ProTeam instructors, teacher mentors, and former Teacher Cadets, Pro-Team students, or Teaching Fellows. In addition to the advisory capacity of these educators to influence CERRA's program design and policies, they serve as positive voices for teacher recruitment, education reform, professional advocacy, and professional growth for all teachers, as well as focusing on student achievement as the goal of teacher leadership.

CERRA'S CONTINUUM OF TEACHER PREPARATION REFORM

During the 2008–2009 academic year, CERRA was invited by the Richard W. Riley College of Education at Winthrop University to participate as a partner in developing and submitting a proposal for a U.S. Department of Education Teacher Quality Partnership Grant.

The grant has five goals: (1) improving student academic achievement in targeted high-need schools, (2) improving professional learning for school–university faculty and teacher candidates, (3) strengthening the prebaccalaureate education of teacher candidates, (4) increasing support for new teachers in the high-need districts, and (5) implementing ongoing and accessible school leadership programs (Rakestraw, Johnson, Williams, & Black, 2009). The proposal was successful, and the $7-million grant was awarded in September 2009. The project is named NetSCOPE—Network of Sustained, Collaborative, Ongoing Preparation for Educators. The grant provides a unique opportunity for CERRA to realize a vision that channels students through the continuum of programs and services from middle school to classroom teaching. Also, the grant extends the induction and mentoring guidelines to formulate a comprehensive induction program, beginning with preservice teacher candidates. NetSCOPE embraces nine districts, five of which are high need, in counties within driving distance of Winthrop University. The structure of the grant implementation encompasses a univer-

sity–school partnership network of professional development schools and partner schools in collaboration with Winthrop's faculty and students. The Grant Management Team, on which CERRA is represented, consists of liaisons for the university, districts, and educational organization partners.

Partnership through the grant enables CERRA to cooperate on several levels with the university and the districts. First of all, encouragement and funding are provided in the grant for the professional development schools and partner schools that do not have ProTeam, FEA, or Teacher Cadets, thereby enabling them to include these CERRA programs in their hometown recruitment portfolio. Winthrop University is a college partner for 20 Teacher Cadets high schools, and it has sponsored Teacher Cadets since the beginning of the program. The grant extends its partnership to include the targeted local education agencies, focusing on underrepresented groups who may be interested in teaching. Winthrop offers three elective credits for students who successfully complete Teacher Cadets. In addition, Winthrop is expanding a Phi Delta Kappa International chapter to encourage the targeted middle schools and high schools to establish FEA chapters with CERRA's assistance.

Second, Winthrop has one of the largest and most successful South Carolina Teaching Fellows cohorts, which recruits heavily from Teacher Cadets. NetSCOPE uses strategies to place and eventually employ Teaching Fellow graduates in the target, high-need schools. Winthrop's Teaching Fellows curriculum offers a unique focus on a limited-English-proficiency teaching component for Hispanic students in local schools, as a form of yearlong community service, and in schools in Costa Rica during spring break, as an opportunity to see how an education system in another country operates.

Third, the grant implements and sustains a high-quality induction and mentoring program, using a "birth to 5" model—that is, from the "birth" of the teaching career (clinical internship) to age 5 (Year 4 as a classroom teacher).

> This approach will ensure our teacher candidates experience a seamless transition as they move from the teacher preparation experience to their teaching careers, successfully spanning the bridge between teacher quality (aptitude, professional preparation, licensure, certification and prior work experience) and teacher effectiveness (student outcomes and engagement). (Strong, 2009, as cited in Rakestraw et al., 2009, p. 41)

Embedded in the concept of seamless transition is a groundwork of common experiences for a community of educators—university supervising faculty and local education agency mentors and administrators—who support both preservice candidates and induction teachers. These experiences include a mentor qualification, application, selection, and assignment process; initial (certified) and advanced mentor training; cognitive coaching; ADEPT evaluator (certified) training; continuous mentor training and support; formative feedback; and professional sharing among the schools, the university, and CERRA. Winthrop is expanding its semester internship to a yearlong design that facilitates the fidelity of the guided transition from student to teacher.

Finally, CERRA's coordinator of research and program development has assisted with providing data for the grant and continues to work with assessment of the effectiveness of CERRA's contributions. This research-based, best-practices partnership is part of the research shaping the South Carolina mentoring and induction platform. The NetSCOPE grant treatment allows CERRA to monitor and assess with Winthrop the ongoing application of CERRA's continuum of teacher recruitment and beginning teacher retention.

CONCLUDING COMMENTS

CERRA's strategic plan, developed by its Board of Directors in 2008, identifies the center as holding a unique niche in the education community, offering a menu of opportunities that serve precollege and college students as well as teachers in the profession. The information, training, and networking opportunities provided by the center are based on the needs of each client group to provide or become successful members of the education profession. Collaborating with school administrators, teacher education institutions, the SCDE, and other education entities throughout the state and nation, CERRA is designed to be an independent, strategic, flexible, and innovative force that unifies efforts to mold and enhance the teaching profession in South Carolina. The future of CERRA's service to the state's students is to focus on new ways to affect high-priority targets of rural schools and hard-to-staff schools with a strong "grow your own" approach of holistic and sustainable recruitment, retention, and advancement efforts for high-quality, effective teachers.

APPENDIX 6.A: CONTINUUM OF PROGRAMS AND SERVICES

The purpose of the Center for Educator Recruitment, Retention, and Advancement (CERRA) is to provide leadership in identifying, attracting, placing and retaining well-qualified individuals for the teaching profession in our state. In doing so, CERRA will respond to changing needs for teachers from underrepresented populations, in critical subject fields and in under-served geographical areas in South Carolina. The Center will work cooperatively with other organizations to promote the education profession.

PRE-COLLEGIATE
Recruitment Programs & Resources

ProTeam

Teacher Cadets

Teacher Educators

PRE-SERVICE
Recruitment & Retention Programs & Services

Teaching Fellows

Job Bank Online App

Teacher Expo

SERVICE
Retention & Advancement Trainings & Resources

Research

Teacher Leaders

National Board

Mentor Training

REFERENCES

Center for Educator Recruitment, Retention, and Advancement. (2009). *Teacher cadet data.* Rock Hill, SC: Author.

Center for Educator Recruitment, Retention, and Advancement. (2010a). *Annual report to the South Carolina Commission on Higher Education.* Rock Hill, SC: Author.

Center for Educator Recruitment, Retention, and Advancement. (2010b). *CERRA annual report 2009–2010.* Rock Hill, SC: Author.

Center for Educator Recruitment, Retention, and Advancement. (2010c). *A report on the special education mentoring grant in South Carolina.* Rock Hill, SC: Author.

Center for Educator Recruitment, Retention, and Advancement. (2010d). *Teacher Educator Handbook.* Rock Hill, SC: Author.

Center for Teacher Quality. (2009). *Strengthening and diversifying the teacher recruitment pipeline: Current efforts.* Washington, DC: National Education Association.

Darling-Hammond, L. (1984). *Beyond the commission reports: The coming crisis in teaching.* Santa Monica, CA: Rand.

Future Educator Association (FEA). (2009). Retrieved July 9, 2011, from www.futureeducators.org.

Graham, P. L. (2009, April). *History of the South Carolina center for teacher recruitment.* Presentation for the Center for Educator Recruitment, Retention, and Advancement, Rock Hill, SC.

Ingersoll, R. (2001). Teacher turnover, teacher shortages: An organizational analysis. *American Educational Research Journal, 38*(3), 499–534.

National Commission on Excellence in Education. (1983). *A nation at risk: The imperative for educational reform. A report to the nation and the secretary of education.* Retrieved from http://www2.ed.gov/pubs/NatAtRisk

National Commission on Teaching and America's Future. (2003). *No dream denied: A pledge to America's children.* Washington, DC: Author.

Rakestraw, J., Johnson, L. E., Williams, D., & Black, A. (2009). *Network of sustaining collaborative, ongoing preparation for educators.* Teacher Quality Partnership Grant, US Department of Education. Winthrop University, Rock Hill, SC: Author.

South Carolina Department of Education (2006). *South Carolina induction and mentoring program: Implementation guidelines.* Retrieved from http://www.scteachers.org/Cert/certpdf/mentor_guide.pdf

III

Closing the Gaps Through Teacher Career Pathways

The multiple pathways idea, even in its nascent form, provides a conceptual framework not only for rethinking the programmatic and organizational design of high schools but also for developing a strategy for doubling the numbers of young adults with a postsecondary credential. It suggests a way to give the preparation for work and citizenship goals of high schools more legitimacy while sending a strong message that all pathways require preparation for further learning.
—Kazis, Vargas, and Hoffman (2004, p. 25)

With diverse populations and locations in many areas in need of teachers, community colleges are an important pool of talent for future classroom teachers. The focus on teaching and the wide variety of programs available make community colleges valuable environments for educating prospective teachers. To help address the need for more teachers, especially minority teachers, the role of community colleges in educating tomorrow's teachers should be emphasized to an even greater extent.
—Gederman (2001, p. 72)

Stakeholders in our schools who seek to design and implement career pathways are faced with addressing many widespread and persistent educational challenges in secondary and postsecondary education. These challenges include increasing college and workforce readiness among high school graduates, closing the gap in achievement and postsecondary degree attainment among first-generation and historically underrepresented students, and responding to workforce supply and demand in a global economy (Harper & Quaye, 2009; Hoffman, Vargas, Venezia, & Miller, 2007; Kazis, Vargas, & Hoffman, 2004).

Specifically, in the design of teacher career pathways, these challenges include reversing the problematic trend of decreased percentages of teachers of color currently employed in the teacher workforce, developing seamless career trajectories across secondary and postsecondary educational institutions leading to teacher licensure, improving projections for teacher supply and demand aligned with trends in workforce development, and increasing financial assistance to minimize the risk of college debt in seeking a degree in a low-wage-earning field, the teaching profession.

In part III, "Closing the Gaps Through Teacher Career Pathways," the historical barriers and contemporary issues in educational policy and practice related to the implementation of teacher career pathways are examined through the diverse perspectives of educational stake-holders in a statewide nonprofit organization, an urban public school district, and an educational policy center within a university system. These perspectives offer three distinct lenses for interpreting the teacher career pathway program models presented here and for engaging in deeper levels of understanding the interrelationships among theory, policy, and practice in designing successful Grade 9–16 career pathway programs.

As a conclusion to the book, the first chapter within this part establishes a conceptual framework for determining the practical applications of teacher career pathways situated within other contemporary reform initiatives in Texas, including Early College High Schools, TSTEM Academies, and the UTEACH program. This discussion is followed by the second chapter, which presents a theoretical framework and a review of the related literature that examines the impacts of social capital and self-efficacy on student engagement, persistence, and success among diverse and historically underserved populations in college settings. It also explores the role of the community college in closing the achievement gap and increasing postsecondary degree attainment for historically marginalized students. The final chapter offers an animated discussion of the changes in educational policy that are needed to support teacher career pathway programs. The discussion of policy support is illustrated with four exemplars of current teacher career pathway programs.

Together, the chapters provide a macroperspective of the institutional and societal challenges in designing and implementing long-term, sustainable career pathway programs for the preparation of teachers. Therein, the authors critically examine the structures and supports necessary for transforming teacher preparation into a responsive and flexible model of teacher workforce development. Together, these chapters offer promising, emergent strategies for evolving teacher preparation, a profession within transition, to respond to the changing needs of schools, advance the ideals of the purposes of education in a democracy, and prepare students to succeed within a rapidly evolving global society.

REFERENCES

Gederman, R. D. (2001). The role of community colleges in training tomorrow's school teachers. *Community College Review, 28*(4), 62–77.

Harper, S. R., & Quaye, S. J. (Eds.). (2009). *Student engagement in higher education: Theoretical perspectives and practical approaches for diverse populations.* New York: Taylor & Francis.

Hoffman, N., Vargas, J., Venezia, A., & Miller, M. S. (2007). *Minding the gap: Why integrating high school with college makes sense and how to do it.* Cambridge, MA: Harvard Education Press.

Kazis, R., Vargas, J., & Hoffman, N. (2004). *Double the numbers: Increasing postsecondary credentials for underrepresented youth.* Cambridge, MA: Harvard Education Press.

Chapter Seven

Building the Teacher Pipeline for College Access, Readiness, and Success

Heather Zavadsky and Kelty Garbee

The recession negatively affected school district budgets across the nation between 2010 and 2011, resulting in a number of teacher layoffs. While this created some excess in the overall supply of teachers nationwide, within states there are still regional shortages of certain types of teachers, particularly in the areas of math, science, special education, and English-language learners. Given the increasing number of Latino students requiring English-language services across the nation, it is problematic that there has historically been an absence of Latino teachers. The solution for effectively teaching English-language learners is hiring qualified teachers from students' own communities because they can better understand the challenges that students face and can communicate with students and their parents. However, there has never been a concerted effort to recruit and train teachers from these underrepresented communities or, to the extent needed, in these other shortage areas.

While there are alternative routes to the teaching profession outside a college degree, students who prepare to enter the workforce by earning a college degree will have the largest number of options in the job market. So, to increase the number of teachers, it is important to ensure that high school students are prepared for college. One strategy for placing more students on a strong postsecondary path is through innovative high school models designed, not only to improve college preparation, but also to connect students with an understanding of how to access postsecondary education and the skilled workforce. Two exemplary models that can prepare and motivate more diverse students to consider college are early college high schools (ECHSs), where students can earn up to 60 hours of college credit in high school, and science, technology, engineering, and mathematics (STEM) academies, which prepare students for success in college and degrees in STEM fields. Both models not only increase academic rigor but reinforce analytical thinking and complex problem solving and, in so doing, increase student engagement. ECHSs and STEM academies also make high school more relevant by providing career pathways for students that can fulfill our workforce needs. By ensuring that students are prepared for college and by providing them with training in math and science, these models could be used as a mechanism for expanding the teacher pipeline in shortage areas such as math, science, bilingual and special education and for recruiting teachers of color.

Both the STEM and ECHS models require teachers to apply skills different from those that are typically employed in traditional classrooms. In addition to being able to deliver standard core knowledge, teachers must be able to increase instructional rigor, differentiate and accelerate instruction, diagnose and address learning problems, work with students in urban settings, teach the self-management skills required for college, and convince students and their families—particularly those with very little exposure to higher education—that college is a viable and feasible option.

This chapter begins with an overview of several programs supported by the Texas High School Project, a public–private alliance focused on improving postsecondary readiness, access, and success in Texas. The examples included here highlight several successful programs that can better prepare a wider range of students for college and in shortage areas such as math and science. The goal of this chapter is to explain the role of teachers and their training in each of these programs and to consider additional ways that teachers could be trained for similar programs.

Additionally, these examples demonstrate how we can attract more diverse students into college and use career pathway school models as an intentional vehicle for targeting regional teacher shortages to provide teachers who can motivate and prepare students for postsecondary success.

The secondary school–level programs include the Hidalgo Early College High School, the Paul and Jane Meyer Public High School, and the H. Ross Perot Texas Science Technology Engineering and Math Academy. Representing a reach from higher education down to the K–12 system, UTeach is a recruiting program for math and science teachers that is delivered through colleges and universities in close collaboration with secondary schools. All four programs represent strong partnerships between higher education and K–12 systems that emphasize meeting school and student needs.

TEACHER TRAINING FOR ECHS AND TEXAS STEM PROJECTS

Through a grant from the Texas Education Agency, all of the ECHSs in the state have access to a comprehensive program of professional development based on the leadership and instructional model of the University Park Campus School in Worcester, Massachusetts, supported by Jobs for the Future.[1] The training focuses on three strands: school leadership, instructional training, and supplementary training for math teachers and teachers new to early college. To increase teachers' skills on providing academics and culture that enable struggling learners to achieve success in college courses, teachers are trained to use a common set of instructional strategies aligned within a coherent instructional framework. The strategies include collaborative group work, writing to learn, literacy groups, questioning, scaffolding, and classroom talk. Teachers at Texas STEM (T-STEM) academies receive specialized training through T-STEM centers and through training opportunities sponsored and produced by the Texas High School

Project. T-STEM centers, which are located at universities and regional education service centers throughout the state, assist T-STEM schools in a number of ways including: designing innovative STEM curricula, delivering professional development, and creating strategic partnerships with businesses and higher education institutions. The centers all use a set of core professional development modules that provide T-STEM teachers with training in project-based learning, gender equity, and the T-STEM design blueprint. Each center also provides its own specialty offerings, ranging from rocketry (Texas Tech T-STEM Center) to biomedicine (Southeast Regional T-STEM Center at the University of Texas, Medical Branch, Galveston).[2] Through specialized professional development, the T-STEM centers seek to improve the performance of math and science teachers across the state of Texas.

HIDALGO EARLY COLLEGE HIGH SCHOOL: HIDALGO INDEPENDENT SCHOOL DISTRICT

Hidalgo Independent School District, located in the Rio Grande Valley border area of Texas, serves over 3,500 students, 99% of whom are Hispanic. Over the past few years, the district has gained national recognition for its academic accomplishments, its ability to keep students in school, and its focus on college and skilled career preparation. The district, which has one high school with an enrollment of 960 students, has garnered this attention through implementation of the ECHS model, which blends high school and college into one coherent program that allows students to earn 2 years of college credit while they earn a high school diploma. Rather than focusing only on the high school though, district leaders made college preparation a function of the entire K–12 program and emphasized the motto that "college preparation belongs in kindergarten."

With a $1.4-million 4-year grant from the Texas High School Project through the Communities Foundation of Texas, Hidalgo Independent School District partnered with the University of Texas Pan American, South Texas College, and Texas State Technical College. The three higher education partners provided academic and career and technical education options for students beginning in middle school. After sampling different career and technical education options in middle school, Hidalgo Independent School District students select a career pathway upon entrance into high school. Sample career pathways include business and management administration, finance, information technology, health sciences, human services, protective services, and engineering. Many of these fields were selected by the district to match critical industry needs to needs within the Hidalgo community. For example, recognizing that the health field was in short supply of bilingual nurses, Hidalgo leaders saw the opportunity to meet an important demand while helping students gain the opportunity to earn a viable income.

College-Going Culture

Teachers, principals, and district leaders do not suddenly change their expectations and instructional approaches for students; changes must be nurtured over time. Hidalgo had one advantage in changing its school culture in that the district already had relatively strong ties to the local community colleges and several higher education institutions. These close partnerships helped district and school staff members become more familiar with postsecondary expectations. However, not all staff members believed that students could perform higher-level work. Dr. Irma Duran, a former Hidalgo principal, explained:

> I spent countless hours meeting with the site-based decision making committee and staff discussing our vision and mission. We often discussed, what did we believe about student learning? What could we do for students? What type of graduate did we want to produce at the end of four years at Hidalgo High School? I remember my first year as assistant principal the math department did not want to commit to 70% of all students to pass TAAS [the statewide assessment at the time].

They did not believe all students could learn and pass the state exam. It took time for teachers to raise their expectations and believe that all of their students could succeed.

Several people at Hidalgo Early College High School mentioned that once students yielded test scores demonstrating that they could reach higher academic levels, it became easier to convince staff that higher expectations were reasonable. As expectations were raised, the staff also learned to collaborate more, and they began to view accountability as a collective effort requiring teamwork.

Parents are a key factor in Hidalgo's approach to cultivating a college-going culture. The district created numerous programs that connect parents to the school. In addition to helping parents better support their children in school, these programs keep college in the forefront of all school activities. The district created parental academies that provide English instruction, GED preparation, and training to understand student reports and data. One administrator described how his school meets with parents to make sure that they understand what their children are learning, to emphasize the importance of grades and tests, and to explain how to interpret achievement data. Additionally, parents are invited to "college pep rallies." These activities have raised awareness of college options for parents and have increased parent involvement in their children's education. Even at the high school level, staff members assert that parent involvement has risen and that parents call them if they do not hear from the school on a regular basis.

Anecdotal evidence collected through parent and student interviews show signs that these parent activities have made an impact. For example, one set of parents at an elementary school pep rally proudly proclaimed that their two older children had started college over the previous 2 years. The mother had volunteered in the district for over 5 years, and the father explained that college was discussed throughout their family's involvement with the school. These parents appeared to be incredibly proud and wore T-shirts from the children's college, Texas A&M University in College Station.

Interviews with students confirmed the same shift in parental attitude. When we asked students if their parents were worried about them going away to college, they said that it was not an issue at all and that their parents expected them to go to college. One student mentioned that he was going to attend a college near home to tend to his sick mother but that he was still planning to enroll the following year in the nursing program.

Student Culture

Changing the expectations for teachers and parents was an important step in setting college as a goal for Hidalgo's students, but motivating students was also a critical component of changing culture. The district purposefully created an environment that emphasized college attendance. Anyone walking into an elementary, middle, or high school in Hidalgo sees college banners hanging everywhere, and the high school posts a list showing the different colleges where students have been accepted. The district does much more than hang banners on the walls. Administrators seek ways to connect students with college and build knowledge about the many different schools they can attend.

Hidalgo Elementary School regularly holds college-themed pep rallies. Administrators explained that each class selects a college to represent and study over the course of the year. Once a week, the class wears T-shirts from that college, and once a year the class hosts a pep rally featuring its college. The district solicits support from each college by requesting items such as T-shirts and pens that display the college's insignia. During a Texas A&M pep rally that we observed, all students and parents wore college T-shirts; kindergarten students presented facts about the college; and four students dressed up as "careers" that could be studied at A&M—engineer, nurse, accountant, and farmer. A video showed recent Hidalgo graduates who were currently attending A&M talking about their experiences in college.

In addition to making college visible in the environment, district personnel work to connect students' interests with careers; this not only motivates students but also helps them understand that what they learn in school can lead to a career with family-sustaining wages. Before students select a career pathway in the eighth grade, they take assessments, participate in experiential courses, and learn about career pathways that can make them employable. During this process, students hear speakers from fields such as robotics, environmental engineering, and various medical professions. Once students select a pathway, their instruction is built around that area. One instructor described how he makes instruction more relevant to his students:

> In my area [pharmacology], when I take them to the hospital, my students say, "The surgeon was speaking to me and I understood all the terms!" They can see how what I teach is applied; it opens their eyes and they can see the relevance. In pharmacology, when teaching about a drug being taken off the market because of adverse effects, I related it back to the scientific method. What's the difference between the experimental and control groups? They have little learning if they just memorize it, no gain of the true concept in the real world.

Teachers in the district assert that once students are interested in a career, they appear to be more invested in their education. At that point, teachers work to help students take charge of their own education by reviewing grades, necessary scores on college entrance exams, and the number of credits they need to graduate. Because students have strict requirements they must follow in their college-level courses, staff members work hard to ensure that students know how to study and to monitor their progress to be successful.

Within all these activities, district and higher education staff members work to continually motivate students and help them feel proud of their accomplishments. Teachers, principals, and professors mentioned that they constantly remind students, "You are taking an actual college course. You are doing things that some young adults cannot do." One principal described a student who had turned around difficult behavior through a nursing course at the college and had become proud of his commitment to his own education. The principal drove him home one day because he had forgotten his stethoscope, a requirement for every class. She stated that she could not figure out why it took him so long to walk from the house and back to the car. Finally, exasperated, she asked him about it, and he responded, "I wanted the neighbors to see me wearing my scrubs."

Teachers also motivated students by telling their own stories, both good and bad, about their experiences in college. They believed that it helped their students understand that if their teacher could overcome some of the obstacles that come along with college and starting a career, they could as well.

We saw the student culture shift in action while observing students in their certified nursing class at a nearby community college. After a full morning of high school classes, 23 students took a 45-minute bus ride to attend afternoon classes from 1 to 4 pm at a local community college. As soon as they arrived at the school, they transformed into young adults. They immediately got busy practicing putting bedpans under each other, checking for joint stiffness, and doing other activities associated with geriatric care. They worked together and were focused and serious for over 3 hours. The community college instructor said that she very much enjoyed working with the students, despite her early skepticism, and she mentioned that the Hidalgo students in particular were very responsible.

When asked if the program changed their attitudes toward school, the students all responded that it had. Most of them said that the nursing program gave them a concrete goal, which motivated them to work even harder in their high school program. A few said that while they knew the high school work was important, they found themselves taking the college courses more seriously.

Teacher Training and Support

In addition to the training and support available from the Texas High School Project, the district is doing some interesting activities to help prepare teachers for creating a strong college-ready environment. One strategy is to connect teachers to the types of careers that students might enter. For example, through a business council partnership, the district provided paid internships to four teachers a year who took summer jobs in engineering, restaurant management, and other professions in area businesses. When teachers returned to school the next year, they were better able to tie instruction to real issues in the business world. One teacher explained how he made writing more relevant to his students, saying, "If you are going into the criminal justice field, you will have to write a report. If one word is left out of the case or it can't be understood, you've got a killer on the loose. Writing is important; I stress a lot of writing."

Another middle school principal invested time motivating his staff to raise expectations and collaborate by focusing on "spiritual, motivational, and theoretical" frameworks. To "help teachers remove the old lens and put on a new one," the principal had teachers each bring the book that most inspired them to be an educator. The teachers then swapped books until they had each read three different books; they liked the books and enjoyed discussing them so much that they did not want to give them back. According to this principal, transforming culture takes "process, concept, theory, and research about ourselves—who we are."

Results

Hidalgo Early College High School has yielded impressive results: Its 2010 graduating class crossed the stage with more than 3,200 hours of college credit, representing an average of 20 to 60 hours per student. Finding these statistics in a district serving a student population that is 99% Hispanic, 90.5% low income, and 56% limited English proficient is more than atypical. Not only did the district create a program that matched its students' needs, but it also changed the mind-set of the schools, parents, and students by convincing them that college and skilled careers are an integral part of their future.

Hidalgo Independent School District has successfully created an entire early college district by instilling the expectation of college and skilled careers into district staff members, parents, and students. Once teachers believed that students could meet higher expectations in school, parents supported their children gaining entrance to career pathways and college courses, and students became motivated to do well. As a result, the ground became more fertile for teachers to change their instructional approaches and continue to ramp up their expectations for students. The district is still working on systemically raising the rigor of its courses and aligning them with college and career content, but that work is well underway. In some places, the ECHS has helped communities increase their workforce—like in a highly impoverished region such as Hidalgo.

PAUL AND JANE MEYER PUBLIC HIGH SCHOOL: RAPOPORT ACADEMY PUBLIC SCHOOL

Rapoport Academy Public School is a preK–12 charter school located in Waco, Texas, where the mission is to foster learning that exceeds national and state standards through rigorous academics, evidence-based practices, and real-world experiences. The charter school opened in response to low standardized test scores among low-income children in East Waco, to provide more choice in public education for students who may not otherwise have access to a high-quality school. While the charter originally opened as a K–8 school, it expanded to include the Paul and Jane Meyer Public High School (Meyer Public High School) in fall 2006. Soon after it opened, this unique high school partnered with Texas State Technical College in Waco and applied for designation from the Texas Education Agency both as a T-STEM academy and as an ECHS.

Through a collaborative partnership with Texas State Technical College, this school not only integrates STEM across its curriculum but also allows students to earn college credit as early as the ninth grade. In addition to providing students the opportunity to earn up to 60 transferable college credit hours along with their high school diploma, Meyer Public High School focuses on developing the critical thinking and problem-solving skills of students so they will be prepared for college and the workforce.

College Preparation

At Meyer Public High School, there are a number of well-designed programs that allow teachers to help students connect high school academics to college and the workforce. Two of the most notable programs include an innovative "mini-mester" program, which creatively aligns the high school and college calendar, and a senior thesis or an internship requirement, which provides students with real-world experiences that connect to college and the workforce.

The mini-mester program actually arose because of a misalignment that frequently occurs in ECHSs in Texas. Whereas colleges and universities have significant latitude about when they may start and end their academic calendars throughout the year, school districts must provide 180 days of instruction between specified dates in August and May. Because of the different requirements of the two systems, there are three times during the school year—in August, December/January, and May—when the school district is in session but the college is not. In an effort to use the schedule misalignment in a productive way, school administrators and teachers developed a mini-mester program that provides all students with two college-readiness courses per year in the time between college semesters.

According to Matthew Polk, the assistant superintendent, "the mini-mester program at Rapoport Academy's Paul and Jane Meyer Public High School is designed to provide students knowledge and skills required for college success in a focused, systematic way." When the mini-mester program was being developed, teachers and administrators identified the knowledge and skills that students need to be successful in college and divided them by grade level. As a result, all students take the same courses in the same sequence, and the courses build on one another. Freshmen take Study Skills and Grammar, which provide a strong academic foundation and prepare them for dual-credit courses.

The mini-mester courses offered to sophomores include Writing and Leadership. The Writing course builds on the Grammar course offered to ninth graders. Meanwhile, the Leadership class prepares students for participation in school and community activities while providing a foundation for the 11th-grade mini-mester classes. Juniors take SAT Preparation and Civic Engagement, which allows students to research, debate, and analyze a topic of real-world relevance. Finally, seniors take two courses designed to help them transition into college and careers—College Planning and Financial Planning. The College Planning course begins with college applications, and once students choose the college that they will attend, the course focuses on building a plan of study at the university, researching the campus layout and student activities, and learning about the school's rules and requirements.

Seniors at Meyer Public High School put the knowledge and skills from their mini-mester courses to use during their senior year when they write a senior thesis or complete an 80-hour internship. The thesis, which is expected to be a college-level research paper, culminates with a presentation to the student body and interested community members; this not only allows seniors to showcase their work and practice public speaking but also sets the tone for younger students by publicly establishing academic expectations. Meanwhile, the internship program—which is coordinated by a staff member who has developed relationships with businesses ranging from the local hospitals, television stations, and police department to academic departments at Texas State Technical College—allows students to explore potential careers. The internship and the senior thesis contribute to academic rigor on the campus while showing students how high school academics connect to college and careers.

Teachers

Because Meyer Public High School is a T-STEM ECHS, teachers on this campus benefit from professional development provided by both programs. In addition to using the ECHS's instructional strategies, they incorporate project-based learning and gender equity training from T-STEM. These resources allow teachers to help students reach their full developmental potential not only academically but also socially and emotionally. To this end, teachers at the school staff two support programs that are designed to help students in all aspects of their development; these programs include an advisory program and a grade-level advisor program that makes creative use of staff time for the benefit of students.

Through the school's advisory program, teachers meet with small groups of 6 to 10 students known as Community Groups. Teachers who serve as advisors and facilitators focus on building a sense of rapport with and among the students. In one activity, teachers talk about their own experiences in college, including how they chose their majors and what obstacles they encountered. This activity not only builds connections between students and teachers but also helps students gain perspective on the college experience. In addition to the individualized attention that students receive through Community Groups, the school provides support that is specific to each grade level.

Each cohort of students is assigned a teacher, or grade-level advisor, who talks with students on a weekly basis to develop a sense of the class and understand the aggregate issues that the class faces. To do this, the grade-level advisor must know what is expected of the grade level and then take time to understand the particular academic and social challenges that it is facing. The grade-level advisor moves up with his or her assigned cohort, so over time he or she is able to personally connect with all the students. Through creative use of staff time, Meyer Public High School enlists teachers to provide an additional level and type of support to students than what is usually available.

Students

Teachers at Meyer Public High School encourage students to take personal responsibility for their educational experience and develop a working knowledge of college culture. For example, tutoring is referred to as *office hours.* In addition to introducing students to the language used on a college campus, office hours are designed to encourage students to take the initiative to approach their teachers for help and guidance just as they would on a college campus. While some students may be required to attend office hours based on their classroom performance or individual educational needs, for many students it is optional. One practice that is not optional at the school is the campuswide policy about homework, which may be turned in 1 day late for partial credit but will not be accepted after 1 day. The uniform grading policy enables teachers to balance support with expectations to prepare students for the rigor of a college environment. While the campuswide grading policy and expectations about office hours introduce students to the culture of college in a subtle way, there are other practices, such as daily announcements, that more overtly encourage students to be responsible for their education.

Daily announcements, referred to as Morning Meeting, are conducted in a way that encourages students to be accountable to one another other. Each morning, all students and teachers meet in the school's commons area. In addition to daily announcements, anyone in the community can raise issues that concern them, and students who have been late or who have broken the school's core values apologize to the community. Morning Meeting also provides a forum for students to learn how to participate in an academic community. Teachers encourage students to form study groups for the dual-credit courses they take through Texas State Technical College. During Morning Meeting, newly formed study groups recruit additional members.

By participating in Morning Meeting, holding office hours, and enforcing the campuswide grading policy, teachers at Meyer Public High School support campuswide efforts to give students both the rigor and the support that will prepare them for college and the workforce.

Results

Making college and skilled careers an attainable and realistic goal for students requires a commitment on the part of teachers and administrators. And at Meyer Public High School, it appears that everyone's efforts are paying off. One hundred percent of students in the first two classes at Meyer Public High School graduated and were accepted to college. In 2009–2010 there were 24 graduates, and in 2010–2011 there were 20 graduates, and both classes graduated with over 500 cumulative college credit hours. Sixty-one percent of students on this campus are economically disadvantaged, and 31.5% are African American. Considering that economically disadvantaged students have lower rates of college attendance and that there are shortages of African American teachers and math and science teachers, it is incredibly meaningful that this campus has been so successful in preparing students for their future endeavors. In addition to affecting individual students, this campus has potential to address shortages in the teacher pipeline.

H. ROSS PEROT TEXAS SCIENCE TECHNOLOGY ENGINEERING AND MATH ACADEMY: TEXARKANA INDEPENDENT SCHOOL DISTRICT

With an enrollment of approximately 7,100 students, Texarkana Independent School District has eight elementary schools, one middle school, one high school, and one alternative high school. The high school houses the H. Ross Perot Texas Science Technology Engineering and Math Academy, which is a small learning community that opened in 2009–2010 with a grant from the Texas Education Agency. Since T-STEM was introduced in Texarkana Independent School District, district leaders have worked to implement the model across the district. In addition to the T-STEM academy in the high school, the middle school, which serves sixth through eighth grades, is divided into two academies—T-STEM and arts and communication—that students choose based on their interests.

In addition, two elementary schools in the district focus on math and science: Martha and Josh Morriss Math and Engineering Elementary School and Innovative Connections Academy at Dunbar (ICA@D). Morriss Elementary, which opened in 2007, features daily engineering classes, hands-on learning, and an accelerated math curriculum. Dunbar Elementary transitioned to the Innovative Connections Academy at Dunbar in 2011 when district leaders decided to apply the best practices and lessons learned from Morriss Elementary to a campus that serves 95% economically disadvantaged students.

By incorporating STEM practices from kindergarten through 12th grade, Texarkana Independent School District has committed to raising levels of academic rigor. In the process, the district has earned a reputation in the community for truly preparing students for college and careers. Through its implementation of the T-STEM model, the district has introduced innovative practices in teacher training and curriculum that enhance the knowledge and skills of math and science teachers in the district.

Teacher Training and Support

When H. Ross Perot Texas Science Technology Engineering and Math Academy opened, the district partnered with Texas A&M University–Texarkana to provide a 1-week training program for teachers in the new school. After the first year of operation, the 1-week training was extended to two graduate-level courses that focus on the design and delivery of an effective research-based T-STEM curriculum. Through these courses, teachers are immersed in the methods that are used in the T-STEM academy (such as conceptual, hands-on, and project-based learning). This not only creates a common framework for teachers and students but also sets expectations for the level of rigor that is required in the T-STEM academy.

According to Ronda Jameson, director of STEM education,

> the partnership with Texas A&M University–Texarkana has been absolutely essential to the success of our T-STEM program. The university has been our "champion" in higher education by opening doors of opportunity that a school district does not have the access to open.

The strong partnership between the university and the school district allows both organizations to leverage their strengths for mutual benefit. The district pays all tuition and fees, so teachers receive high-quality professional development from the university, which is able to increase its enrollment through the partnership. Meanwhile, district administrators are confident that teachers understand the level of rigor that is necessary for a student-centered, project-based classroom. And, most important, students have the opportunity to learn from teachers who use a variety of research-based and effective teaching methods. As the success of the partnership has expanded, so has its reach.

Initially, only teachers in the middle school T-STEM academy were required to take these classes and to have or obtain a master's degree. Now, this is required for all middle and high school T-STEM teachers. The concept has also been extended to the Martha and Josh Morriss Math and Engineering Elementary School, where teachers are required to obtain a master math teacher certification and to complete four graduate-level mathematics education courses.

The goal is to ensure that teachers have deep content knowledge and are using the T-STEM teaching methods. In addition to changing teacher preparation, the T-STEM model has affected math curriculum across the district.

College Preparation

H. Ross Perot Texas Science Technology Engineering and Math Academy provides students the opportunity to enroll in two dual-credit engineering courses during their junior and senior years. When the school opened, administrators realized that to be prepared for these courses, students would need to take Algebra I by the 7th grade to complete precalculus by the 10th. District leaders piloted a model called Link, Learn, Extend at Morriss Elementary School, which is designed to accelerate math instruction up to 2 years. For example, a kindergarten student is introduced to kindergarten and first-grade math in the same year. When the student enters first grade, the teacher links to what was taught in kindergarten (first-grade standards), ensures that the student learns second-grade math, and, if the student is ready, extends to third-grade math. The model ensures that the mathematics curriculum is accelerated yet taught to mastery with no gaps in vertical alignment. After 3 years of Link, Learn, Extend, sixth-grade students were completing eighth-grade math, and the approach was deemed so successful that it became the model for teaching math in the district.

T-STEM was the impetus for developing Link, Learn, Extend, but it would not have been possible without ensuring that teachers were trained to teach vertically. According to Ronda Jameson, district leaders realized that master teachers have vertical knowledge of their subject area. So the requirement that elementary math teachers obtain a master math teacher certification and the focus on hiring math teachers with master degrees are strategies for supporting Link, Learn, Extend. In addition to developing intentional professional development strategies that support curriculum and instruction, the district has been strategic about the way that students develop their interpersonal skills to prepare for college and careers.

Culture

While planning the curriculum for Morriss Elementary, Ronda Jameson and Lori Ulmer, the curriculum coaches for the campus, conducted research on the strengths and weaknesses of engineering students at the university level. After reviewing the literature, they learned that engineering students often have high levels of academic performance but are weak in their ability to articulate discoveries and findings. Meanwhile, the district also took a group of STEM students to a local company, International Paper, for a roundtable discussion with the company's engineers. When students asked what traits the company seeks from potential employees, they learned that what differentiates applicants is the ability to lead a team and articulate findings. As a result, district administrators decided that leadership and articulation would the hallmarks of STEM students from Texarkana Independent School District.

Leadership and articulation are instilled in the school culture and reinforced by teachers in a number of ways. One particularly visible way that students are reminded to practice leadership and articulation is through classroom visitor questions, which are posted in all T-STEM classrooms. Teachers encourage students to serve as ambassadors of the school whenever they have visitors. In keeping with the visitor questions protocol, students introduce their projects and explain the following: what they planned, what actually happened, what was successful and unsuccessful, how they will improve their work, and what lessons they learned. This not only encourages students to communicate with others but also gives them practice articulating their findings.

There have been challenges in the process of introducing T-STEM to the district. One of the initial challenges was obtaining buy-in from various stakeholders, including teachers. Because the T-STEM academy was developed as a small learning community within the comprehensive high school, it was inevitable that staffing patterns were going to change. In addition, the requirement that all T-STEM teachers have master degrees meant that those teachers who wanted to work in the T-STEM academy but did not have such a degree would need to go back to school. The district gave teachers the option to participate in the T-STEM academy, but those who did not want to join were able to pursue other opportunities within the district. In spite of the extensive time required to fulfill the T-STEM professional development requirements, feedback from teachers enrolled in the program has been overwhelmingly positive.

Parents and community members are another group of stakeholders whose support is critical. According to Joanne Rice, assistant superintendent of student and community development, "parents have really loved T-STEM and they appreciate the opportunity for their children to have access to higher level thinking, learning, and math." Now that the T-STEM model is maturing and being diffused across the district, though, the challenge is maintaining the standard of quality. However, according to Ronda Jameson, "the graduate courses offered by Texas A&M Texarkana and the relationship with the university have been tremendously helpful. Without the courses it would have been difficult to hold the bar."

The T-STEM academy is in its third year of operation, so it is still too early to determine how this program will affect college preparation and attendance among students. However, according to district officials, preliminary results indicate that 89% of students in the STEM academy passed math on the Texas Assessment of Knowledge and Skills, as compared to 76% of students in the comprehensive high school.[3] Meanwhile, the partnership with Texas A&M University–Texarkana that provides Texarkana with teacher training is a major accomplishment because it is specifically tailored to the needs of math and science teachers in the district. In addition to increasing the capacity of teachers who are already working in the district, this partnership has the potential to affect the teacher pipeline throughout the region, as teachers move between districts or if other districts decide to request similar training from the university.

UTEACH: THE UNIVERSITY OF TEXAS AT AUSTIN

UTeach was established in 1997 at the University of Texas at Austin in the Colleges of Natural Sciences and Education, in collaboration with Austin Independent School District, to reform STEM education by reforming STEM teacher preparation. UTeach introduces undergraduate math and science majors to secondary school teaching with the goal of attracting and retaining more and better students in K–12 science and math education career paths. Much in the same way that school districts implementing the ECHS and STEM models demonstrated creativity and flexibility in their approach to education reform, UTeach is an innovative program that provides a streamlined pathway to teacher certification. By drawing on the resources and capacities of the College of Natural Sciences and the College of Education, UTeach allows interested students to explore teaching, to work with experienced mentors, and, ultimately, to receive both a bachelor's degree and teacher certification in 4 years.

Teacher Training and Support

The training and support that UTeach provides occurs in phases, beginning with recruitment to the program, continuing with support during the program, and ending with induction for new teachers. One of the most innovative aspects of UTeach is the way that the program recruits students with strong math and science skills and allows them to decide if it is an appropriate career path before making a full commitment. The College of Natural Sciences covers tuition for the first two 1-hour courses. When students begin working in the classroom, they may also receive scholarships and paid internships. While the financial support is particularly notable, another very important aspect of UTeach is classroom support during the program and after graduation.

As early as their first semester, UTeach students participate in a variety of field experiences to gain an understanding of student development and school culture. UTeach participants are mentored by master teachers, and "in carefully calculated steps, each student's teaching experience becomes progressively longer and more independent." Students who enter the UTeach program at the same time are encouraged to function as a cohort so they can learn from and support one another. When students graduate and begin teaching, they have access to induction services, which provide personalized support and resources for new teachers, ranging from lesson planning and grant writing to responding to the unique needs of students. The goal of providing induction services is to increase retention of UTeach graduates in the classroom, to increase student achievement in new teachers' classrooms, and to ensure that new teachers move along a continuum from novice to expert.

The UTeach program combines the support and resources of a university and local school districts to create an organization that is devoted to preparing teachers. UTeach actively recruits students who join a learning community that provides support and resources not only during the program but also after they have graduated and moved into the classroom.

Results

Of the more than 600 students enrolled in UTeach at the University of Texas at Austin as of fall 2011, 516 are from the College of Natural Sciences. While the majority of students who participate in UTeach are from natural sciences, the program draws students from across the university in majors ranging from engineering and business to nursing and fine arts. The program has grown exponentially, with enrollment increasing from 9 students in 2000 to 675 in 2011. In addition to expansion at the University of Texas at Austin, the program has been replicated at 21 sites in Texas and across the country.[4]

The significant expansion of UTeach over the past 10 years demonstrates that there is both interest in and a need for programs that train math and science teachers with a deep understanding of their content area. By bringing together the content knowledge of the College of Natural Sciences with the theoretical and pedagogical experience of the College of Education, this program capitalizes on the university structure in a very productive way.

DISCUSSION

To ensure that we have an ample supply of minority teachers and teachers who are prepared to work in the most high-need teaching subjects, there are three areas that require attention. First, we must provide professional development and support for teachers, both preservice and practicing, to enable them to teach in ways that support college-focused student learning, particularly math and science. Second, we must make certain that postsecondary education is a desirable and viable option for all students. This means ensuring that a diverse range of students (particularly Latino students) are prepared to attend college and succeed in all areas, specifically in math and science. Third is to provide opportunities for high school and college students to observe and gain exposure to the teaching profession as a possible option for their future. The examples in this chapter illustrate the importance of preparing students, academically and socially, for their choice postsecondary experience, whether it is a 2 or 4-year college, a certificate program, or a skilled career. How teachers are developed and supported to implement these programs is also addressed.

Teaching in a program designed to foster college readiness needs to increase academic rigor, connect students to actual careers and problem- or project-based learning, and teach the "soft" skills associated with college, such as organizing study time, keeping schedules, and asking for assistance. The soft skills are often addressed within high school programs, sometimes with the assistance of counselors focused on college advising or a principal who has made the presence of a college culture a priority, where the adults discuss their college experiences, hang college banners, and have pep rallies, as we heard about in Hidalgo. The instructional part can pose more challenge for teachers and likely will require more training and support. Project-based learning, for example, is a skill that is difficult for students to grasp and teachers to teach. It takes focused and repetitive training, the ability to engage in cross-discipline planning that connects to real-world problems, and follow-up support, which is what the Texas High School Project provides to the schools it supports.

Programs that focus on increasing college readiness often forget that simply providing the academics does not mean that college will automatically become a feasible and desirable option for students or their families. It is important that schools focus on a college-going culture and to work with parents as well as with students to help them see college in their future, as our three high school examples did. The Texas High School Project has put in a number of ECHS and T-STEM programs that have helped many Latino families in Texas not only see the benefits of college but also feel more comfortable letting their children consider it (often the first in their family to do so). Additionally, those programs have helped students build confidence in math and science and encouraged them to consider math- and science-related college majors and professions.

UTeach was the only specific teacher recruiting program provided, which represents a reach from a postsecondary institution out to students interested in becoming math or science teachers. To date, UTeach has graduated 675 students, including 296 students in math and 244 students in science education.[5] We would love to see additional teacher career pathways built within high school programs the same way that ECHS programs provide training in nursing, for example. However, the policies in most states do not provide credits in teaching at the high school level, due to credentialing issues.

Several activities in these programs could go far in promoting the teacher profession. For example, programs such as Rapoport could have students do educational community projects, such as being a reading buddy to a struggling or younger reader or tutoring other students. Other programs, such as the ECHS programs, have students do "career cruising," which means observing and interviewing other adults in their job setting, and could include teaching as a profession to explore as well. Additionally, just as teachers connect students to higher education by describing their personal experiences in college, they could motivate students into the education field by discussing why they wanted to become a teacher, what types of courses they needed to take, and how they felt about it as a profession.

Meanwhile, UTeach, which has been in operation in Texas since 1997, began nationwide replication in fall 2008 and is currently being implemented at 25 universities in 12 states. This program, which has the potential to dramatically influence STEM education, provides opportunities for school districts and 4-year universities to build or expand options for teacher preparation. At its current rate of growth, graduates of UTeach programs are expected to teach more than 3.5 million secondary STEM students by 2019.

CONCLUSION

When considering how to motivate students to consider the teaching profession, we need to identify ways to better prepare the current teacher labor market and to creatively fill the gaps in high-need areas. Models such as ECHS, T-STEM, and UTeach, which provide structures that support students as well as teachers, can be used to positively affect the teacher labor market.

All of the programs featured in this chapter demonstrate how school districts and colleges can strategically create career pathways that will engage students, increase their earning potential, and infuse their communities with needed skills. The ECHS and T-STEM models aim to increase access and success by providing an academically rigorous program that connects high school to college and career pathways. To date there are 49 ECHSs, 54 T-STEM academies, and 5 hybrid T-STEM ECHSs serving approximately 25,000 students in Texas. Meanwhile, the UTeach intentionally sets out to fill gaps in the teacher pipeline by recruiting students to train as math and science teachers and by ensuring that they have high levels of training and a viable career pathway. These programs represent some of the most promising ways to strategically guide students into high-wage, high-need fields: a win-win situation for students and families, businesses, and communities.

NOTES

1. Jobs for the Future identifies, develops, and promotes education and workforce strategies that expand opportunity for youth and adults who are struggling to advance in America today. See http://www.jff.org for more information.

2. For more information on Texas science, technology, engineering, and mathematics academies and centers, see http://thsp.org/programs/t-stem-centers/.

3. E-mail correspondence with Ronda Jameson (October 13, 2011).

4. See http://uteach.utexas.edu/sites/default/files/UTeach%20Replication%20Talking%20Points%202007.pdf .

5. To date UTeach has graduated 675 students, including 296 students in math and 244 students in science education.

Chapter Eight

The Role of Social Capital in Student Persistence and Retention in Career Pathways: A Theoretical Framework

Gregory M. Bouck

INTRODUCTION

Looking to the partnerships and initiatives necessary for the successful creation of teacher pipelines and career pathways, one must have a working knowledge of the theoretical underpinnings of student success for crossing of the bridges designed to assist in progression from high school to the 4-year university. In attempting to accurately portray the importance of student access and persistence at each level of teacher career pathways, one must also examine various theories and their possible shortcomings in relation to students who have been historically underserved due to race or economic disadvantage. At the center of the preK–16 transitional process is the 2-year or community college. In recognition of its increasingly centralized role in the process of creating teacher career pathways, the experiences of community college students transferring to 4-year universities will provide the backdrop for this inquiry.

This chapter examines contemporary research associated with postsecondary transfer, including a close-up examination of the theoretical underpinnings of student engagement, persistence, and success within 2- and 4-year institutions of higher learning. This examination is situated within critical theory and closely explores internal and external factors that influence student persistence, such as educational goals, intentions, and the level of commitment to a particular institution (Tinto, 1987). Social cognitive theory and the role of self-efficacy are offered as interpretive lenses for developing an understanding of internal factors that enhance student persistence and success, which in turn have a significant bearing on student retention. Next, external factors affecting the success and persistence of first-year students, such as minority status and social capital, are explored. Finally, a review of literature focuses on the role of community colleges in promoting and supporting the persistence of traditionally marginalized or disenfranchised students through preK–16 career pathways.

STUDENT RETENTION AND PERSISTENCE

In investigating student retention, one need look at several theories concerning attrition, student involvement, and social learning. This examination begins with Tinto's (1987) model of student departure and its focus on the importance of student commitment to an institution in predicting persistence to degree obtainment. A student's level of academic and social integration is directly affected by her or his commitment to a particular institution. Tinto's model "highlights the important interplay between the social and intellectual components of student life" (p. 119), and the theory stresses that academic and social components are necessary not only to student persistence but also to the "process of social and intellectual development that are the very basis for higher education" (p. 120). In fact, "Tinto proposed analogously, that college students are more likely to withdraw if they are insufficiently integrated or if they maintain values sufficiently different from the college they are attending" (Christie & Dinham, 1991, p. 412). Also important to note is the fact that individual students may become integrated into one system but not the other (Tinto, 1987). For example, "a person can conceivably become integrated and establish membership in the social system of the college, largely comprised of one's peers, and still depart because of an inability to establish competent membership in the academic domain of the college" (p. 107). On the other hand, "a person may perform more than adequately in the academic domain of the college and still come to leave because of insufficient integration into its social life" (p. 107).

Successful students are by and large fully integrated into both systems to function as a whole (Sanford, 1962; Tinto, 1987). However, the prevalence of these systems is not necessarily equal. For example, some colleges may heavily promote the intellectual aspects of their institutions, effectively undermining social facets, whereas the social systems of some schools may dominate academics (Tinto, 1987). Whatever the case, students must be integrated into both systems to become committed to a particular institution.

While Tinto's initial work in this arena is criticized by many (Braxton, 2000; Pascarella & Terenzini, 1991; Townsend, 2007) as being limited by student and institution type, Tinto (2006–2007) revised his theory in recent writings. In looking to the works of Allen (1992), Borglum and Kubala (2000), Padilla and Pavel (1986), and Pascarella and Chapman (1983), Tinto posited, "We have come to understand how the process of student retention differs in different institutional settings, residential and non-residential, two- and four-year" (p. 4). Tinto also stated that his early work in student retention failed to consider historically underserved students.

In adapting his model and adopting those of others in the field, Tinto (2006–2007) maintained that "involvement, or what is increasingly being referred to as engagement, matters and it matters most during the critical first year of college" (p. 4). Describing the longitudinal process of full integration into the college experience, Tinto (1987) applied Van Gennep's (1960) "rites of passage" to the process. According to Christie and Dinham (1991), there are three steps involved:

(1) Separation from past communities (high school friends and family), (2) transition into the new, college community through learning the values and expectations of that community (for example by building friendships through on campus living and extracurricular participation), and (3) incorporation into the college community through actually adopting the norms and behavioral patterns of the new community. (p. 431)

However, Tinto's (1987) model appears to minimize other external variables, such as self efficacy, socioeconomic status (SES), social capital, ethnicity, and involvement, as they relate to students' persistence in their first year of attendance at 2- and 4-year colleges or universities.

Astin (1985) supported Tinto's (1987) premise in his theory of student involvement. The theory of student involvement "provides a unifying construct that can help to focus the energies of all institutional personnel on a common objective" (Astin, 1985, p. 152). However, Astin posited that before that objective can become the impetus of an institution's efforts, student involvement must be defined:

Student involvement refers to the quantity and quality of the physical and psychological energy the student invests in the college experience. Such involvement takes many forms: absorption in academic work, participation in extracurricular activities, interaction with faculty members and other institutional personnel, and so forth. (p. 157)

Schools that increase student involvement in all areas of the campus create a connectedness with students and provide an atmosphere that promotes student retention (Astin, 1985; Tinto, 1987).

Finally, social cognitive theory and its major component, self-efficacy, are used as a lens to guide the investigation into student retention and persistence. According to Kahn and Nauta (2001), "persistence is influenced by a student's confidence in his or her academic ability (self-efficacy), the anticipated consequences of persisting and graduating, and the determination to persist and graduate" (p. 635). Self-efficacy drives the other components of social cognitive theory and is defined as "individuals' confidence in their ability to successfully complete a task" (DeWitz, Woolsey, & Walsh, 2009, p. 19).

DeWitz and colleagues (2009) go on to explain that "self-efficacy and goal orientation (defined as students' reasons for approaching an academic task) have been linked to success in many areas, including college" (p. 19). This view of self-efficacy supports Bandura and Locke's (2003) idea that "self-efficacy beliefs are rooted in the core belief that one has the power to produce desired effects" (p. 87). With this, students see educational challenges as a hill to be conquered rather than a task to be avoided. Through the scope of these theories, one may better understand the interrelationship among all factors affecting student retention and persistence, including commitment, academic and social integration, student involvement and intention, SES, ethnicity, social capital, and self-efficacy.

Commitment

Tinto (1987) drew a correlation between student commitment and departure from higher education. While he stated that there are those in any collegiate cohort "who simply are unable or unwilling to commit themselves to the task of college completion and expend the level of effort required to complete a college degree program" (p. 44), there are those whose levels of commitment are adversely affected by the failure to integrate academically or socially within the institution. Identified as two of the primary components of a student's decision to persist or leave a university, the social and academic integration of students is pivotal to the success of these institutions. According to Bitzer (2009), "the successful academic and social integration of 'new' students in to higher education settings remains important with regard to study commitment, study success and preventing early student departure" (p. 226). However, the relationship between integration and student persistence is complex, and a simplified explanation is problematic, especially if generalized across all student populations. Bitzer posited, "the close relationship between successful integration and student motivation remains a challenge, while the complex relationships among personal, academic and social factors will continue to prevent any simplified explanation of or interventions towards first-year integration" (p. 242).

Bitzer (2009) warned that

> student integration is the function of as wide a range as possible facets of a program of study and elements of contact between an institution and its students, irrespective of whether these elements of contact are of an academic, an administrative or a social nature (p. 226)

Institutions of higher learning play a pivotal role in developing and nurturing integration and its resulting persistence. According to Paulsen and St. John (1997), persistence at a particular institution is ultimately the product of ongoing behavioral and perceptual interactions between the student and various aspects of the campus environment. It is crucial, then, that institutions begin involving new students as soon as they arrive on campus. Berger and Milem (1999) posited, "Early involvement in the fall semester positively predicts spring involvement and has significant indirect effects on social integration, academic integration, subsequent institutional commitment, and persistence" (p. 654).

The resulting positive opinions of institutional and peer support "tend to lead to lower levels of noninvolvement in the spring and greater levels of academic and social integration" (p. 659). Recent changes in financial aid availability and budget cuts have left many institutions of higher learning in financial straits. Accordingly, "institutions have come to view the retention of students to degree completion as the only reasonable course of action left to ensure their survival" (Tinto, 1987, p. 2). Therefore, it is crucial for higher education leaders to have an understanding of integration and the purpose it serves.

Academic integration. According to Tinto (1987), academic integration centers on perceived congruency between a student's academic ability and the institution's expectations, as well as perceived individual accomplishments at the postsecondary level. Tinto (1987) continued,

In the formal academic realm of the college, incongruence may take the form of a quantitative mismatch, if you will, between the skills, interests, and needs of the individual and those which are characterized by the demands of academic life. (p. 55)

This does not mean that a preponderance of students are leaving universities due to academic failure or expulsion; only a small percentage leave for this reason (Tinto, 1987). To the contrary, "some students leave because they think that their schools' academic demands are too easy, in which case many able students end up withdrawing from one college to transfer to another" (Baker & Velez, 1996, p. 92). Unsatisfactory academic performance is oftentimes related to "students' lack of commitment" (p. 92). In this instance, "withdrawal, then, is usually a voluntary decision, reached after a student fails to become integrated in the intellectual life of his or her college" (p. 92).

While it may appear that this lack of congruence is fostered by the actions or inactions of the institution, Tinto (1987) warned that, though this is often the case, "it is also true that some students are unable or unwilling to avail themselves of the full range of academic resources available to them" (p. 56). This may be the result of external factors, initially ignored by Tinto, such as self-efficacy, social capital, or involvement. These external issues are discussed in a later section. Academic integration may also be affected by a student's failure to integrate socially, or as discussed earlier, the student may have integrated into one system but not the other.

Social integration. While Tinto's (1987) model does not state that full integration into both systems is a requirement for student persistence, it does state "that some degree of social and intellectual integration must exist as a condition for continued persistence" (p. 119). In other words, it is necessary for students to become integrated academically to remain in an institution. Institutions have minimum standards for maintaining enrollment, as well as the power to expel (Tinto, 1987). However, membership in at least one form of social or intellectual community is important for student persistence. In fact, "in the institutional environment, Tinto asserted, if a student does not establish sufficient social ties with the institution—that is, if the student feels isolated—then she or he will be more likely to drop out than will less isolated students" (Christie & Dinham, 1991, p. 429).

This is not to say that a student must be involved in mainstream campus activities to be connected to a particular institution. To the contrary, Tinto (1987) argued that as in any organization, colleges' possess "a variety of communities or subcultures, each with its own distinct view of the world" (p. 121). Tinto posits,

Deviancy from the social and intellectual mainstream of institutional life does not in itself ensure withdrawal. Insofar as individuals are able to find some communal niche on campus, then it is possible for a person to be seen as deviant from the broader college environment and still persist to degree completion. (p. 121)

Nevertheless, this type of connection to a university may not be as likely to aid in student persistence, as is an identification with a more dominate campus community. According to Tinto (1987) "the more central one's membership is to the mainstream of institutional life the more likely, other things being equal, is one to persist" (p. 123). Bean and Bradley (1986) linked social integration to satisfaction and, ultimately, performance. Their research looked at students' social lives and memberships in campus organizations as indicators of social integration.

According to Bean and Bradley (1986) "students who view their social lives positively are expected to be more satisfied with their college experience" (p. 396), which corresponds with Bean's earlier work that positively linked social life and institutional fit. According to Christie and Dinham (1991) "two types of institutional experiences stood out in their effects on social integration: living on campus in residence halls, and participation in extracurricular activities" (p. 419). These experiences influence social integration in similar ways. Students view both campus living and extracurricular activities as influences that "increased opportunities to meet and develop friendships with other students" and as "explicitly linking them to the college environment" (p. 422). Current research in this area recognizes the impact of social underpinnings on student persistence and the need for institutional involvement in this area. In fact, "the research field generally agrees about the importance of social integration with regard to student retention and the fact that students have difficult time persisting when they are not socially integrated into campus life" ("A Framework for Retention," 2003, p. 78). Closely linked to social integration is the level of student involvement and intention.

Student involvement and intention. Student intention and involvement also affect overall student commitment. According to Astin (1985) "the extent to which students are able to develop their talents in college is a direct function of the amount of time and effort they devote to activities designed to produce these gains" (p. 143). In applying Astin's theory of student involvement to the study of student persistence, those environmental factors that both positively and negatively affect student achievement are directly related to student involvement. The most significant factor identified—and one discussed in relation to social integration— has to do with students residing on campus. According to Astin, "living in a campus residence was positively related to retention, and this positive effect occurred in all types of institutions and among all types of students regardless of sex, race, ability, or family background" (p. 145). The benefit of residing on campus was mainly related to time and opportunity. Those students who were not using time to commute to and from school were able to become involved in the activities an institution provided.

As Astin (1985) posited, "simply by virtue of eating, sleeping, and spending their waking hours on the college campus, residential students stand a better chance than do commuter students of developing a strong identification with and attachment to undergraduate life" (p. 145). It stands to reason, then, that the theory of involvement is greatly affected by university type. As such, "the most consistent finding—reported in virtually every longitudinal study of student development—is that a student's chances of dropping out are substantially greater at a two-year college than at a four-year college" (p. 146). However, this theory may not apply to today's community college students, as "community colleges have been magnets for a generation of professionals with new ideas about campus life, involvement, activities, and the culture of the community college" (Miller, Pope, & Steinmann, 2005, ¶ 3).

Student intentions also provide insight into student persistence. Tinto (1987) posited that "generally speaking, the higher the level of one's educational or occupational goals, the greater the likelihood of college completion" (p. 40). This is not to imply that student intentions and goals do not change over time. In fact, many students are unsure of their educational goals when entering college (Tinto, 1987). This uncertainty is not necessarily linked to attrition. However, the longer students remain uncertain about the formation of their careers or identity, the more likely they are to depart. As Tinto noted,

> when those careers and identities are crystallized, that is, when individuals are more certain as to their futures, they are more likely to finish college. When plans remain unformulated over extended periods of time, that is, when uncertainty persists for several years, they are more likely to depart without completing their degree programs. (p. 44)

Student intention may even be more difficult to discern in community colleges, as there seems to be a wider range of goals among these students (Voorhees & Zhou, 2000, p. 220). As such, the American Association of Community Colleges created a framework of indicators "that support the community college mission" (p. 220). In an effort to predict student outcomes, the first of these indicators measures student intent.

According to Voorhees and Zhou (2000) "understanding student intention as it affects individual student outcomes is the essential element of [the association's] indicator system because goal attainment cannot be understood independently from student intent" (p. 220). Therefore, while the issues of involvement and intention have bearing on student retention and persistence at both 2- and 4-year institutions, how they manifest themselves may be quite different. In fact, it becomes necessary to look at how external factors such as SES, social capital, and ethnicity have an overarching effect on student commitment.

Historically Underserved Students

Those students who have been historically underserved have different academic and social experiences on the campuses of higher education institutions. In fact, "in highlighting the differences in college experiences for economically and educationally challenged students, the negative implications for persistence and for students' post college opportunities become clear" ("College Experiences," 2007, p. 41). A review of the literature reveals that economically disadvantaged students are required to work more during their college tenures and, as such, participate less in student activities and organizations (Finkelstein, 2000; Oldfield, 2007).

According to Weidman (1989), informal interactions with faculty and peers play an important role in the undergraduate socialization process. However, when economically disadvantaged students reported spending time with faculty outside the classroom, it was "in more structured settings, such as working on a research project, while high-SES students were more likely to report visiting faculty in their homes" ("College Experiences," 2007, p. 42). Economically disadvantaged students also tend to choose vocational majors rather than those within the liberal arts ("College Experiences," 2007). According to Oldfield (2007), "for first-generation poor and working-class college students, surviving the social challenges of higher learning can be at least as demanding as achieving a high grade point average" (p. 3).

However, many school officials fail to recognize the effects of social class bias on student persistence. Efforts to address the needs of economically disadvantaged students will also benefit economically advantaged students and faculty in their quests to promote social justice. For example,

> democratizing higher education so that it represents a more complex reality and more diversity in terms of socioeconomic status will help privileged groups gain a greater respect and appreciation for the values and survival skills their fellow travelers bring to campus. (Oldfield, 2007, p. 3)

Many first-generation, low-income students have difficulty entering 4-year universities and describe "the shock of arriving with far less academic preparation, money, and confidence than their peers with college educated parents" (Cushman, 2007, p. 44). For this reason, many choose to attend community colleges initially and then transfer. Cushman (2007) posited,

> First-generation students at community colleges will probably find many fellow students who share their backgrounds, because these colleges typically serve large numbers of low-income students and students of color. At a state university or private college, however, first-in-the-family students are often taken aback by the social and academic climate. (p. 44)

It is important for institutions of higher education to develop an understanding of economically disadvantaged students and their specific needs to support retention and persistence. With this, it becomes necessary to look into those areas that contribute to or result from economic disadvantage categorization such as race and social capital.

Race and Student Persistence

Nationwide, a large percentage of students who earn a high school diploma do not acquire the requisite skills required to be successful in postsecondary endeavors (ACT, 2009; Boser & Burd, 2009; National Center for Public Policy and Higher Education, 2008). Roderick, Nagaoka, and Coca (2009) posited,

> Over the past several decades, high school students' college aspirations have increased markedly, and gaps in educational aspirations across race and ethnicity and income have fallen dramatically. But significant, and in some cases widening, gaps remain in college readiness, access, and success across these groups. (p. 186)

College readiness and success are usually predicted by students' levels of content knowledge, core academic skills, and noncognitive skills. Institutions of higher learning measure these skills by looking at "students' high school coursework, their performance on achievement exams, and their relative class rank and grade point average" (Roderick et al., 2009, p. 190). Those students who are admitted to colleges but fall short in any of these areas must complete a series of remedial coursework. Although 50% of students who are admitted to institutions of higher learning college graduate within 6 years, only around 30% of high school graduates required to take remedial courses go on to earn a degree (Graves, 2008). The problem is worse among African American and Hispanic students (National Center for Public Policy and Higher Education, 2008).

According to the National Center for Education Statistics (NCES) (2009), students of all ethnic backgrounds have shown some growth in the areas of completion, transition to college, persistence, and progress. For example, 88% of 25- to 29-year-olds received high school diplomas or their equivalent in 2008 (NCES, 2009). In addition "during the period of 1971 to 2008, the gap in high school attainment between Blacks and Whites decreased from 23 to 6 percentage points" (Completions section, ¶ 1). However, the fact remains that a gap still exists between minorities and nonminorities in high school degree attainment, college enrollment rates, and postsecondary persistence.

According to NCES (2009), "gaps in immediate enrollment rates by family income, parents' education, and race/ethnicity have persisted over time" (Transition to College section, ¶ 1). The latest statistics available from NCES show that "in 2007, White students accounted for 64 percent of college student enrollment. In that year, 13 percent of college students were Black, 11 percent were Hispanic . . . and 3 percent were non resident aliens" (Characteristics of Postsecondary Students section, ¶ 1). In looking to persistence, statistics show that in 2008, 60% of Whites, 49% of Hispanics, and 42% of African Americans graduated with a bachelor's degree within 6 years of entering a postsecondary institution (NCES, 2009).

While Tinto (1987) linked college persistence to academic preparedness, a growing body of research is focused on the examination of differences between minority and nonminority adjustment processes. This research indicates that predictors of cognitive and persistence outcomes between the two are basically the same (Cabrera & Nora, 1994; Eimers & Pike, 1997; Nettles, Thoeny, & Gosman, 1986; Nora & Cabrera, 1996). Cabrera and Nora (1994) conducted a study into the effects of race on student persistence. According to their research, "though African American students reported that they had less preparation for college than their White counterparts, prior ability exerted at most an indirect effect on their decisions to persist" (p. 152).

The findings of their study revealed that minorities and nonminorities alike adjust to higher education in similar ways. Cabrera and Nora stated,

> For both groups, persistence is determined by preparation for college, positive academic experiences, strong parental encouragement, and academic performance in college. For both groups, exposure to a campus climate of prejudice and intolerance lessens commitment to the institution and, indirectly, weakens decisions to persist. In view of this commonality it stands to reason that institutional policies and practices that address the students' needs rather than his or her ethnicity would be effective not only in fostering tolerance among students but in retaining all students, be they minorities or non-minorities. (p. 153)

This is not to say that practices that harm minorities—such as underrepresentation, racism, and discrimination—no longer exist, just that they are not a prevalent factor in student persistence. As Tinto (1987) noted, the classroom is the best tool for overcoming racial tensions and forwarding social and academic integration of students.

By creating acceptance and understanding in the classroom, the hope is that these attitudes will exude into other areas of campus life and student interactions. This sentiment is mirrored by Cabrera and Nora (1994). In a call to action of higher education institutions, they posit, "Because stereotypes can be overcome through information, college administrators can effectively diffuse racial tension on their campuses by creating a climate that fosters tolerance among students, faculty, and staff" (p. 154). While minority status may not have direct effect on student persistence, a review of the literature indicates that social capital does.

Effects of Social Capital on Student Persistence

In entering college, many students may encounter personal and institutionalized barriers that hinder or prevent their retention or persistence. Wells (2008) posited,

> Such barriers may be associated with low family income or wealth, low parental education, or the poor, ill resourced schools that students from low-socioeconomic (SES) backgrounds often attend, all of which may result in less access to the financial, social, cultural, and academic resources that aid in the college-going process. (¶ 3)

To better understand how these barriers affect student outcomes, it is necessary to first explore the concept of social capital.

Social Capital Theory

Constructs of social capital. The construct of social capital is a fusion of the interactions, relationships, opportunities, and intangible resources that guide and support both groups and individuals within a particular social organization or relationship. As Putnam (2000) defined it,

> by analogy with notions of physical capital and human capital—tools and training that enhance individual productivity—the core idea of social capital theory is that social networks have value. Just as a screwdriver (physical capital) or a college education (human capital) can increase productivity (both individual and collective), so too social contacts affect the productivity of individuals and groups. (pp. 18–19)

Although there is wide acceptance of the fact that the structural and economic influences of neighborhoods affect the learning outcomes of students within them, social capital requires acknowledgement of social practices as well (Woolley et al., 2008, p. 133).

According to Israel and Beaulieu (2004), "an expanding body of work suggests that social capital—the set of supportive interpersonal interactions that exists in the family, community, and school—plays a decisive role in promoting educational achievement" (p. 261). It therefore becomes necessary to look at not only the social capital with which one is born but that which is gained, positively or negatively, from communities, schools, and associations. Beaulieu, Israel, Hartless, and Dyk (2001) elaborated:

> If the child has strong, dependable and extensive interactions with individuals in these three social environments (i.e., family, school, and community), then that child has access to high social capital. Being embedded in such a rich social capital environment is likely to translate into higher educational achievement for that child. (p. 122)

Social capital at its core, then, is one's connections and relationships with other human beings. As pointed out by Stockard and Mayberry (1992) "it embraces obligations, behavioral expectations, and trust that develop from strong ties among individuals in a group, channels of information that help individuals be more informed, and norms and sanctions that facilitate and constrain certain actions" (p. 74).

This is not to say that social capital benefits only individuals. To the contrary, "social capital has both an individual and a collective aspect—a private face and a public face" (Putnam, 2000, p. 20). For example, individuals form relationships that will further their personal agendas. For example, one may utilize a relationship or friendship to secure employment, a business loan, and so on. In addition, capitalizing on one's membership in a particular group or organization is a widely accepted form of networking, "for most of us get our jobs because of whom we know, not what we know—that is, our social capital, not our human capital" (p. 20).

However, individual relationship building is not the only aspect involved in procuring individual success. The broader communities from which individuals hail directly affect them. Putnam (2000) illustrates this point in his statement that "a well-connected individual in a poorly connected society is not as productive as a well-connected individual in a well-connected society" (p. 20). This also brings into question the converse effects of being a poorly connected individual in a well-connected society. One may look to the concept of "White privilege" in explaining how cultural capital allows those Whites who may not be well connected to still enjoy the benefits of simply being White.

It then stands to reason that those individuals who retain the social capital associated with a well-connected society may be able to ameliorate their own poor connectedness. As Siisiäinen (2000) explained, "Putnam's idea of social capital deals with collective values and societal integration, whereas Bourdieu's approach is made from the point of view of actors engaged in struggle in pursuit of their interests" (p. 10).

Bourdieu (1986) acknowledged the politics surrounding social capital:

> The aggregate of the actual or potential resources which are linked to possession of a durable network of more or less institutionalized relationships of mutual acquaintance and recognition—in other words, to membership in a group—which provides each of its members with the backing of the collectively owned capital, a "credential" which entitles them to credit, in the various senses of the word. (pp. 248–249)

According to Siisiäinen (2000), this view differed from Putnam's idea of social capital in that "Bourdieu's concept of social capital puts the emphasis on conflicts and the power function (social relations that increase the ability of an actor to advance her/his interests)" (p. 2). Siisiäinen argued that in Bourdieu's viewpoint, "social capital becomes a resource in the social struggles that are carried out in different social arenas or fields" (p. 2).

Attempting to maintain cultural capital, Bourdieu (1986) explained that the dominant class works to ensure that its network of power is transmitted to subsequent generations. Therefore, efforts to prevent this transmission of capital are met with resistance and underhanded attempts to promote the status quo. In fact, "the more the official transmission of capital is prevented or hindered, the more the effects of the clandestine circulation of capital in the form of cultural capital become determinant in the reproduction of the social structure" (p. 254). Education reproduces social capital, and its range "tends to increase, and together with this increase is the unification of the market in social qualifications which gives rights to occupy rare positions" (p. 255). While education has often been viewed as an equalizer of class inequities by providing opportunities for students to "overcome their socioeconomic origins and move up the social ladder. . . . Postsecondary education overall has also been characterized as one of the forces in society that may serve to reproduce existing hierarchies" (Wells, 2008, ¶ 1).

According to Wells (2008), "researchers have almost always recognized the effects that SES has when studying educational outcomes, and persistence research is no different" (Determinants of Persistence in Postsecondary Education section, ¶ 1). Wells found that "accumulated social and cultural capital will likely have an influence on college student decision making, and the effects that this may have on student decisions are likely to be especially strong during the first years of postsecondary schooling" (Theoretical Grounding section, ¶ 3). In addition, "cultural capital is often inherited from one's family and therefore may sustain SES stratification based on families passing the torch of societal privilege and advantage" (Theoretical Grounding section, ¶ 2). One way that students accumulate social capital is through the associations and acquired social capital of their parents, which may be directly linked to parental income, wealth, and educational levels.

Parental influence on social capital. Parents have great influence on how students perform within the culture of their chosen institutions. It is becoming more evident that what students "bring with them" to a college or university environment determines how well they integrate into and function within that environment. According to Wang (2008), "social capital within the family—discussions with children, monitoring and helping with homework, number of siblings, and so forth—helps the children to take advantages of the financial, cultural, and human resources available to them in the family" (p. 122). It also prepares them to form relationships and ties with the surrounding community and the schools they attend. As Haghighat (2005) pointed out, "social capital therefore refers to social networks available to parents that enhance a pupil's ability to benefit from educational opportunities" (p. 215). "Parents and schools that 'possess' more social capital (e.g. stronger relationships, ties and a strong sense of connectedness) promote a higher level of pupil achievement" (p. 215). While Wang (2008) recognized the importance of these social networks and resulting social capital, he questioned terminology that confounded the issue, asking, "Why not simply use 'parental involvement' or 'family support' which may carry more intuitive meaning than the term 'social capital'?" (p. 120).

Stewart (2007) discussed this parental involvement and support: "overall, the research has shown that parents are instrumental to the academic success of their children, and that parental involvement has a positive impact on student achievement" (p. 21). Stewart reinforced this by stating,

Parents' behavior with or on behalf of their children is a major domain of influence on children's school success. Parents not only influences what the child brings to the school setting when he or she begins school but also can influence how well the child acquires school-related skills throughout the school years and can influence other behaviors, such as study habits, that are likely to affect the child's achievement and attainment. (p. 21)

Therefore, it appears that parents directly affect the type and amount of social capital their children possess. This review of literature now turns to exploring how social capital, SES, involvement, intention, and commitment affect student retention and persistence at both 2- and 4-year institutions.

RELATIONSHIP AMONG SES, SOCIAL CAPITAL, AND SELF-EFFICACY

SES and social capital play an important role in student self-efficacy and ultimately student persistence. SES determines the amount and type of exposure that students have to cultural and educational opportunities, familial support, and skills development. As such, "students hailing from less supportive environments may bring with them deficiencies in their self-esteem and efficacy, especially as they relate to academics when compared with students from more advantaged backgrounds" ("A Framework for Retention," 2003, p. 79). As discussed earlier, social cognitive theory closely links behavior and self-influence (Bandura, 2003). Self-influence or "self-efficacy, outcome expectations, and performance goals are influenced by one's ability/past performance, and these three factors in turn affect subsequent performance" (Kahn & Nauta, 2001, p. 635). If one's past experiences have been limited, it stands to reason that self-efficacy would be low.

According to Kahn and Nauta (2001) "theoretically if academic self-efficacy is low, outcome expectations regarding finishing college are not favorable, and/or performance goals are discordant with persisting, then a student would be at risk for leaving college" (p. 635). In a study of general self-efficacy and subjective well-being of economically disadvantaged college students, Tong and Song (2004) found that levels were significantly lower for economically disadvantaged students than for other students and that the reason may be linked to inadequate social support. These students require support in areas concerning stressors that vary greatly from those of economically advantaged students. For example, in addition to stresses commonly related to college life, such as academic requirements or social obligations, economically disadvantaged students often have the additional anxiety of financial difficulty.

The Role of Community Colleges in Increasing Student Persistence

According to Wells (2008), social capital has "a positive effect on student persistence in postsecondary education" (Discussion and Implications section, ¶ 1). However, it appears that community colleges may play a crucial role in reaching those students with low social and cultural capital. In his study of 2- and 4-year institutions, Wells found,

For full-time students, the probability of a high-capital student persisting when beginning at a four-year institution is 45 percentage points higher than the probability for a low-capital student, but this difference is only 13 percentage points when beginning at a community college. (Discussion and Implications section, ¶ 1)

It is difficult to measure persistence on community college campuses due to the fact that students have varying intentions upon entering the college. Nevertheless, these schools have been historically saddled with extremely low persistence rates. Miller and colleagues (2005) identified a "rising schism between types of students enrolling in community colleges" (Who Are Community College Students? section, ¶ 3). They explained,

One group of students enrolls at the local college for a variety of reasons that have nothing to do with transfer intention. These reasons might include that they desire an occupational education, they lack fundamental skills necessary for entry into the workforce, or that they want some exposure to higher education, but do not yet have the maturity or commitment to enroll on a full-time basis or at a four-year institution. The second group of students is using community colleges to earn a general education that can transfer to a four-year institution. (Who Are Community College Students? section, ¶ 3)

Regardless of motivating factors, low-capital students who begin their journey into higher education at community colleges "appear to be more successful in persisting into the second year than their low-capital peers beginning at four-year institutions" (Wells, 2008, Discussion and Implications section, ¶ 4). For this reason, it is important that higher education provide services for historically underserved students who possess a heterogeneous range of intentions. However, this undertaking is not without its critics. While many view the education of those who have previously been denied as an act of forwarding democratic ideals and promoting social justice, there are those who accuse these institutions of promoting rather than quelling "prevailing patterns of social and class inequity" (Karabel, 1986, p. 18). According to Kisker (2007), this criticism arises from the fact that only a quarter of students transfer from community colleges to 4-year universities.

This criticism has brought about a "greater demand for community colleges to document their claims of success and allay continuing concerns over low transfer and degree attainment rates" (Dougherty & Townsend, 2006, p. 6). However, it is a difficult challenge for community colleges to focus their missions on one specific curriculum when they serve the needs of so many individuals, including individuals who attend for reasons other than ultimate degree attainment. Nevertheless, those who criticize the function of community colleges point out that "the majority of community colleges' many disadvantaged students do not receive a degree, and if they do, it carries a lower reward than a four-year degree" (p. 7).

Conclusion

Recent educational statistics appear to point to the fact that a greater number of students are receiving high school diplomas or the equivalent and that although a gap continues to exist between minority and nonminority enrollments at institutions of higher learning, more students are entering college. However, the fact remains that persistence rates of historically underserved students continue to be disproportionately low. Through this examination of the internal and external factors that contribute to student attrition as viewed through the lens of Tinto's (1987) model of student departure with constructs from Astin's (1985) theory of involvement, one is able to utilize a combined model of persistence in developing an understanding of why students who hail from backgrounds of economic disadvantage and low social capital are more likely to leave institutions of higher learning than realize degree attainment. In reviewing the related literature, one comes to understand the importance of student commitment and its underpinnings of academic and social integration. It is here that Astin's idea of student involvement and Tinto's premise of student intention merge and provide clear insight into the relationship of these external factors to the overarching idea of integration and its position in fostering and supporting student commitment.

In developing an understanding of the relationship between student commitment and persistence, it becomes increasingly important to factor in those defining social and/or cultural characteristics shared by many who have been historically underserved. Those identified as historically underserved include first-generation poor, working-class, and ethnic minority students. Historically underserved students often possess low social capital and, as a result, describe associative personal and institutional barriers to persistence at the collegiate level. In many cases, these barriers result from the fact that students simply have less access to supports that facilitate the collegial process, such as financial, social, cultural, and academic resources.

Another barrier arising from economic disadvantage and low social capital is poor self-efficacy. Students who have had less exposure to educational and cultural experiences and opportunities during their lifetimes demonstrate deficiencies in efficacy. Low self-efficacy often translates into expectations or goals that fail to align with student persistence. In a study of the general self-efficacy of economically disadvantaged students, Tong and Song (2004) found that these students have significantly lower self-efficacy than do students from advantaged backgrounds. While economic disadvantage and low social capital and resulting low self-efficacy may negatively influence the educational pursuits of many students who begin their studies at 4-year universities, Wells (2008) found that persistence rates are higher for low-capital students who begin school at community colleges.

The review of literature suggests that the goals and intentions of students attending community colleges are difficult to discern and that persistence is not easily measured, because students attending these schools may take courses in an effort to further career goals or acquire fundamental skills or as a foray into higher education (Provasnik & Planty, 2008). Nevertheless, historically underserved students who matriculate into programs at community colleges are more likely to persist to a second year of study than are their peers who begin at 4-year institutions.

It appears then that the increasing role of community colleges needs to focus on the provision of quality education, whether vocational, remedial, or prebaccalaureate, to equitably serve the myriad needs of students in attendance (Cohen & Brawer, 2008). As financial aid awards increasingly leave gaps between costs and funding and as tuition at 4-year universities continues to increase at alarming rates, groups of students across the country are being denied access. In the current economic climate, community colleges are in a position to become promoters of social justice and equity by providing greater access to education for individuals who might otherwise be denied.

REFERENCES

ACT. (2009). *The condition of college readiness.* Iowa City, IA: Author.

Allen, W. (1992). The color of success: African-American college student outcomes at predominantly white and historical black colleges and universities. *Harvard Educational Review, 62*, 26–44.

Astin, A. W. (1985). *Achieving educational excellence: A critical assessment of priorities and practices in higher education.* San Francisco: Jossey-Bass.

Baker, T., & Velez, W. (1996). Access to and opportunity in postsecondary education in the United States: A review. *Sociology of Education, 69*(2), 82–101.

Bandura, A. (2003). Role of mechanisms of selective moral disengagement in terrorism and counterterrorism. In F. M. Mogahaddam & A. J. Marsella (Eds.), *Understanding terrorism* (pp. 121–150). Washington, DC: American Psychological Association.

Bandura, A., & Locke, E. (2003). Negative self-efficacy and goal effects revisited. *Journal of Applied Psychology, 88*, 87–99.

Bean, J. P., & Bradley, R. K. (1986). Untangling the satisfaction-performance relationship for college students. *Journal of Higher Education, 57*(4), 393–412.

Beaulieu, L., Israel, G., Hartless, G., & Dyk, P. (2001, April). For whom does the school bell toll? Multi-contextual presence of social capital and student educational achievement. *Journal of Socio-Economics, 30*(2), 121–127.

Berger, J., & Milem, J. (1999). The role of student involvement and perceptions of integration in a causal model of student persistence. *Research in Higher Education, 40*(6), 641–664.

Bitzer, E. (2009). Academic and social integration in three first-year groups: A holistic perspective. *South African Journal of Higher Education, 23*(2), 225–245.

Borglum, K., & Kubala, T. (2000) Academic and social integration of community college students: A case study. *Community College Journal of Research and Practice, 24*, 567–576.

Boser, U., & Burd, S. (2009). *Bridging th e gap: How to strengthen the pk– 16 pipeline to improve college readiness.* Washington, DC: New America Foundation.

Bourdieu, P. (1983). Forms of capital. In J. G. Richardson (Ed.), *Handbook of theory and research for the sociology of education* (pp. 241–258). New York: Greenwood Press.

Braxton, J. M. (2000). *Reworking the student departure puzzle.* Nashville, TN: Vanderbilt University Press.

Cabrera, A. F., & Nora, A. (1994). College students' perceptions of prejudice and discrimination and their feelings of alienation. *Review of Education, Pedagogy, and Cultural Studies, 16*, 387–409.

Christie, N., & Dinham, S. (1991). Institutional and external influences on social integration in the freshman year. *Journal of Higher Education, 64*(2), 412–436.

Cohen, A., & Brawer, F. (2008). *The American community college* (5th ed.). San Francisco: Jossey-Bass.

College experiences. (2007). *ASHE Higher Education Report, 33*(3), 41–45.

Cushman, K. (2007). Facing the culture shock of college. *Educational Leadership, 64*(7), 44–47.

DeWitz, S. J., Woolsey, M. L., & Walsh, W. B. (2009). College student retention: An exploration of the relationship between self-efficacy beliefs and purpose in life among college students. *Journal of College Student Development, 50*(1), 19–34.

Dougherty, K. J., & Townsend, B. (2006). Community college missions: A theoretical and historical perspective. *New Directions for Community Colleges, 136*, 5–13.

Eimers, M. T., & Pike, G. R. (1997). Minority and nonminority adjustment to college: Differences or similarities. *Research in Higher Education, 38*(1), 77–98.

Finkelstein, J. (2000). Maximizing retention for at-risk freshmen. *Community College Week, 13*(5), 4.

A framework for retention. (2003). *ASHE-ERIC Higher Education Report, 30*(2), 75–112.

Graves, L. (2008, May 2). The gap in graduation rates. *U. S. News and World Report.*

Haghighat, E. (2005). School social capital and pupils' academic performance. *International Studies in Sociology of Education, 15*(3), 213–235.

Israel, G., & Beaulieu, L. (2004). Laying the foundation for employment: The role of social capital in educational achievement. *Review of Regional Studies, 34*(3), 260–287.

Kahn, J., & Nauta, M. (2001). Social-cognitive predictors of first-year college persistence: The importance of proximal assessment. *Research in Higher Education, 42*(6), 633–652.

Karabel, J. (1986). Community colleges and social stratification in the 1980s. In L. S. Zwerling (Ed.), *The community college and its critics: New directions for community colleges* (pp. 13–30). San Francisco: Jossey-Bass.

Kisker, C. (2007). Creating and sustaining community college—university transfer partnerships. *Community College Review*, *34*(4), 282–301.

Miller, M., Pope, M., & Steinmann, T. (2005). A profile of contemporary community college student involvement, technology use, and reliance on selected college life skills. *College Student Journal*, *39*(3), 596–603.

National Center for Education Statistics. (2009). *The condition of education 2009*. Washington, DC: U.S. Department of Education. Retrieved from http://nces.ed.gov/programs/coe/2009/section3/indicator22.asp

National Center for Public Policy and Higher Education. (2008). *Measuring up 2008*. San Jose, CA: Author.

Nettles, M. T., Thoeny, A. R., & Gosman, E. J. (1986). Comparative and predictive analyses of Black and White students' college achievement and experiences. *Journal of Higher Education*, *67*(3), 119–148.

Nora, A., & Cabrera, A. F. (1996). The role of perceptions of prejudice and discrimination on the adjustment of minority student to college. *Journal of Higher Education*, *67*, 119–148.

Oldfield, K. (2007). Humble and hopeful: Welcoming first-generation poor and working-class students to college. *About Campus*, *11*(6), 2–12.

Padilla, R., & Pavel, D. M. (1986). *Successful Hispanic community college students: An explanatory qualitative study*. Tempe, AZ: Arizona State University, Hispanic Research Center.

Pascarella, E. T., & Chapman, D. (1983). A multi-institutional, path analytic validation of Tinto's model of college withdrawal. *American Educational Research Journal*, *20*, 87–102.

Pascarella, E. T., & Terenzini, P. T. (1991). *How college affects students: Findings and insights from twenty years of research*. San Francisco: Jossey-Bass.

Paulsen, M. B., & St. John, E. P. (1997). The financial nexus between college choice and persistence. In R. A. Voorhees (Ed.), *Researching student aid: Creating an action agenda* (pp. 65–82). San Francisco: Jossey-Bass.

Provasnik, S., & Planty, M. (2008). *Community colleges: Special supplement to "The condition of education 2008."* Washington, DC: U.S. Department of Education, National Center for Education Statistics, Institute of Education Sciences.

Putnam, R. D. (2000). *Bowling alone: The collapse and revival of American community*. New York: Simon & Schuster.

Roderick, M., Nagaoka, J., & Coca, V. (2009). College readiness for all: The challenge for urban high schools. *The Future of Children*, *19*(1), 185–210. Retrieved from http://www.princeton.edu/futureofchildren/publications/Docs/19_01_policybrief.pdf

Sanford, N. (1962). The development status of entering freshmen. In N. Sanford (Ed.), *The American College* (pp. 253–282). New York: Wiley.

Siisiäinen, M. (2000, July). *Two concepts of social capital: Bourdieu vs. Putnam*. Paper presented at the ISTR Fourth International Conference, Dublin, Ireland. Retrieved from www.istr.org/Conferences/Dublin/workingpapers/Siisiainen.pdf

Stewart, E. (2007). Individual and school structural effects on African American high school students' academic achievement. *High School Journal*, *91*(2), 16–34.

Stockard, J., & Mayberry, M. (1992). *Effective educational environments*. Newberry Park, CA: Corwin Press.

Tinto, V. (1987). *Leaving college: Rethinking the causes and cures of student attrition*. Chicago: University of Chicago Press.

Tinto, V. (2006–2007). Research and practice of student retention: What next? *Journal of College Student Retention*, *8*(1), 1–19.

Tong, Y., & Song, S. (2004). A study on general self-efficacy and subjective well-being of low SES college students in a Chinese university. *College Student Journal*, *38*(4), 637–642.

Townsend, B. (2007). Interpreting the influence of community college attendance upon baccalaureate attainment. *Community College Review*, *35*(2), 128–136.

Van Gennep, A. (1960). *The rites of passage* (M. Vizedon & G. Caffee, Trans.). Chicago: University of Chicago Press.

Voorhees, R., & Zhou, D. (2000). Intentions and goals at the community college: Associating student perceptions and demographics. *Community College Journal of Research & Practice*, *24*(3), 219–233.

Wang, D. (2008). Family–school relations as social capital: Chinese parents in the United States. *School Community Journal*, *18*(2), 119–146.

Weidman, J. C. (1989). Undergraduate socialization: A conceptual approach. In J. Smart (Ed.), *Handbook of theory and research in higher education* (Vol. 5, pp. 289–322). New York: Agathon.

Wells, R. (2008). The effects of social and cultural capital on student persistence: Are community colleges more meritocratic? *Community College Review*, *36*(1), 25–46.

Woolley, M., Grogan-Kaylor, A., Gilster, M., Karb, R., Gant, L., Reischl, T., et al. (2008). Neighborhood social capital, poor physical conditions, and school achievement. *Children & Schools*, *30*(3), 133–145.

Chapter Nine

Teacher Career Pathways and Educational Policy: A Quick Fix or Long-Term Solution?

Leslie Huling and Virginia Resta

School success is inextricably intertwined with the economic and cultural vitality of a society, and the quality of the teaching force is arguably the most important contributor to school success. Given these important links, policymakers have the political authority and responsibility to support, regulate, and cultivate teacher recruitment, preparation, and retention efforts.

In recent decades, policymakers have responded with a wide variety of initiatives to attract and retain teachers. In spite of these efforts, high teacher turnover continues to result in the inequitable distribution of quality teachers and thwart efforts to close the achievement gaps that have for decades plagued American schools. The National Council for Teaching and America's Future observed that

> a massive amount of scarce capital—both human and financial—is consumed by the constant process of hiring and replacing beginning teachers, who leave before they have mastered the ability to collaborate with their colleagues to create a successful learning culture for their students. (Carroll, 2009, p. 2)

Quick fixes, such as alternative preparation programs, teacher pay increases, and signing bonuses, have failed to solve school staffing challenges. Increasingly, there is a realization that what is needed are long-term solutions that involve systemic change in how teachers are recruited, prepared, mentored, and retained. One of the most promising long-term strategies involve "grow your own" partnerships, through which local residents are identified and recruited into teacher preparation programs to serve as teachers in their local communities. Often, these teacher candidates are already working in the schools as paraprofessionals, or they may be high school students who will become the first in their families to complete a college degree. These pipelines are also typically developed in response to critical teacher shortages in educational fields—namely, bilingual education, special education, mathematics, and science (Carnegie Corporation of New York, 2009; Snyder & Burgener, 2007; Stallings, 2007).

This chapter examines a number of demographic and societal trends that further necessitate the establishment and sustainability of teacher career pathway programs. Among these trends are the increasing demands for more highly skilled and educated workers, the discrepancy in the diversity between the student population and the teaching force, the tendency for high-need schools to be assigned less experienced and less highly qualified teachers, and the increase in the number of first-generation college students who can benefit greatly from mentoring and academic/career support programs. The policy supports for different models of teacher career pathway programs are discussed, specifically those targeted at recruiting teacher aides into teacher certification programs and those targeted at recruiting secondary teachers. The chapter concludes with suggestions for how policymakers can support the establishment and sustainability of teacher career pathway programs.

A CLOSER LOOK AT CONVERGING TRENDS

Never has the need been greater for highly competent and committed teachers. The profile of the typical classroom in the United States has undergone dramatic changes in the recent past. Many more students today come from impoverished homes, speak English as a second language, and have identified or suspected disabilities (Persky, Daane, & Jin, 2003).

In 1970, at the peak of baby boomer enrollments, the student population was 79% non-Hispanic white, 14% African American, 1% Asian and Pacific Islander, and 6% Hispanic. In 2003, in contrast, the elementary and high school population was 60% non-Hispanic white, 16% African American, 4% Asian and Pacific Islander, and 18% Hispanic.

The growth in minority populations is projected to continue and ultimately transform the face of the country. The nation's Hispanic and Asian populations are projected to triple over the next 50 years, but the non-Hispanic White population would drop to about 50% by 2050. In 2005, it was estimated that 45% 445% of children younger than 5 years belong to a racial or ethnic minority group and also 1 in 10 U.S. counties has a population that is more than 50% minority (Crouch, 2007). Between 2000 and 2008, the number of minority children grew by 4.8 million. Minorities represented 47% of the population under the age of 5 years in 2008 (Johnson & Lichter, 2010). Minority births accounted for nearly 48% of all U.S. births in the year ending in July 2008 (U.S. Census Bureau, 2009). These changing demographic factors increase the complexity of the classroom and the crucial role of the teacher in facilitating learning in rapidly changing educational settings. In light of these complex demographics, all teachers, regardless of preparation pathway, will need to be prepared to serve students from diverse backgrounds.

At the same time that schools face increasing challenges, the complexity of a global workplace demands that today's students not only be literate but also be prepared to be creative problem solvers who can work collaboratively with others to solve problems that have not yet been encountered. In today's economy, there are fewer job opportunities for students who do not enter and complete postsecondary education. It has been reported that almost 90% of the new jobs being created today require more than a high school level of literacy and math skills (Nondestructive Testing Resource Center, 2010) and between one-half to two-thirds of new jobs in the future will require a college education (Graham & Hebert, 2010). Earnings projections based on data from the Current Populations Survey indicate that the projected lifetime earnings of a college graduate in 2000 is almost double of that of a high school graduate ($2.1 million vs. $1.2 million; Day & Newburger, 2002).

In spite of the increasing need for larger percentages of students to enroll in and complete postsecondary education, the school dropout problem persists, and the student pipeline is hemorrhaging students along the way. Three out of every 10 students in America's public schools fail to finish high school on time with a regular diploma (Greene & Winters, 2005). That amounts to 1.3 million students falling through the cracks of the high school pipeline every year, or more than 7,000 students lost every day (Pinkus, 2006). Most nongraduates are members of historically disadvantaged minority groups. Dropouts are also more likely to have attended school in large urban districts and come from communities plagued by severe poverty and economic hardship (Editorial Projects in Education, 2010).

The dropout problem is not confined to high schools. Of the students who enter college, only about half complete college within 6 years. The college completion rates are lower for African American and Hispanic students, with only about one-third completing college within 6 years (Bonner, 2010). As expected, high school grades and test scores are among the best predictors of college completion status (College Completion Declining, 2003). Based on these sobering statistics, there is an undeniable need for highly trained teachers who can help students develop the critical skills necessary for postsecondary success, especially in high-need schools that have traditionally had fewer graduates matriculating into postsecondary education.

Yet, schools that serve the largest percentages of economically disadvantaged students traditionally have had the least prepared teachers and the highest teacher turnover rates. Children in the highest-poverty schools are assigned to novice teachers almost twice as often as children in low-poverty schools, and students in high-minority schools are assigned to novice teachers at twice the rate as students in schools without many minority students (Peske & Haycock, 2006). High turnover is a central factor driving the inequitable distribution of quality teaching (Carroll, 2009). This results in young, inexperienced teachers often facing assignments in the most challenging schools because that is where the openings are—but with little support, they burn out in a few years, feeding the churn of attrition and teacher turnover in these schools (Carroll, 2010). The teacher turnover rate continues to be high and is even more so in the high-need schools where students have the greatest need for highly skilled teachers. Moreover, a teacher's own performance is affected by the quality of her or his peers. Jackson and Bruegmann (2009) found that "changes in the quality of a teacher's colleagues (all other teachers in the same school who teach students in the same grade) are associated with changes in her students' test score gains" (p. 21). More simply stated, where one teaches and with whom one teaches affects one's effectiveness as a teacher (Fuller, 2010).

Depending on new, young, novice teachers to replace those who have just left, these schools have contributed to the achievement gap in high-need schools because students lose the value of being taught by an experienced teacher (Carroll, 2010). Teacher recruitment will not solve the staffing problems of schools if they do not also address the problem of teacher retention (Ingersoll, 2001). Participants in teacher career pathway programs typically plan to teach in the same neighborhoods where they live.

Not only does high teacher attrition contribute to the achievement gap in high-need schools, but it is also a very costly endeavor. A conservative national estimate of the cost of replacing public school teachers who have dropped out of the profession is $2.2 billion a year. If the cost of replacing public school teachers who transfer schools is added, the total reaches $4.9 billion every year. For individual states, cost estimates range from $8.5 million in North Dakota to a whopping half a billion dollars for a large state such as Texas (Alliance for Excellent Education, 2005).

The National Commission on Teaching and America's Future estimates that the national cost of public school teacher turnover could be more than $7.3 billion a year. This new estimate is significantly higher than the most recent estimate of $4.9 billion in annual costs, which was made in a report by the Alliance for Excellent Education in 2005 and takes into account recent increases in the size of the teacher workforce and the rate of teacher turnover. Stemming the teacher attrition rate, a primary goal of teacher career pathway programs, could create resources that could be devoted to other educational priorities, including efforts to attract and retain teachers who have a desire to make a positive difference in high-need schools.

Recognizing these various yet converging factors, astute policymakers understand the benefits of teacher initiatives to attract and retain diverse candidates who can be successful in rapidly changing schools and who will be committed to teaching in high-need schools. Many participants in these specialized recruitment programs are first-generation college students who typically need extra financial, academic, and social support to be successful. Teacher career pathways hold the promise of being win-win-win situations, as (1) first-generation college students are provided with support to complete their education for a career in teaching and (2) public school students will receive teachers who have the cultural competence and dedication to help them succeed beyond high school, while (3) communities and families receive the economic and societal benefits of a more highly educated workforce.

DIFFERENT MODELS OF TEACHER CAREER PATHWAY PROGRAMS

Teacher career pathway program initiatives most frequently arise out of partnership endeavors involving school districts, community colleges or universities, and other community or professional organizations. The majority of programs have some type of grant or external funding, and a few states have made funding available to support projects that address state-developed guidelines. Teacher career pathways programs typically target a specific population of prospective teacher candidates, though some provide services to different groups of participants. The two most common types of programs are (1) those that target secondary students (typically high school, though sometimes middle school) and provide services to them as they progress through their college years and into teaching and (2) those that target paraeducators who are nondegreed individuals working in schools who are provided with financial, academic, and social support to enroll in college to earn their degrees and teacher certification. Some programs also target community members who wish to become teachers and who have cultural or language competencies well suited to the needs of local students and schools.

Targeted Recruitment of Secondary Students

Academy of Urban Education. Philadelphia Public Schools operate three urban education academies to introduce high school students to careers in teaching (Burgess, 2010). The Academy of Urban Education is designed to serve as an introduction to the teaching profession and other educational careers for students, and it is dedicated to preparing students both academically and emotionally for college. The academy offers students opportunities to interact with their community to help bring about effective change in their schools.

Students in this academy have the opportunity to do the following: take advantage of a Job Guarantee Agreement that specifically guarantees every graduate of the program a teaching position upon completion of a college degree and Pennsylvania teacher certification; participate in an instructional internship in which they observe mentor teachers and practice planning and teaching lessons; participate in programs designed to enhance leadership skills and students' ability to serve the community in meaningful ways; attend summer enhancement programs; and gain dual-enrollment credit for college while still in high school.

The program has partnerships with the education departments of area colleges and universities, and it helps prepare academy students for college while giving them an introduction to the teacher-training curriculum. The academy's Industry Advisory Board and other partners support the program by providing practice interviews, speakers, tours, and internships for students and by working with academy staff to develop curriculum and train teachers. Board members for the Academy of Urban Education currently include representatives of the Community College of Philadelphia, Pennsylvania State University-Brandywine, School District of Philadelphia, Temple University, and the Philadelphia Federation of Teachers (Philadelphia Academies, 2010).

Wichita Grow Your Own Teachers Program. The Wichita (Kansas) Public School District operates a Grow Your Own Teachers Program to increase diversity in the district's teaching staff. The locally funded program was launched in 1989 and is a collaborative effort of public education, higher education, and the private/business sector, designed to provide financial assistance in the form of forgivable loans to outstanding graduates of Wichita Public School to encourage them to pursue full-time teaching careers (Wichita Public Schools, 2010). To date, more than 150 participants have completed their college education, and 96 of these individuals are currently teaching in the Wichita Public Schools. Participating universities include Wichita State University, Friends University, Newman University, and Southwestern College. Graduates are eligible for loan forgiveness if they begin teaching in the Wichita Public Schools the semester following graduation and continue teaching for 3 consecutive years.

Targeted Recruitment of Paraeducators Working in Schools

Latino Teacher Project. There are many innovative teacher career pathway programs emanating from universities. One well-known program is the Latino Teacher Project at the University of Southern California. The project provides financial, social, and academic support to promising paraeducators to enable them to successfully complete a teacher education program and become successful bilingual teachers (University of Southern California, 2010). Project partic.ipants are employed as bilingual paraeducators who work daily in the classrooms of eligible schools throughout the Los Angeles area while attending classes full-time at one of four participating project universities.

The Teacher Pipeline Project. The Teacher Pipeline Project at St. Edward's University in Austin, Texas, is another example of a university that is investing in a teacher career pathway program. The project is coordinated by the university and is a consortia of Austin Independent School District, Austin Community College, Huston-Tillotson University, Capital IDEA, Austin Interfaith, and Education Austin. In this program, teaching assistants in Austin Independent School District are provided with financial and academic support to earn a bachelor's degree and teacher certification in high-need content areas (St. Edward's University, 2010). Bilingual education candidates in the program attend St. Edward's University, while special education candidates attend Huston-Tillotson University. Funding support for the program has been provided by the Ford Foundation, the Houston Endowment, and the KDK Harman Foundation.

The four teacher career pathway programs highlighted here are representative of the types of teacher pipelines that are emerging across the nation. Most of these programs are designed to recruit and prepare teachers for schools that have had difficulty attracting and retaining an adequate supply of highly qualified teachers. Furthermore, most of these programs aspire to provide educational opportunities and academic, social, and financial support to prospective teachers who may be the first in their families to pursue higher education. Both of these program goals address high-priority policy issues related to school staffing and equity in educational opportunities.

Policymakers who provide resources for such programs ascribe to a number of underlying policy assumptions. One underlying assumption is that failure to act will perpetuate the school staffing and educational equity status quo, an unacceptable alternative that has a number of undesirable consequences. It is this compelling belief that motivates policymakers to provide financial and human resources in this environment where increasing social needs are competing for declining resources. Another underlying assumption is that high-need schools serving highly diverse student populations will benefit from having a teaching force that more closely resembles the demographics of the student population. This assumption is based on the belief that teachers who have lived in these communities will have a better understanding of the challenges that students face, will have a greater stake in helping such students succeed, and will serve as important role models for students.

A third underlying assumption is that teachers who are products of these communities will be more likely to remain in neighborhood schools than teachers who have little experience or affinity for the community. And a fourth underlying assumption is that multiple stakeholders must work together to achieve goals as complex and long-range as the ones being addressed by teacher career pathway programs. Communities help recruit participants; school districts provide candidates with laboratories in which to learn about teaching; and universities provide the academic coursework required in teacher education. Numerous stakeholders must work together to provide the resources necessary to operate such programs and provide candidates with the various services required to successfully complete teacher preparation and enter the teaching profession.

These underlying assumptions often guide the actions of policymakers but have not, for the most part, been tested empirically. The assumptions provide rich possibilities for future research efforts, but in the meantime, policymakers believe in the promise that such programs possess to address critical goals that cannot be placed on hold. For this group of policymakers, the following recommendations can help inform their decisions and actions.

RECOMMENDATIONS FOR POLICYMAKERS TO ESTABLISH, SUPPORT, AND SUSTAIN TEACHER CAREER PATHWAY PROGRAMS

From a policy perspective, teacher career pathways offer a partial and highly promising solution to recruiting, preparing, and supporting a new generation of teachers. A key strength of career pathway programs is the increased likelihood that teachers entering the profession through such avenues will choose to serve in high-need schools and remain in the communities where they are needed most. Even though policymakers are not typically the front-line providers of such programs, they are critically important in providing resources and policy supports to establish and sustain programs. The following policy recommendations can help in this endeavor.

Recognize and Illuminate the Complexity of the Situation

Astute and well-informed policymakers recognize that there are no "quick fixes" or "magic bullets" to solve the complex issues facing today's students, schools, and teachers. Many of the school reform efforts already underway to support student success and access to postsecondary education dovetail and complement the goals of teacher career pathway programs. State and local teacher recruitment and induction efforts can be intertwined with program support activities designed to facilitate the transition from student to teacher. Similarly, many state and local data systems include valuable information that can be mined to help identify problems in the educational pipeline and help gauge the impact of various educational interventions. During hard economic times, it will be difficult but especially important for policymakers to provide resources for research and evaluation efforts that continue to advance our understanding of complex educational issues in need of innovative solutions.

Communicate Clear Expectations to Stakeholders and Support Partnerships

As problems are identified in the educational and student-to-teacher pipelines, policymakers need to clearly communicate their expectations for improvements while making targeted resources available to fund these improvements. Such an approach might be called the "pressure plus support" model of school improvement (Hall & Hord, 2011). Policymakers should also recognize that some improvements necessarily require multiple entities that have not previously worked together to form partnerships and work in new and collaborative ways. An example of such a situation is the "academic gap" that often exists between high schools and colleges, resulting in many students who have successfully completed high school finding that they do not have the academic skills necessary to succeed in college. These educational challenges require, at a minimum, the collaboration of schools and universities and ideally would also involve parents and community/business partners. Policymakers can support these efforts by facilitating the formation of partnerships, establishing articulation agreements, providing resources, and monitoring progress while understanding that substantive change is an evolving process that takes time and ongoing commitment.

Help Elevate the Attractiveness of the Teaching Profession

If schools are to be successful in producing students who have the skills necessary to succeed in college and in the workplace, it will be necessary to attract talented and committed individuals into teaching. Such persons are more likely to be enticed into teaching if they view the profession as making an important societal contribution. Schools and universities should work together using a preK–16 approach to communicate a consistent message about the importance of teachers and their value to society. Competitive teacher salaries are critically important, but in addition to the financial compensation provided to teachers, policymakers and community members can promote teacher recognition events that help "craft" a consistent message that teachers are respected professionals who are highly valued for their professional knowledge and service.

Educational leaders can ensure that workplace conditions are favorable for both student and teacher success and that teachers are involved as key decision makers at the campus and district levels. Teacher career pathway programs can provide positive, enthusiastic teacher role models for program participants, but their ultimate success in attracting teacher candidates will be largely dependent on the message being sent to prospective teachers from society and the community at large.

Understand and Embrace the Long-Term Nature of Student-to-Teacher Initiatives

Teacher career pathway initiatives, by their very nature, are long-term endeavors. Some programs start with students as young as middle school and provide services throughout their high school and college years and into their first years of teaching. Programs can and should be evaluated in an ongoing way using multiple measures, but depending on the program, it may be years before participants complete their teacher preparation programs and enter teaching. It will take even more years to track the retention of these teachers in high-need schools and communities.

Deliberately Plan for Program Sustainability

As policy priorities shift and staff changes occur, it will take a deliberate commitment to maintain an ongoing focus on these long-range programs. All stakeholders—including educators, community members, and policymakers—need to recognize this on the front end and understand that each subsequent investment is necessary to protect the initial investment and ultimately realize the dividends from these efforts. Given this situation, it would probably be a wiser investment to allocate resources over a longer period than invest in a well-funded but short-lived program. Partnership agreements executed at the beginning of the program can help clarify expectations and contributions and avoid confusion and disagreements when resources become scarce.

Recognize the Special Challenges and Strengths of Program Participants

The diverse participants in teacher career pathway programs bring new strengths to the teaching profession. Many of them are local residents who possess valuable cultural information about their local communities that will allow them access to students and their families. Program participants may also face some special challenges, especially if they will be the first in their families to attend college. They will likely need financial assistance in the form of scholarships, grants, or loans to pay for the cost of higher education. They may need extra encouragement, careful advising, and mentoring, and some will need academic support as they navigate an unfamiliar academic setting.

Understand That Making College Accessible Is Necessary but Not Sufficient

First-generation college students often lack the "social capital" that enables more privileged students to successfully navigate the bureaucracy known as higher education. As a group, first-generation college students tend to be more tentative and less self-directed and assertive about seeking assistance. College-educated parents have firsthand experiences that make them a valuable asset to their children when they experience difficulty or frustration. First-generation college students are not the beneficiaries of these same advantages and therefore need educators to provide more guidance, encouragement, and academic support to enable their success (Jenkins, Miyazaki, & Janosik, 2009; Merritt, 2008).

The Association of American Colleges and Universities has embraced the challenge of serving first-generation college students through its Making Excellence Inclusive initiative (Williams, Berger, & McClendon, 2005). In explaining this initiative, the authors of a commissioned paper on the topic wrote,

> If we do not commit to discovering what does and does not work for historically underserved students, we run the very real risk of failing a significant portion of today's college students—even as we diversify our campuses to a greater extent than ever before. (Bauman, Bustillos, Bensimon, Brown, & Bartee, 2005)

First-generation college students can benefit from services such as one-stop centers where students can get assistance with advising, registration, and financial aid; summer "bridge" programs; and advisors who continue with the student throughout his or her college career and carefully monitor the student's academic and personal progress. Student support services are not without costs, but the cost-to-benefit ratio of this investment can be enormous as student matriculation increases, in turn increasing the efficiency of expenditure by the university.

Because the earning potential of the recipients of these services dramatically increases, the community will benefit from taxpayer contributions and consumer purchases. In the case of teacher career pathway initiatives, the community is the beneficiary of years of service from a talented educator who has chosen to remain in the community. Policymakers can be advocates for student support services that not only help students enroll in college but also foster their successful completion of college and entry into the teaching profession, where they can be a positive force in helping future generations of students become academically prepared to succeed in college or the 21st-century workplace.

Provide Resources for Programs and Participants

Many participants in teacher career pathway initiatives will be first-generation college students with limited financial resources and a high degree of apprehension about the workings of college financial aide. Policymakers can provide resources for students in the form of scholarships, grants, and forgivable loans. Financial resources are also needed to provide the staff to coordinate student-to-teacher initiatives, to produce recruitment materials, to finance student visits to area universities, and to support other program operating expenses. Community organizations are often willing to contribute to educational programs that develop community capacity, and policymakers who are frequently leaders in their communities often have the contacts necessary to help channel community resources to worthy causes.

Highlight Model Programs and Promote Positive Dialogue

A number of different teacher career pathway initiatives are in operation across the country, and many of these are beginning to generate positive evaluation findings and have much to share about "lessons learned." Policymakers can advance the important work being accomplished by teacher career pathway programs by looking for opportunities to highlight and recognize these programs in high-visibility contexts, such as board meetings, public hearings, and other events for policymakers and educators. Policymakers can also encourage state and regional conferences focused on promoting the quality and stability of the teacher workforce, including teacher career pathway programs, or they can suggest that teacher workforce solutions be included as a programmatic strand in educational conferences that are sponsored annually by professional organizations or state entities.

Examine Existing Policies and Revise Those That Hinder Student and Teacher Success

Policymakers have a financial interest in students matriculating through college in a timely fashion and, because of this, have established policies that encourage students to do so. Examples of such policies include requiring students to take a minimum number of hours to qualify for financial aid, charging tuition/fee penalties for students who drop courses too frequently or who take too many years to complete college, and requiring students to complete all developmental education requirements before they can begin credit-bearing courses. At the same time, some students who must work part-time (or full-time) jobs to support themselves and their families may find it difficult to progress through college at the typical pace. Policymakers need to be sensitive to the plight of these students and make sure that policies are achieving the intended goals without creating an undue hardship for students who are struggling with academic or financial challenges.

Similarly, educational policies that affect teacher job satisfaction and retention should receive careful and ongoing attention. Policymakers can help ensure that salary incentives are used to help attract and retain teachers where they are most needed and that teacher compensation packages are structured fairly and, in fact, function to positively motivate teachers rather than discourage faculty collaboration or diminish faculty morale. In short, policymakers need to continually monitor and evaluate policies to ensure that they are stimulating positive change and not being counterproductive by creating unintended consequences.

CONCLUSION

Teacher career pathway initiatives contribute to the larger cycle of attracting and preparing high-quality teachers who will remain in high-need schools and help students develop the academic skills they will need for college and career success. Changing student demographics have increased the complexity faced by teachers and schools, and never has it been more important that schools be staffed with highly competent and dedicated professionals.

Teacher career pathway programs help students explore teaching as a career option and provide the academic, financial, and social support to help these students enter college and successfully complete their college degrees and earn teacher certification. As a result, teachers who are the products of such programs tend to have many of the cultural and life experiences that will help them relate to, and be advocates for, the diverse student populations that are prevalent in high-need schools. Various configurations of teacher career pathway programs are initiated by partnerships involving stakeholders, including school districts, universities, professional organizations, community organizations, and, in some cases, state departments of education. These programs provide models and examples of what is possible when stakeholders commit to a common goal and provide human and financial resources to support the development of the next generation of teachers.

Policymakers have a vested interest in promoting teacher career pathway programs, and there are a number of ways that that they can create the conditions for such programs to thrive. By understanding the complexity of the related social, educational, and economic issues that contribute to the need for teacher career pathway programs, they can provide leadership and resources to create partnerships for the common good. They can help elevate the teaching profession through their day-to-day actions that communicate that teachers are valued professionals. By continually examining and refining existing policies that can facilitate student and teacher success, policymakers can remove barriers that prevent students from realizing their full potential. No doubt teacher career pathway programs are long-term investments, but given all that is at stake for students, teachers, and communities, they are definitely an investment worth making.

REFERENCES

Alliance for Excellent Education. (2005). *Teacher attrition: A costly loss to the nation and to the states.* Retrieved from http://www.all4ed.org/files/archive/publications/TeacherAttrition.pdf

Bauman, G., Bustillos, L. T., Bensimon, E., Brown, C., & Bartee, R. (2005). *Achieving equitable educational outcomes with all students: The institution's roles and responsibilities*. Washington, DC: Association of American Colleges and Universities.

Bonner, J. L. (2010). *States to fight college completion rates*. Retrieved from https://verify1.newsbank.com/cgi-bin/ncom/APAB/ec_signin

Burgess, S. (2010). Philadelphia grooms future teachers at Parkway West High School. *Philadelphia Public School Notebook*. Retrieved from http://www.thenotebook.org/teacher-academy

Carnegie Corporation of New York, Institute for Advanced Study Commission on Mathematics and Science Education. (2009). *The opportunity equation: Transforming mathematics and science education for citizenship and the global economy*. New York: Author.

Carroll, T. (2009). *Learning teams: Creating what's next*. Retrieved from http://www.nctaf.org/resources/research_and_reports/nctaf_research_reports/index.htm

Carroll, T. (2010). *Who will teach? Experience matters*. Retrieved from http://www.nctaf.org/resources/research_and_reports/nctaf_research_reports/index.htm

College completion declining, taking longer, study shows—noteworthy news. (2003, April 24). *Black Issues in Higher Education*. Retrieved from http://findarticles.com/p/articles/mi_m0DXK/is_5_20/ai_101413754/?tag=content;col1

Crouch, R. (2007). *Changing demographics: At a glance*. Retrieved from http://www.centerforpubliceducation.org

Day, J. C., & Newburger, E. C. (2002). *The big payoff: Educational attainment and synthetic estimates of work-life earnings*. Washington, DC: U.S. Census Bureau.

Editorial Projects in Education. (2010, June 10). Diplomas count 2010: Graduation by the numbers. *Education Week, 29*(34).

Fuller, E. (2010). *Study on the distribution of teacher quality in Texas schools*. Austin, TX: Association of Texas Professional Educators.

Graham, S., & Hebert, M. (2010). *Writing to read: Evidence for how writing can improve reading*. Washington, DC: Alliance for Excellence in Education.

Greene, J. P., & Winters, M. A. (2005). *Public high school graduation and college-readiness rates: 1991–2002* (Education Working Paper No. 8). New York: Manhattan Institute. Retrieved from http://www.manhattan-institute.org/html/ewp_08.htm

Hall, G. E., & Hord, S. M. (2011 *Implementing change: Patterns, principles, and potholes* (3rd ed.). Upper Saddle River, NJ: Pearson Education.

Ingersoll, R. (2001). A different approach to solving the teacher shortage problem (Teaching Quality Policy Brief No. 3). Seattle, WA: Center for the Study of Teaching and Policy.

Jackson, K., & Bruegmann, E. (2009). Teaching students and teaching each other: The importance of peer learning for teachers. *American Economic Journal: Applied Economics, 1*(4), 1–27.

Jenkins, A. L., Miyazaki, Y., & Janosik, S. M. (2009). Predictors that distinguish first-generation college students from non-first generation college students. *Journal of Multicultural, Gender and Minority Studies, 3*(1), 1–6.

Johnson, K., & Lichter, D. (2010). Growing diversity among America's children and youth: Spatial and Temporal Dimensions. *Population and Development Review, 36*(1), 157.

Merritt, C. R. (2008). First-generation college students: Then and now. *Human Architecture: Journal of the Sociology of Self-Knowledge, 1*(1), 45–52.

Nondestructive Testing Resource Center. (2010). *Education means more opportunity and earning potential*. Retrieved from http://www.ndt-ed.org/Careers/Placement&Pay/CollegeIsImportant.htm

Persky, H. R., Daane, M. C., & Jin, Y. (2003). *The nation's report card: Writing 2002*. Washington, DC: U.S. Department of Education, National Center for Education Statistics.

Peske, H., & Haycock, K. (2006). *Teaching inequality: How poor and minority students are shortchanged on teacher quality* (ERIC Document No. ED494820). Retrieved from http://www.eric.ed.gov/ERICWebPortal

Philadelphia Academies. (2010). *Academy of urban education*. Philadelphia, PA: Author. Retrieved from http://www.academiesinc.org/program_urban.html

Pinkus, L. (2006). *Who's counted? Who's counting? Understanding high school graduation rates*. Washington, DC: Alliance for Excellent Education.

Snyder, J., & Burgener, J. (2007). *The 31 st annual AAEE educator supply and demand research study*. Columbus, OH: American Association for Employment in Education.

St. Edward's University. (2010). *Teacher pipeline*. Retrieved from http://www.stedwards.edu/educ/access/index.html

Stallings, D. T. (2007). *The math and science teacher pipeline in North Carolina.* Chapel Hill, NC: Center for the Study of the American South.

University of Southern California. (2010). *Latino and language minority teacher projects.* Retrieved from http://www-bcf.usc.edu/~cmmr/LTP.html

U.S. Census Bureau. (2009). *2008 national demographic components of change.* Retrieved from http://www.census.gov/popest/national/asrh/NC-EST2008–compchg.html

Wichita Public Schools. (2010). *Grow your own teacher program.* Retrieved from http://www.usd259.com/employees/humanresources/grow/default.html

Williams, D. A., Berger, J. B., & McClendon, S. A. (2005). *Toward a model of inclusive excellence and change in postsecondary institutions.* Washington, DC: Association of American Colleges and Universities.

Coda: An Emerging Portrait of Responsive Teacher Preparation

Realizing the potential efficacy of teacher education as a transformative agency requires us to understand the function of education in a democracy, and more specifically, to understand the transformative nature of teacher education in a democratic society.
—Jenlink (2005, p. 236)

Although we now appear to have consensus about the importance of teacher quality, there is no parallel consensus about how to define it: How to conceptualize teacher quality in ways that account for the complexities of teaching and learning, how to identify which characteristics of teacher quality are linked with desirable educational outcomes, how to decide which educational outcomes are desirable in the first place, and how to recruit, prepare, and retain teachers who provide rich academic learning opportunities but also prepare their students for participation in a democracy.
—Cochran-Smith (2004, pp. 3–4)

In schools, colleges, and universities today, the emergence of the teacher career pathway model, as a means of addressing persistent challenges in teacher workforce development and school staffing in America, signals a transition within the profession. Learning environments continue to change, and as societies became closer linked through technology, so too must the teaching profession evolve to respond to the changing needs of schools and communities. As teaching and learning advance in the 21st century, a new set of challenges will emerge as educational systems are affected by global influences in standards and curriculum design, economic interdependence, and an increasing presence of virtual schools, campuses, and university systems. The challenges of the 20th century that offered a backdrop to this book—challenges regarding equity, access, and representation in postsecondary education—may be diminished or lose some of their urgency as newer challenges surface.

How the issues of teacher quality, capacity, and licensure will be influenced by these changes remains to be seen, but as evidenced in the teacher preparation programs presented here, the teacher career pathway model introduces several new elements into the current order of teacher preparation; namely, it is community based, learner focused, and strategic. Spanning Grade 9–16 partnerships among high schools, community colleges, and 4-year universities, the teacher career pathway model represents an emerging paradigm in teacher preparation in the 21st century. Teacher career pathways offer a model of social agency, one that is focused on addressing historic injustices and closing the gaps through responsive teacher recruitment, preparation, and induction. By design, teacher career pathways are self-transforming. In this sense, they exemplify the ideals of democracy within an educational system, an associated form of living and working together to develop a strong and advanced citizenry. It is likely that they will be around for a long time.

REFERENCES

Cochran-Smith, M. (2004). Taking stock in 2004: Teacher education in dangerous times. *Journal of Teacher Education, 55*(1), 3–7.

Jenlink, P. M. (2005). Coda. In P. M. Jenlink & K. E. Jenlink (Eds.), *Portraits of teacher preparation: Learning to teach in a changing America* (pp. 235–238). Lanham, MD: Rowman & Littlefield Education.

About the Editor and Contributors

ABOUT THE EDITOR

Karen Embry Jenlink is professor of doctoral studies in educational leadership in the James I. Perkins College of Education at Stephen F. Austin State University. Currently, her teaching emphasis is in higher education administration and research methodology, and she serves as an advisor in dissertation research. She received her bachelor degree with a dual major in Spanish and elementary education from East Texas Baptist University in Marshall, Texas; her master degree in education from the University of Texas at Tyler; and a doctorate in education from Texas A&M University at Commerce. In higher education, she has served as a program coordinator, professor, and academic dean. Her university teaching and administrative assignments include East Texas Baptist University, Stephen F. Austin State University, and St. Edward's University. Nationally, she has served as an educational consultant and evaluator in curriculum development and evaluation of federally funded programs in photonics, telecommunications, and science, technology, engineering, and mathematics–related career and technical education.

Throughout her career, Dr. Embry Jenlink has worked to promote greater opportunity and equity for teachers and students in schools and in colleges and universities. Her current research interests include access and representation in higher education, career pathways, leadership preparation, and democratic pedagogy. She has published over 30 articles and book chapters related to these topics and coauthored two books: *Portraits of Teacher Preparation: Learning to Teach in a Changing America* and *The Ultimate Test Guide to Praxis I and II*. Dr. Embry Jenlink has conducted research related to teacher and leadership preparation and educational systems in England, Ireland, the Czech Republic, Hungary, and China. She has served as the president of the Consortium of State Organizations for Texas Teacher Education and is a past president of the Texas Association of Teacher Educators. In 2005, Dr. Embry Jenlink received the Outstanding Alumnus Award from the College of Education at Texas A&M University at Commerce. She currently serves as associate editor of *Teacher Education and Practice* and on several state and national advisory boards related to college and career readiness, teacher quality, and science and mathematics education.

ABOUT THE CONTRIBUTORS

Gregory M. Bouck earned a doctoral degree in educational leadership from Stephen F. Austin State University in May 2012. His research interests and efforts have focused on issues of social justice and democratic education, especially in the area of student persistence. As a scholar–practitioner, he seeks to ensure that his educational practice is grounded in theory and research, informed by experimental knowledge, and motivated by personal values, ethics, and political commitments. His work with students of low socioeconomic status with exceptionalities has allowed him to promote diversity and differentiate instruction in an effort to reach all students. He currently serves as special education compliance specialist for Caddo Parish Public Schools in Shreveport, Louisiana.

Kelty Garbee is the associate program officer for the Texas High School Project's Teacher Effectiveness initiative. Before joining the Texas High School Project, Ms. Garbee worked at the Texas Education Agency, where she served as the early college high school program manager. In this capacity, she developed expertise in dual-credit and preK–16 partnerships and was responsible for creating a designation process that allows school districts and colleges to join the statewide network of early college high schools. Before working at the Texas Education Agency, Ms. Garbee served as assistant manager of grants and sponsorships in the Development Office at the John F. Kennedy Center for the Performing Arts in Washington, DC. Ms. Garbee earned a bachelor degree in English and studies in women and gender from the University of Virginia and a master degree in public affairs from the LBJ School at University of Texas–Austin. She is currently pursuing a doctorate in education administration with a specialization in higher education from University of Texas–Austin.

Paula Griffin taught prekindergarten and kindergarten for 22 years in Texas public schools and is currently employed as an instructor in the EC-6 (early childhood–sixth grade) Online Completer Program at Stephen F. Austin State University in the Department of Elementary Education. She holds a bachelor degree in elementary education and a master degree in early childhood education and is currently pursuing a doctorate in educational leadership at Stephen F. Austin State University.

Anne C. Hallett serves as director of Grow Your Own Illinois, an innovative partnership that supports nontraditional candidates to become highly effective teachers. She founded and served 11 years as executive director of the Cross City Campaign for Urban School Reform, a network of school reform leaders in large cities. She serves on the Board of Directors of the Interfaith Youth Core and the Center for Neighborhood Technology. She cowrote the successful Chicago Annenberg Challenge proposal, which provided $49.2 million to Chicago's school reform efforts. As executive director of the Wieboldt Foundation in Chicago for 7 years, she cochaired the Neighborhood Funders Group and chaired Chicago Women in Philanthropy. She served as the founding executive director of the Chicago Panel on School Policy and chaired the Governing Board of the National Committee for Citizens in Education. She was executive director of Citizens Education Center in Seattle, Washington.

Leslie Huling is a professor in the College of Education at Texas State University–San Marcos, where she directs the Education Policy Implementation Center, a research entity of the Texas State University System. Her areas of research expertise include teacher recruitment, induction, and mentoring. For the past 25 years, she has been continually engaged in collaborative research involving universities and public schools. She is the author of more than 50 professional publications, including two books on mentoring and teacher induction.

Virginia Resta is the assistant dean for academic affairs in the College of Education at Texas State University–San Marcos. Dr. Resta's research interests include teacher induction and mentoring. She has served on two national commissions on teacher induction and mentoring for the Association of Teacher Educators and is a frequent presenter at national conferences.

Gayle Sawyer is the executive director of CERRA (Center for Educator Recruitment, Retention, and Advancement of South Carolina). Sawyer's interest in recruitment and retention of highly effective teachers began with her responsibilities as a middle and high school administrator, grew as while she was director of human resources for a rural school district, and expanded statewide through her leadership at CERRA. She is a past president of the Personnel Division for the South Carolina Association of School Administrators and was recognized as South Carolina's Personnel Administrator of the Year in 2004. Sawyer received her undergraduate degree with a double major in English literature and music (organ performance) at Coker College. She also earned a master degree in reading education at Clemson University and education specialist degree and doctoral degree in educational policies and leadership from the University of South Carolina.

Deborah L. Voltz is dean of the School of Education, director of the Center for Urban Education, and professor in the Department of Curriculum and Instruction at the University of Alabama at Birmingham. She received her bachelor degree in elementary education and special education at the National College of Education in Evanston, Illinois; her master degree in special education at the University of Alabama at Birmingham; and her doctorate of education from the University of Alabama. Dr. Voltz began her career as a special education teacher at Gate City Elementary School in Birmingham, Alabama. She also has taught in teacher preparation programs at several universities across the country, including Alabama State University, the University of Wisconsin–Milwaukee, and the University of Louisville. Throughout her professional career, Dr. Voltz has had a passion for the education of diverse learners in inclusive urban schools. She has engaged in an active research agenda related to this area and has published dozens of articles and book chapters devoted to the topic of teaching diverse learners.

Melva L. Ware has primary responsibility for developing equity and access strategies that improve opportunities for students from a range of backgrounds to pursue degrees in education. As director of ASPIRE (Academic Support Program Inspiring Renaissance Educators) at the University of Delaware, Dr. Ware has focused an interest on longitudinal guidance interactions to establish outreach into schools and the broader community. In 2010, she received the Louis Lorenzo Redding Diversity Award for contributions to promoting diversity in Delaware. Prior to assuming responsibilities at the University of Delaware, Dr. Ware was an assistant professor in the Division of Teaching and Learning at the University of Missouri–St. Louis. Her research has examined the impact of urban education policy, and she was a 1998 recipient of an National Science Foundation Early Career Investigator Award from the Professional Opportunities for Women Researchers program.

Dawn Michelle Williams taught special education for 20 years, served 10 years as a middle and high school administrator in Kansas and Texas, and is currently employed as an assistant professor and coordinator of the middle-level grade online completer program at Stephen F. Austin State University in the Department of Elementary Education. She holds master degrees in special education and educational administration and a doctoral degree in educational leadership from Stephen F. Austin State University.

Heather Zavadsky, director of research and implementation for the Texas High School Project, has over 15 years of experience in education research and practice, with an emphasis on urban education, district data and accountability systems, teacher quality, systemic district/school reform, and special education. She recently published a book entitled *Building School Reform to Scale: Five Exemplary Urban Districts* and is completing a second book, on scaling turnaround to the district level. Prior to coming to Texas High School Project, she was the director of policy at the University of Texas System Institute for Public School Initiatives. From 2002 to 2006, she managed the Broad Prize for Urban Education for the National Center for Education Accountability. She also conducted research for the Charles A. Dana Center and led the charter renewal process for the University of Texas–University Charter School. Additionally, she taught for 6 years as a special education teacher and worked extensively with students with autism.